THE "REASON" OF SCHOOLING

WITHDRAWN

Problematizing the "reason" of schooling as historical and political, in this book leading international and interdisciplinary scholars challenge the common sense of schooling and the relation of society, education, and curriculum studies. Examining the limits of contemporary notions of power and schooling, the argument is that the principles that order school subjects, the curriculum, and teaching reforms are historical practices that govern what is thought, acted on, and talked about. Highlighting the dynamics of social exclusion, the normalizing of people through curriculum, and questions of social inclusion, The "Reason" of Schooling underscores the urgency for rethinking curriculum research.

Thomas S. Popkewitz is Professor, Department of Curriculum and Instruction, University of Wisconsin–Madison, USA.

STUDIES IN CURRICULUM THEORY
William F. Pinar, Series Editor

Reid   **Curriculum as Institution and Practice: Essays in the Deliberative Tradition**

Pinar (Ed.)   **Queer Theory in Education**

Huebner   **The Lure of the Transcendent: Collected Essays by Dwayne E. Huebner. Edited by Vikki Hillis. Collected and Introduced by William F. Pinar**

For additional information on titles in the Studies in Curriculum Theory series visit **www.routledge.com/education**

THE "REASON" OF SCHOOLING

Historicizing Curriculum Studies, Pedagogy, and Teacher Education

Edited by
Thomas S. Popkewitz

Routledge
Taylor & Francis Group

NEW YORK AND LONDON

First published 2015
by Routledge
711 Third Avenue, New York, NY 10017

and by Routledge
2 Park Square, Milton Park, Abingdon, Oxfordshire OX14 4RN

First issued in paperback 2016

Routledge is an imprint of the Taylor & Francis Group, an informa business

© 2015 Taylor & Francis

Library of Congress Cataloging-in-Publication Data
The "Reason" of schooling : historicizing curriculum studies, pedagogy, and teacher education / edited by Thomas S. Popkewitz.
     pages cm. — (Studies in curriculum theory series)
  Includes bibliographical references and index.
  1. Curriculum planning—Philosophy.   2. Education—Philosophy.
3. Teachers—Training of.   I. Popkewitz, Thomas S., editor of compilation.
  LB1570.R372 2014
  375′.001—dc23
  2014008558

ISBN 13: 978-1-138-69059-2 (pbk)
ISBN 13: 978-1-138-01746-7 (hbk)

Typeset in Bembo
by Apex CoVantage, LLC

CONTENTS

PREFACE

The book focuses on the "reason" of schooling. This problematizing of the "reason" takes the common sense of school subjects, its psychologies of learning, reform-oriented research, and teacher education to consider the conditions that make possible the educational objects seen, thought about, and acted on. Further, it provides ways of thinking about the political in schooling through focusing on its knowledge (and language) as the governing of conduct. In focusing on the reason of schooling, the collection provides ways of thinking about the materiality; and of schooling different from what is found in structural Marxist traditions without reducing differences into oppositional categories of the real/context and text and discourse.

The contributions work across North America, Europe, Asia, and Latin America to provide an international and historical context to the study of schooling. In many ways, the chapters translate a range of European and North American philosophy and cultural history. These works include those of Giorgio Agamben, Gilles Deleuze, Jacque Derrida, Ian Hacking, Michel Foucault, Martin Heidegger, Jacques Rancière, and the Cambridge Historical School, among others. These literatures travel in the texts to play with the problematic of knowledge, questions of the relation of epistemology and ontology, and systems of reason as "actors" in the making of the self and world. The issue of translations that I speak of is not just changing of languages. It is the moving of scholarship (French and German) into other cultural spaces. That traveling is never merely of the author herself but becomes "traveling libraries" to enunciate particular research approaches that are different from the originating academic field (see Popkewitz, 2005). The result, as indicated in this volume, is the assembly and connections to provide sets of problems, methods of study, and ways of thinking about the phenomena of schooling that open up different avenues of critical thought about politics, power, and change in education than those embodied in current orthodoxies.

The focus on *the reason* as the study of schooling goes against the grain in at least two ways.

First, reason is generally considered a natural property of the mind (psychology), the method by which humans can interrogate themselves and "nature," or as the universal logic through which the truthfulness of statements are determined. Yet when examined as a social and historical phenomenon, there is nothing natural about how people "reason" through conceptions of childhood and stages of growth and development. Nor should it be assumed that the translation of disciplinary knowledge related to history, science, mathematics, and music is logically formed through psychologies about learning. Questions of school equality and performances are formed through the inscription of identities that then produce comparative distinctions and divisions that paradoxically the reforms were to erase. The comparativeness is given in the name of equality but, as argued in multiple chapters, produces exclusions within the reason of inclusion itself. To problematize the rules and standards of reason is to consider the productive side of how power operates through the principles generated about reflection and action.

Second, the contributions provide alternative modes of analysis to the instrumentalism of reform-oriented research that speaks through the language of the New Public Management of benchmarks, standards, and numerical ranking as comparative tools. The book also provides ways to reformulate and problematize the political of schooling which has dominated critical studies related to structural questions of identity and representation. If one examines contemporary research on school learning and the social organization of classrooms, for example, that research takes as its object the child who "learns" and the school subjects replicating the logic of science, mathematics, music, and literacy. The problems taken in research, from one ideological stance, are how to get teachers to be more effective in what they teach (didactics) and how to develop standards and best teaching practices for children to learn more efficiently; and, in critical studies, to understand the social structures, institutional forms, and organizational qualities to form "the hidden curriculum" that reproduces inequalities and an unjust society. To ask about the historical and social conditions that make possible what is seen, thought about, and acted on is to open up other possibilities, making the taken-for-granted objects of reflection and action as social facts amenable for study, critique, and resistance.

The last point about resistance is important as it throws into light the very question of change that underlines the social and educational sciences since their formation in the 19th century.[1] The orthodoxy of science is to provide for mastery of the world (social and physical) and with that mastery to enter its processes to produce change. The latter was joined with the theme of progress to link science to the hopes of the Enlightenment in creating a future that assumes the name of human progress, freedom, and liberty. That future was to occur through the intervention of the philosophy (and philosophers) through the 19th century and be replaced by social science by the turn of the 20th century to produce what is desired for in the present.

As discussed in Chapter 1 and throughout the book, this notion of regulating social change through governing the present re-inscribes the alchemist's philosopher stone as modernity's elixir. The reforms and the sciences of education assumed as strategies to produce a better world are the political of modernity. Political in the sense of generating principles that govern thought and action. The paradox of this notion of change, discussed in the volume, is conservative. It leaves unscrutinized the very rules and standards that order and classify the present and its possibilities. It is with this critique that the volume provides an alternative to think about the present and the questions of change and resistance, but with no guarantees.

Contribution of the Book

Challenging the common sense of schooling and (re)visioning certain central notions about the relation of society, education, and what is viewed in North America as "curriculum studies," this book:

1. Examines the limits of contemporary notions of power and schooling through exploring the role of language and discourse as simultaneous processes of constructing/construing the world and self.
2. Re-introduces history in thinking about the governing of the present through the knowledge that people have about self and others.
3. Provides ways of exploring questions of social inclusion as simultaneous practices of exclusion and abjection.
4. Extends and challenges the notion of "critical" studies beyond that of the Frankfurt School in contemporary Anglo-American social and educational studies. Drawing on interdisciplinary scholarship from both sides of the Atlantic, the book focuses on the critical in research as denaturalizing what seems natural in schooling, making fragile the causality of daily life in education, so as to make possible other options than those interred and enclosed in the boundaries of the contemporaneous frameworks.
5. Explores the international and interdisciplinary quality of the new curriculum studies. I use the word "new" in the sense of bringing together European, North and South American, and Asian scholars to provide original ways of thinking about present-day schooling.

Central to the connections in the studies in this volume has been the Wednesday Group, an ongoing seminar of graduate students and visiting fellows in the Department of Curriculum and Instruction at the University of Wisconsin–Madison, and my collaboration and dialogue with multiple researchers in Scandinavia,

Iberia, Latin America, continental Europe, and East Asia, much of whose work is present in this volume. The specific origin of the book was my Visiting Research Professorship at the French ENS research Institute on the Sociology of Education in Lyon, 2010. When there, I was asked to prepare a special issue of the journal *Éducation et Sociétés* to bring the tradition of scholarship related to knowledge and "reason to the French sociology of education." This volume is drawn from that special issue with additional papers prepared specifically for this volume.

Thomas S. Popkewitz

Madison, Wisconsin

February 16, 2014

Note

1. I use this phrase to think about uneven historical movements that come together at certain times to produce particular objects of thought and action. The social sciences comprise one such example: what is institutionalized in the United States at the turn of the century requires understanding different historical trajectories that move unevenly from the late 18th century through the beginning of the 20th century. These different historical trajectories have no single origin but connect to make possible what is taken for the formation of disciplinary fields, such as that of biology and history.

Reference

Popkewitz, T. S. (Ed.). (2005). *Inventing the modern self and John Dewey: Modernities and the traveling of pragmatism in education.* New York: Palgrave Macmillan.

ACKNOWLEDGMENTS

Growing up, I lived the caricature of the *New Yorker* magazine cartoon: standing in the big space of the city and looking across the Hudson River to the narrow plot of land left to fulfill the nation/continent. The only thing I knew of Wisconsin was its professional football teams that played in cold-cold weather. Once I crossed the Hudson to work at the University of Wisconsin–Madison, a particular charmed life began to appear that made this volume possible. The book is a collaborative effort that emerges through the PhD students who, during and after degree time, engage me in continual conversations that I always benefit from; the visiting fellows who braved the cold and enjoyed the delicious springs and summers to become a part of the conversations; and the accidents of life of meeting people whom I enjoy talking with and whose scholarship I enjoy reading. These accidents and conversations are this volume.

This volume began with an invitation from Jean-Louis Derouet (Director) and Romuald Normand (Associate Director and now professor at the University of Strasbourg) of the then Sociology of Education Section of the French Ministère de L'Éducation Nationale, De L'Enseignement Supérieur et De La Recherche, Institut National de Recherche Pédagogique in Lyon, where I was the Guest Researcher Professor. Their kindness and conversations are deeply appreciated. While there, they asked if I would edit a special issue of their journal, *Éducation et Sociétés* (2013, *31*[1]). Many of the chapters in this book were initially prepared for that issue and then revised for this volume.

Bill Pinar, the editor of the Studies in Curriculum Theory series, has been gracious in his support of this project and including the book in his series. I can only hope that this volume contributes to the play of ideas that characterizes his own work in curriculum studies.

Naomi Silverman of Routledge is a rare person in the publishing field. In the days of dwindling support for book preparation, she is a ray of sunshine in her caring and thoughtfulness in organizing the process of publication.

Chris Kruger is my secretary who has helped in the book preparation. She is as much a friend and my lifeline in the world of academia. She continually works with the contributors and publishers in ways that allow my chaos to seem orderly to the outside world.

And finally but also first is Lea Aschkenase, who wakes up in the morning to the sound of "Will you read something for me?" and then suffers through numerous drafts. Her heavy pen and dwindling patience as she derides my locutions are invisibly present in the reworking of my contributions to this and other books that I have written.

A version of Chapter 10, "Numbers in Grids of Intelligibility: Making Sense of How Educational Truth Is Told," appeared in H. Lauder, M. Young, H. Daniels, M. Balarin, & J. Lowe (Eds.) (2012), *Educating for the Knowledge Economy? Critical Perspectives* (pp. 169–191). London: Routledge. It is reprinted with permission.

1

CURRICULUM STUDIES, THE REASON OF "REASON," AND SCHOOLING

Thomas S. Popkewitz

An Introduction

The contemporary world of education constantly casts its problems and formulas of reform in the language of finding useful and practical knowledge: useful for helping the policy maker be wiser in solving educational problems; helpful to the teacher in becoming more effective and efficient for all children and identifying the practical knowledge for children to find the paths to a righteous and future happiness. Evoking practical and useful knowledge as the educational panacea of change is filled with irony. That irony is that the very principles that organize the hopes of practical knowledge are impractical. They are impractical in that the desire to find practical knowledge assumes a consensus and harmony to organize change that conserves the contemporaneous frameworks that are the object of change (see Popkewitz, 2013).

The case studies in this volume give visibility to what are taken as the practices of schooling and its irony as a strategy of change. The studies direct attention to the knowledge or systems of reason that order and classify the objects of schooling—what is seen, thought about, and acted as the child, school subjects, and individuality in teaching, teacher education, the psychologies of learning, and the sciences of education. Notwithstanding the current *topoi* of the Knowledge Society, a particular "fact" of modernity is that power is exercised less through brute force and more through systems of reason that order and classify what is known and acted on.[1] This "fact" is not new. From at least the late 18th century, the social and political principle of government was the making of the citizen; and that kind of person was governed through organizing the rules and standards of conduct linked to collective belonging and the codes of civic virtue. Modern schooling is the social space to make "the reasonable" individual who participates, is motivated to act, and believes in human agency to effect change.

This quality of knowledge—or more accurately, the systems of reason that govern reflection and action—are often overlooked in educational studies. Yet schools are places to make children into particular kinds of people that they would not be if they did not go to school! And central to this making of kinds of people are the principles about how one should know (didactics and learning theories) and what one should know (the school curriculum). These principles are, as I will argue, an effect of power that intern and enclose the (im)possibilities of the present.

This focus on knowledge, or the systems of reason, is the concern of this volume and a strategy with which to consider the problematic of curriculum studies. The focus can be expressed in the following questions addressed throughout this volume:

> What principles of "reason" historically order what is thought about and acted upon in schooling, its sciences, and reforms?
>
> What are the historical conditions that make possible the subjects of schooling—its curriculum and human kinds?
>
> How can the political of schooling and the problems of exclusion and abjection be rethought?

The notion of social epistemology organizes this chapter as a way to think about "reason" as historically produced and changing principles about what is done, thought about, and hoped for in schools. The first section of the chapter discusses social epistemology to think about the "reason" and "reasonable person" of schooling (Popkewitz, 1991, 2008; Popkewitz & Fendler, 1999). That section plays on the words "the reason of reason" to explore the intersections of different historical trajectories that make possible what is seen, thought, and acted on. The second section focuses on the sciences of education as social projects to change social conditions that change people. The third section considers the school subjects to explore how the "reason" of reform and the sciences of education embody comparative qualities that exclude and abject in the very impulses of schooling to include. In the fourth section of this chapter, I turn to the particular question of history in thinking about the problematic of social epistemology, focusing on understanding the past as part of the present to ask how the child, the teacher, and the curriculum are made into objects of reflection and action—what is considered as the decentering of the subject. The final and concluding section discusses the social epistemology as a strategy that (re)visions the social and political in the critical studies of education.

The concern of social epistemology is a strategy of curriculum studies. It is a critical approach that can be called "the new materialism" (Deleuze, 1968/1994)—that is, how knowledge "acts" in shaping and fashioning the (im)possibilities of the present. Rather than separate context and text, discourse and practice, subjective and objective, the volume brings to the fore "reason" as political. Political in the sense that the principles that order and classify the objects of schooling—the child who learns or the qualities of the expert teacher—embody cultural boundaries that police the present, protect its insularities, and conserve, enclose, and intern the boundaries of the present.

Social Epistemology and the Reason of "Reason"

In some ways, to ask about "reason" and knowledge as historical is difficult. The knowledge that we inherit makes the world sensible and connects us to others. If we use fish swimming in water as an analogy, knowledge is the medium that surrounds us. As the fish in the water, "our" knowledge provides the background and the procedures to order and classify things that make daily life manageable, stable, and seemingly natural. It gives us an unspoken basis from which to make decisions and navigate the complexities of things. Knowledge is a security blanket. Yet the irony of that security is it can elide the limits of the present by policing the boundaries of possibility and alternatives other than those already existing.

One way to denaturalize knowledge is to historically link epistemology with the social conditions that make possible what is known. *Epistemology* directs attention to the rules and standards of reason that order and classify what is seen and acted on. How is it possible to think of the child as having a "childhood," a stage of life as "youth," humans as separate from nature, or even the abstractions of "the social" and "society" as concepts for constituting our most intimate relations about who we are? Concurrently, *social* epistemology considers different historical patterns and principles assembled in different times and spaces to make possible the "objects" of reflection and action (see Popkewitz, 1991).

This notion of "reason" goes against the grain. Analytic traditions of philosophy tend to view epistemology as questions about the underlying and transcendent logic of knowledge. The sociological traditions of Emile Durkheim and Karl Mannheim during the past century gave emphasis to knowledge as tied to collective goals of society, an emphasis also found in the cultural Marxism of Antonio Gramsci and later by Louis Althusser, Raymond Williams, and the social philosopher Jürgen Habermas. Knowledge is an epiphenomenon to some inherent social structure or transcendent human interest that becomes the material and the origin of change through empowerment, voice, and resistance.

Social epistemology, in contrast, is to historicize the present to understand the complex historical relations and changes in ideas, knowledge, and "reason" organizing the practices of making the self and social worlds. Knowledge is material in that it entails a complex dynamic that responds to things happening (the ontic) but is given expression in particular ways in knowing and constituting the objects of reflection and action. Social epistemology is a critical project to explore the rules of formation and enunciations that are given as true and false (Popkewitz & Fendler, 1999). And as I argue throughout this chapter, social epistemology is a strategy of change through denaturalizing the seeming causality of the present and thus as the potential of opening up possibilities outside the existing framework.

Systems of Reason

If I turn to the inscription of "the social" in sociology and critical theory, the social can be understood as something not naturally "there" to explain the workings of power. That is, the inscription of the social is an abstraction and effect of power through the particular rules and standards to order, classify, and differentiate kinds of people. Historically, the notions of the social and society can be found as autonomous categories in the French philosophes of the 18th century. They gave reference to the abstract relations through which individuality was linked with Enlightenment notions of the cosmopolitan and later brought into the political theories of the citizen and collective belonging in the new republics. Prior to that time, the social and the idea of society were about particular groups of people or associations and not an abstract idea to explain the collective spaces in which one lived.

Tröhler's chapter explores this inscription of the social in responses to fears of urban moral disorder at the end of the 19th century. He argues that the theories and visions of political life in the emergent sociological and educational sciences were not merely about the restraints on individuals. The "social" in the Social Question that was posed by reformers embodied themes of salvation and redemption that were to guide reforming the perceived moral disorder of urban life. Tröhler argues that German evangelical Lutheranism, French Catholicism, and the Baptist church and Congregationalism in the United States brought together different cultural differences in narrating "the social" as constituting a normalizing element of life and community directed to national ideologies in the sociologies of education.

If we think of "the social" as not given in the study of schooling, as does Tröhler, it then is possible to consider another element embedded in its classifications, that is, as a category that fabricates particular kinds of people. The categories of people are produced to act on as the object of schooling and for people to act themselves. In this way, it is possible to explore how power operates through generating principles about modes of life. Lesko's chapter, for example, explores "youth" as particular historical categorizations to measure and calculate differences in kinds of people as if they existed (also see Lesko, 2001; Lesko & Talburt, 2011). Youth as a particular kind of person is produced in a grid of practices that link biology, medicine, psychology, physiology, and culture. Youth as a way of thinking and acting about kinds of people is a response to anxieties in which psychological and sociological attributes are given to describe the danger points that adults need to watch for in youth, and, as Lesko argues, is a set of values and norms for children to think of their own normality/abnormality. The object of "youth," however, is not a stable or natural quality but an effect of power and object of scrutiny and administration that changes over time and space. Lesko focuses on the changing subject of youth after World War II that is formed through the logic of an actuarial imaginary, neuroscientific plasticity, and the emotional pull of risk-taking behavior.

The historicizing of the "reason" in how judgments are formed, experiences of life are organized, and problems are given an existence and made manageable is also the focus of Martin's chapter. It explores the emergence of the notion of genius that makes possible the subject of the artist and artistic education. Genius is given form as a particular kind of person in the late 19th century within the development of eugenic theory about cultural theses of human types—the genius, idiot, insane, and normal. The categories, Martin argues, were given scientific reality through statistical means. The artist and art education embodied these distinctions to think about and act on particular kinds of people at the intersection of art, schooling, and the human sciences, particularly psychology and psychometrics. Martin explores how the qualities and characteristics about people engender cultural theses about modes of life, define principles of "freedom," and frame a comparative mode of thought to differentiate and divide the genius from other social and cultural distinctions in society.

In a different but related problematic of the reason that organizes the common sense of education, Sloane's chapter starts with the ongoing efforts to remake the New Orleans public school system after the devastation of Hurricane Katrina. She focuses on the reasoning of reformers and critics in the rebuilding efforts. Drawing on the work of Giorgio Agamben and to a lesser extent Foucault, Sloane argues that there was a particular epistemological shift about the relation of nature and humans that becomes apparent in the latter half of the 18th century. That shift to divide human and nature produces a paradox. The paradox appears as the impossibility of knowing a real, true nature, yet with the presupposition of an interior power that humans can use to fill that void of finding that nature. This logic is brought into the educational programs in New Orleans to talk about the hurricane as the inseparability of the disaster with the opportunity for the educability of the student. The particular historical paradigm presupposes, at the level of ontology, the potential of education and the social that re-inscribes broad, profound social inequities and asymmetries in the context of public schooling.

There is a certain conservatism that becomes visible in the reforms of schools. That conservatism is in the unquestioned inscription of the contemporary frameworks that order and classify what has been as well as what should be. The system of reason that is named as a radical reform but conserves the boundaries of the possible is given attention in Friedrich's chapter on teacher education. Attention is given to programs that offer alternative routes to teacher certification (ARTC) in the United States and are increasingly part of global reforms. Friedrich calls the alternatives a "boot-camp" style of teacher education that are designed to provide quick access to teaching licenses through on-the-job training in schools rather than in university programs. The paradox of the "alternatives," Friedrich argues, is that they leave unquestioned the foundational assumptions that circulate in traditional and critical approaches to teacher education reform. Learning and developmental psychologies are connected to assumptions of separating and privileging "experience" over theory, differentiating teaching methods and content knowledge, and conceptualizing diversity as something that is found through looking at differences in the "experiences" of different social groups. The assembly of these principles and technologies serves as a self-authorizing system that interns and encloses boundaries to the issues, problems, and solutions given to education. It is here, in the principles of reason, that the politics of schooling is explored. A determinism is produced that elides the indeterminacy of the disciplinary fields brought into the teaching of the various school subjects of history or mathematics. The naturalizing of experience places differences within predetermined spaces that divide those who are the same from those who are "different." The inscription of difference and exclusion in the reason that orders school subjects is pursued as well as in later chapters the historicizing of mathematics, music, and indigenous education.

In pursuing "reason" and its questions of social epistemology, it is important to recognize that "reason" is plural rather than singular both inside and outside of the West. Tröhler's comparative historical studies of the formation of the modern European and American schools, for example, explore differences at the intersection of religious salvation themes and republican notions of the citizen (also see Tröhler, 2011; Tröhler, Popkewitz, & Labaree, 2011). The chapter by Caride about catholic salvation themes in the making of the Argentina citizen in the 19th century and the work of Wu (2013) and Zhao (2014, and in this volume) help consider different historical and cultural sites in the making of people.

The "Reason" of Progress, Agency, and Governing the Present

Reading one of the more famous sculptures of the turn of the 20th century, Rodin's *The Thinker*, cast in 1901 (Photo 1.1), provides a way to historicize the particular "reason" of modernity that circulates in the school. As Martin's chapter suggests in

PHOTO 1.1 *The Thinker*

examining the notion of genius, the statue is the representation of aesthetic value that is not intrinsic to itself. That value entails an historical question about the range of practices, theories, narratives, and stories that make it possible to think about its "modern" cosmopolitan image of reason and reflection. To pursue this briefly, Rodin's statue inscribes a particular European Enlightenment notion of human reason as an actor of change that replaces prior conceptions of theological certainty. Embedded in the gaze of *The Thinker* is the application of "reason" as a force of change, with humans as its agent, and the idea of progress as the ultimate purpose of "thought" itself. Rodin's statue becomes a metonym of the role of human consciousness to assess and analyze the distinct worlds of nature and of the self in the desire to control and plan for the future.

Moving within the gaze of *The Thinker* is the idea of progress. It is the interior of the self in which human agency is enacted as a social project that orders the past and present in order to secure the future. Rodin's *The Thinker* symbolizes the project of change as a problem of planning—human agency is the planning of biography as one's life assumes stages and careers, of parents' moral responsibility for planning for the upbringing of their children, and of the welfare state as planning to ensure the health and cultural and moral qualities of its citizens (see Tröhler, Popkewitz, & Labaree, 2011).

The privileging of "reason" in the statue also has a particular quality that becomes visible. The notion of "reason" embodies the technological sublime in which science and technology are given as the apotheosis of reason at the turn of the 20th century.[2] Science becomes a cultural value about finding wisdom itself. The new scientific psychologies, for example, mark the times of moral as well as physical transitions that served to organize the pedagogy of the progressive school. The sociologies of community and society are to provide the theories and social technologies that relate the capabilities and characteristics of individuality to the values and norms of collective belonging and the nations. In different disciplines, continuums of values are established between the modern and the traditional with the former as the most advanced in wisdom.

The sculpture, then, can be read not only as being about the individual artist but also as embodying a particular assembly and connections of events that make *The Thinker* intelligible. It also provides a way to reverse the conventional question of curriculum asked through the Spenserian one of "what knowledge is of most value?" A different question can be posed about the conditions that make possible the objects given value in reflection and action. And as Friedrich argues in making visible the principles of "the reason" in teacher education, the critical study is a strategy of change through opening up the possibilities for other conceptions of educating.

The Double Space of "Reason" in Science and Making People

Science, at least from the 19th century, occupies a double cultural and social space. First, science is the salvation narrative of modernity. It is the promise of the mastery of the conditions of social life through its principles of calculation and adminis-tration. Brought into the social realm, science embodied a millennialist belief in rational knowledge as a positive force for action and the progress that was called forth as part of the heritage of the Enlightenment. Science was the technology of reform in American Progressivism at the turn of the 20th century. It was used to describe, explain, and give direction for solving social problems by changing the conditions of the new urban city and to enable social improvement. The changing of social conditions, as I discuss later, also entailed changing people.

Second, science embodied a way of ordering, classifying, and acting in the world. Daston (2000) has detailed how the modes of observing in science pro-duced a particular cultural thesis about the scientific "self." The disciplining of conduct in science was also taken into cultural realms as a mode of living for a generalized ordering of life to bring about individual happiness, freedom, and social progress (Rudolph, 2005). The genius of Dewey's pragmatism, for example, was to provide a way to take the elite notions of the Enlightenment's cosmopoli-tan "reason" and science into organizing daily life. Progressive education in the United States and more broadly in the New Education Fellowship pursued a gen-eralized philosophical notion of science as providing the rules and standards for the processes of the mind to work. G. Stanley Hall, a founder of American child studies at the turn of the 20th century, argued that scientific psychology was to replace moral philosophy and theology as the method to produce moral principles for ordering the life of the child. The theories and concepts about motivation, development, and problem solving, among others, "acted" in school programs to order experience, reflection, and action as principles for individuals to plan and order daily life itself (see Danziger, 1990, 1997; Rose, 1989).

The sciences of schooling were designed as technologies of the self to act on the spirit and the body of children and the young (Ó, 2003). Pedagogy was to cultivate, develop, and enable the reason necessary for human agency and progress that was never only of the individual or as merely cognitive and rational. French and Portuguese pedagogy at the turn of the 20th century was to observe and "register" the inner physical and moral life in order to map the spirituality of the educated subject ("the human soul"). The sources of the pedagogical sciences in France and Portugal "are related to the moral faculties of man; pedagogy contains all the parts of the soul and must use always psychology" (cited in Ó, 2003, p. 106).

Today, the principles of governing the self through the abstraction of science are naturalized and made into a universal characteristic of Interest in Science. Policy initiatives are to increase student participation in the fields of science, tech-nology, engineering, and mathematics (STEM). Bang and Valero's chapter histori-cally explores the changing norms and values given in the abstraction of scientific interest and how it is given empirical reality in schooling as principles of the mind and morality in educational reforms. Exploring initially the meaning in Herber-tian and then Deweyan thought at the turn of the 20th century, they then focus on the notion of interest that is placed within psychologies of science education.

Scientific interest is an abstraction formatted through cognitive psychology to measure what is imagined as science and which "acts" to determine science learning, teaching, and curriculum. They argue that a causal relation between students' attitudes is projected and measured as attainment of interest in tests. This imaginary of science is embodied in the practical knowledge of science measured in the Organisation for Economic Co-operation and Development's (OECD) Programme for International Student Assessment (PISA).

The modes of reasoning associated with science connected with narratives and images of the citizen to instantiate norms of collective belonging and progress (Popkewitz, 2008). Science signifies "the soul" as the mind in what is thought of as secularization that unties people from the determinism of the Church. Caride's chapter challenges the division of secularization and religion in modernity through examining the grid of practices that form the cultural thesis of the citizen in Argentina during the 19th century. The formation of the Argentinean republic, he argues, entailed overlapping principles of the Enlightenment's cosmopolitanism and salvation themes connected with the Catholic Church. Caride further examines how the discourses of national identity and the citizen are unstable as they connected with 19th-century Jewish immigrant narratives of freedom and liberty. The narratives of belonging and "home" revise and give different nuances in the notions of the citizen than do merely replicating or adding to what existed.

In these and others chapters in the book, the practices of pedagogy, the organization of the curriculum, and the psychologies of learning come together as a grid of practices directed to making certain kinds of people. The sciences of pedagogy are "actors" in this governing through linking the interior of the child with abstractions of "society" and the nation.

School Subjects: Alchemies and the "Reason" of Exclusions/Abjections

The school subjects are part of the common sense of what schools do! When it comes to reform, they are like the cultural monuments. The school subjects stand as the objects that have less to do with the cultural practices of the natural and social sciences, for example. The models of curriculum and the psychologies of the children are to order conduct; to measure the health of schools and children's achievement; and to serve as the foundation of teaching and teacher education programs. Current teacher education reforms, for example, emphasize teachers learning more disciplinary knowledge so that they can become more competent (see Friedrich's chapter in this volume). The school subjects are the objects of international assessments to gauge the nation's modernization through tests of the proficiency of children's skills and content knowledge in science, mathematics, and reading.

The organizing of school subjects is, in one sense, an invention of the 19th century. Prior to that, the school curriculum was linked to the names of the books read. For example, high school students were to read two books of Caesar and three of Virgil for the study of Latin. American colleges prescribed what books students should read in English for their admission and for the examinations that were given for entrance up to at least 1885. By the first decades of the 20th century, school subjects formed around particular disciplinary knowledge, translated into the curriculum with the new science of psychology.

If these school subjects are treated as historical events that are not naturally there to act on in schooling, then it is possible to ask about the principles that govern their practices. This entails recognizing that school subjects require transportation and translation tools that bring disciplinary fields concerned with knowledge production into the social and cultural spaces of schooling. Children are not physicists or historians, so something needs to be done with the disciplines so children can work with the ideas, narratives, and approaches to understanding. To put this a different way, the school subjects entail alchemic processes. Like the 16th- and 17th-century alchemists and occult practitioners who sought to turn base metals into pure gold, the school subjects magically translate disciplinary fields through the languages of classroom management and theories of learning and communication.

The fact of alchemies is not surprising, as the social and cultural spaces of schools cannot replicate those of the discipline's pedagogical models. While the imaginaries of schoolwork carry the names of science and mathematics, the models of curriculum are transmogrifications and are not replicas of the original. Translation is always a creation. And the translations of curriculum revision mathematics and music, for example, into particular images, words, ideas, and experiences related to learning, children's motivation, and problem solving (Popkewitz, 2004). This organizing, selecting, and evaluating of curriculum as subservient to the governing of conduct should be evident, as well, in the previous discussions of "teaching" youth and the genius.

What is less evident in the alchemy and explored in this volume is how the school subjects embody principles of representation, identity, and difference. The epistemological principles that order the selection, organization, and evaluation of school subjects (the curriculum) and their human kinds carry a comparative style of thought in their thrusts to include. Even with the expressions of the value of diversity and equality, the paradox of the epistemological principles in policy and research is that they inscribe difference and divisions (see, e.g., Popkewitz, 2008). This comparativeness can be located as a part of the European Enlightenment. Cassirer (1932/1951) argues, for example, that the crumbling of the classical and medieval conception of the "cosmos" was accompanied with the different notions of the human mind and reason that emerged in the Enlightenment of Europe to measure, compare, combine, and differentiate the things in the world, including humanity's nature.

This comparing and dividing had a particular and productive quality in the natural sciences and medicine from the 19th century. When brought into the social and psychological sciences associated with schooling, a particular way of normalizing and differentiating the qualities of people on a continuum of value was produced. The most radical was the eugenics movements that were prominent in the United States but also taken up in European political regimes. While eugenics is continually questioned, less noticed are the comparative systems that made eugenics possible as cultural theses about people. With a seemingly more benign classification system, the divisions are taken as nature in the psychologies about conceptual "misconceptions" in the curriculum and the assigning of capabilities and qualities to the child who lacks self-esteem and motivation. The latter inscribes the unspoken normalization of the righteous child who has esteem that particular children don't have and are classified as different. The comparativeness is also in differentiating "fragile families" from some notion of what is not fragile and the use of "community" to direct attention to why children don't succeed in schools. Without identifying "the other" who has esteem, motivation, and the secure family, the categories perform as comparative distinctions that exclude and abject in the impulse to include.

The inscription of comparative styles of thinking is the focus of Diaz's chapter on mathematics education. She begins with a seemingly simple "given" of the logic of equivalences expressed in the mathematical equal sign (=). Focusing on the Back to Basics curriculum movement of the 1970s, Diaz explores how that seemingly universal logic of the equal sign (=) leaves, unnoticed, the alchemy of mathematics attaches political theories of equivalence, difference, and identities about kinds of people. The narrative about the logic of equivalence appears as children learning a particular kind of mathematics about identities of equivalence that place unequal quantities (2 and 3) in a relationship of difference. Yet this relation can also be treated as producing an equivalence when the equal sign (=) is used to express that there is a harmony ($2 + 3 = 5$) between both sides of the equation. A harmony is produced as equivalence, so difference becomes sameness.

When mathematics education is examined as a system of reason, the reason of mathematical equality is assembled and connected with cultural theses about modes of living as the alchemy disconnects it from the logic in the field of mathematics. When seen in relation to the principles of the psychological theories of learning, the equal sign (=) becomes part of classifications that naturalizes the hierarchy of norms and values around which social and cultural differences are produced. These differences are ascribed as distinctions of learning mathematics that elide the cultural theses of equality/inequality through which such learning is made intelligible.

The comparative style of reason that produces differences and divisions that Diaz explores is embodied in the formation of the curriculum subjects. As with mathematics education, music education entails an alchemy that disconnects it from the originary cultural and social spaces of music and assembles it as a content designed to perform within the rules and standards of design in models of curriculum. The models of curriculum are organized through psychologies of learning and instruction that embody cultural theses about modes of living that include norms of belonging and fears of dangers and dangerous populations. Children's singing and music appreciation at the turn of the 20th century, for example, were concerned with fears of moral decay and degeneration if the child is not "civilized" (Gustafson, 2009). The physical activities of children's singing were to remedy the risks epidemic disease posed to civil society and to provide the latest regimens for the stimulation of circulation that was to prevent poor health. Teaching the proper songs was to remove the emotionalism of tavern and revival meetings and serve to regulate the moral conditions of urban life with a "higher" calling related to the nation. Gustafson's chapter in this volume considers the uneven topography in which the borrowing from the European tradition of concerts and manuals of etiquette form comparisons between musical tastes and perception that are linked to race and ethnicity. The consumption of music via radio and gramophone produced new classifications of the listener of music that entailed double gestures. Gustafson argues that they produced social barriers, but the classification of compositions and audiences disrupted the stark differences and their normalizations.

The inscription of comparative styles of reasoning in questions of difference and diversity is explored in Kowalczyk's discussion of Italian intercultural education. The chapter gives focus to an important social and cultural commitment in contemporary policy and research to honor difference and "the other." Through focusing the discourses about the inclusion of immigrants, Kowalczyk argues that there is the double gesture of the hope of integration and fears of these populations to the future. To achieve *convivenza* (civic participation and democracy) in Italy is to manage differences through establishing common values and norms to govern and thus accept and conserve/preserve the particular "cultural thesis" of the "original" community to be saved from conflict and dissolution. The immigrant student is tasked with the impossible: to become an Italian cosmopolitan child and to represent the internal borders of national belonging that the presence of the immigrant transgresses. Yet in the creating of borders, Kowalczyk draws on Foucault's notion of transgression to consider how the cosmopolitanism itself opens up new possibilities in integration policy within schools.

The double gestures of hope and fear are entangled in the Social Question and "the social" as a historical object implicated in questions of power, differences, and moral order. An earlier discussion of "the social" by Tröhler is taken up in a different way by Petersson, Olsson, and Krejsler. They study European educational policy and Swedish teacher education to consider the philanthropic focus on urban economic and moral disorganization in the late 19th century that is today (re) visioned as salvation themes of social redemption. From a future predetermined by Providence in the Social Question of the 19th century, today's dangerous groups are constructed in terms of the social dimension and living as lifelong learners, as entrepreneurs, and with a wide concept of poverty. The Swedish reforms entail a double gesture of the Enlightenment hope of the future and fears of those who do not "fit" the values associated with cosmopolitanism in lifelong learning.

In these studies are reform efforts to honor difference and create political and cultural equality that inscribe its opposite as part of the same phenomenon. Lopez pursues this general problem of reason as a comparative system through exploring the projection and protection of indigenous populations as the social "problem" from the end of the 19th century and into the 20th and 21st centuries, drawing the notion of problem from the writing of the French philosopher Derrida. Lopez focuses on the style of reasoning that historically and today in progressive policies, laws, and documents justifies the importance of respecting diversity to protect and to correct social wrongs as the aspirations of equity and equality. She argues that the principles of indigenousity embody a comparativeness that does violence to the Indian-Other. Bringing in visual cultural theories, the photographs of the indigenous Indian are seen as giving intelligibility to the complex dynamics and shifting centers of borders, temporizations, and spatializations in the social, political, and ontological problem of the Indian. To ask why the problem of change, why indigenous people have not moved from where they were, is to ask, Lopez suggests, to look at the thesis, principle, and logic that historically create closures even when, she says, the desire is for opening.

In these chapters, focusing on the reason of school subjects and curriculum reforms is to ask about the complex historical relations through which what is seen, talked about, and acted on as school knowledge. But it is also to ask about the political aspect—that is, how the very system of reason that orders the common sense of schooling embodies comparative principles that exclude and abject in the impulse for equality and inclusion.

Historicizing "Reason"

Central to the studies related to social epistemology is historicizing. As should be obvious at this point, the history spoken about is a family of resemblance, to borrow from Wittgenstein, that gives attention to the conditions that make possible what is "seen" and acted on as the objects and subject of schooling (see Popkewitz, 2011, 2013; Popkewitz, Franklin, & Pereyra, 2001; Tröhler, 2011). In particular, the question of history is not of the past but about how the past is intricately woven in constituting the present through generating principles about who "we" are and should be but also about who is not that kind of people.

This historicizing brings into focus, first, history as the decentering of the subject. Historicizing is to cut into and denaturalize the givenness of the autonomous subjects of schooling through historically asking about how such a subject got to be "there" in the first place. The decentering of the subject is to treat the given categories of people and things in schools as monuments, things that seem to exist as natural memorials to who we are and should be (see, e.g., Foucault, 1971/1977; Popkewitz & Brennan, 1998).[3] The notions of youth and the relation of man and nature discussed earlier are such monuments. The study of curriculum is to disassemble the rules of formation and enunciations of what is given as the subjects of schooling.

The decentering of the subject, however, should not be seen as doing away with Enlightenment commitments to reason and rationality or with the possibilities of agency and change. Just the opposite! It is to recognize that what has come to be taken as natural and "logical" as the reason and loci of social change is itself a particular historical logic, rationality, and effect of power. This is a continual theme of the various sections that focused on youth, intercultural education, or the indigenous population, among others. The inscription of the actor as the ahistorical subject is to conserve the very framework of its contemporaneity and to substitute activity and motion as change. To think of possibilities outside of the contemporaneous rules is to understand the limits that inhere to the rules and standards of reason.

Historicizing is to understand how multiple different and unrelated events and trajectories come together as a grid in particular times to give intelligibility to the self and its objects of reflection and action. What Foucault calls thresholds and Deleuze and Guattari "plateaus," the notion of grid is analogous to a recipe for baking a cake. The cake is made from ingredients mixed together. The outcome is "the cake," an object or a determinant category that appears as having its own ontological existence! Bang and Valero, for example, bring this notion of grid into view when talking about the making of the scientific self in schooling and the notion of interest in science as the vivisection of different "strata" that are entwined in making Interest in Science. This ordering of different parts into a "whole" has no singular origin; nor are the parts merely a sum of the whole. What is produced is something different.

Curriculum and Critical Studies of Schooling

Curriculum studies, as exemplified throughout this volume, are to ask about the conditions that make the objects of schooling possible and the limits of the principles that order how we find out, recognize, and distinguish the objects to illuminate our predicaments. It is a critical practice that is

> [t]o disturb what was previously considered immobile, to fragment what was thought unified, and to show the heterogeneity of what was imagined. To identify how memories are engraved on things and bodied.
>
> *(Foucault, 1971/1977, p. 151)*

Curriculum studies is a critical history. It is critical in the refusal to take the subject as transcendental and thus outside of history. It is critical in problematizing what is taken as natural and outside of "time." It is to make fragile the causality of the present and the possibilities of alternatives that are outside of the existing inscriptions of the past that govern the future.

The collection, with different approaches to historicize the reason of schooling, is paradoxically a strategy to think about change that rejects the dogma of science as planning people. The decentering of the subject is depriving the self of the reassuring stability of life and its "nature" given as dependent on the calculation and administration of the subject. Freedom is to make visible the historical and human-made qualities of the present to open up the possibilities of alternatives other than those that are interned and enclosed by the existing frameworks.

This rethinking (revisioning) of change goes against the grain of Anglo-American social and educational traditions. The latter posits power in the given-ness of the subject—the oppositions of the rulers and ruled, given in Pierre Bourdieu's notions of field and habitus, neoliberal notions of human interests, and the notion of praxis in critical theories of pedagogy. Agency is inscribed in the theories of the subject as the origin of power. Change is sociologically the shifting of the valences of power inherent in social structures. Knowledge is the planning of the subject to correct the social wrongs.

The commitments to correct social wrongs in this notion of power are important and helpful to understand inequities but tell little about the given concrete forms that generate the principles of differences and divisions. What is constituted politics, if I draw on Rancière (2007), is the policing of the boundaries of the present rather than changing or challenging them. Efforts for change assume a consensus on the existing representations, distinctions, and classification in settling political conflicts through negotiation and agreement, such as the current use of stakeholders to speak about including different political interests. The difficulty of the social assumption of consensus is "conflicts are turned into problems that have to be sorted out by learned expertise and a negotiated adjustment of interests" (Rancière, 2007, p. 306).

To engage the political element that Rancière speaks about is to disturb the consensus and its partitioning of the sensible, its given subjects and the comparative systems of reason that differentiate who the child is, the pedagogical models that organize the kind of person who learns mathematics, environmental education, or music, and the epistemological principles that order difference and diversity that inscribe a hierarchy of values. The decentering of the subject is a strategy to disrupt the practices of consensus and to make possible alternatives for change without guarantees.

Earlier I evoked the notion of materialism to speak about a critical strategy. That materialism recognizes the elisions produced through the separation of theory and practice, objective and subjective, and text and context. The focus is on the complex sets of ideas, images, narratives, and technologies through which the self and world become objects of reflection and action. It problematizes by giving attention to the reason of practice in historical sets of relations. Deleuze argues, for example, that power cannot be explained within institutions, as they are not sources, essences, and mechanisms, since they presuppose the relations that make them intelligible, fixing them in ways that reproduce and conserve rather than make new possibilities (Deleuze & Guattari, 1991/1994). Although with differences but in a family of resemblances, the chapters in this book pose a problematic of educational research as considering the "strategies that transmit or distribute particular features through which forms of knowledge are possible and becoming the integrating factors or agents of stratification that make up institutions" that are not just the state but inscribed in the family, religion, market, art, and morality (Deleuze & Guattari, 1991/1994, p. 75).

Notes

1. I am using the notion of modern and modernity to signal particular epistemological principles that order what is seen, talked about, and acted on that intersect with schooling during the long 19th century in the West, and particularly Western Europe and North America. The discussion of modern, as will be clearer as the argument proceeds, is about the particular historical sets of principles generated about who a person is and should be. It is not to talk about an epoch or to place the present in some hierarchy of difference from something prior to that is "premodern."
2. Steedman (1995) discusses this opening of the interior of the child as coinciding but with different trajectories than the invention of modern history in the 19th century. In both cases, a new temporality appears that gives humanity its own sequential relation of past, present, and future.
3. This notion of decentering the subject has been subject to a range of discussion. Often its critiques are ordered through the principles of historicism that take for granted the actor as the source of humanism. This reduction qua critique misses the substantive arguments being engaged (see Veyne, 1971/1998, for a discussion of history and the limits of this reductionism as critique).

References

Cassirer, E. (1932/1951). *The philosophy of the Enlightenment* (F. Koelln & J. Pettegrove, Trans.). Princeton, NJ: Princeton University Press.

Danziger, K. (1990). *Constructing the subject: Historical origins of psychological research.* New York: Cambridge University Press.

Danziger, K. (1997). *Naming the mind: How psychology found its language.* London: Sage.

Daston, L. (Ed.). (2000). *Biographies of scientific objects.* Chicago: University of Chicago Press.

Deleuze, G. (1968/1994). *Difference and repetition* (P. Patton, Trans.). New York: Athlone Press of Columbia University.

Deleuze, G., & Guattari, F. (1991/1994). *What is philosophy?* (H. Tomlinson & G. Burchell, Trans.). New York: Columbia University Press.

Foucault, M. (1971/1977). Nietzsche, genealogy, history (S. Simon, Trans.). In D. F. Bouchard (Ed.), *Language, counter-memory, practice: Selected essays and interviews by Michel Foucault* (pp. 139–164). Ithaca, NY: Cornell University Press.

Gustafson, R. (2009). *Race and curriculum: Music in childhood education.* New York: Palgrave Macmillan.

Lesko, N. (2001). *Act your age: A cultural construction of adolescence.* New York: Routledge.

Lesko, N., & Talburt, S. (Eds.). (2011). *Youth studies: Keywords and movement.* New York: Routledge.

Ó, J. R. do. (2003). The disciplinary terrains of soul and self-government in the first map of the educational sciences (1879–1911). In P. Smeyers & M. Depaepe (Eds.), *Beyond empiricism on criteria for educational research* (pp. 105–116). Leuven: Leuven University Press.

Popkewitz, T. (1991). *A political sociology of educational reform: Power/knowledge in teaching, teacher education and research.* New York: Teachers College Press.

Popkewitz, T. S. (2004). The alchemy of the mathematics curriculum: Inscriptions and the fabrication of the child. *American Educational Journal, 41*(4), 3–34.

Popkewitz, T. S., & Brennan, M. (Eds.). (1998). *Foucault's challenge: Discourse, knowledge, and power in education.* New York: Teachers College Press.

Popkewitz, T. (2008). *Cosmopolitanism and the age of school reform: Science, education, and making society by making the child.* New York: Routledge.

Popkewitz, T. (2011). Curriculum history, schooling, and the history of the present. *History of Education, 40*(1), 1–19.

Popkewitz, T. S. (2013). The sociology of education as the history of the present: Fabrication, difference, and abjection. *Discourse: Studies in the cultural politics of education, 34*(3), 439–456.

Popkewitz, T. S., & Fendler, L. (Eds.). (1999). *Critical theories in education: Changing terrains of knowledge and politics.* New York: Routledge.

Popkewitz, T. S., Franklin, B., & Pereyra, M. (2001). *Cultural history and education: Critical essays on knowledge and schooling.* New York: RoutledgeFalmer.

Rancière, J. (2007). *The hatred of democracy* (S. Corcoran, Trans.). New York: Verso.

Rose, N. (1989). *Governing the soul.* New York: Routledge, Chapman & Hall.

Rudolph, J. L. (2005). Turning science to account: Chicago and the general science movement in secondary education, 1905–1920. *Isis, 96*(3), 353–389.

Steedman, C. (1995). *Strange dislocations: Childhood and the idea of human interiority, 1780–1930.* Cambridge, MA: Harvard University Press.

Tröhler, D. (2011). *Languages of education: Protestant legacies in educationalization of the world, national identities, and global aspirations.* New York: Routledge.

Tröhler, D., Popkewitz, T. S., & Labaree, D. F. (Eds). (2011). *Schooling and the making of citizens in the long nineteenth century: Comparative visions.* New York: Routledge.

Veyne, P. (1971/1998). Foucault revolutionizes history. In A. I. Davidson (Ed.), *Foucault and his interlocutors* (pp. 146–183). Chicago: University of Chicago Press.

Wu, Z. (2013). Chinese mode of historical thinking and its transformation in pedagogical discourse. In T. S. Popkewitz (Ed.), *Rethinking the history of education: Transnational perspectives on its questions, methods, and knowledge* (pp. 51–74). New York: Palgrave.

Zhao, W. (2013/2014). Teaching with *liangxin* (virtuous heart) held in hands or not: Untangling self- and state-governmentalization of contemporary Chinese teachers. *Special Issue: Governmentality: Governing in the Curriculum and Making People. Journal of European Education. 45*(4), 75–91.

PART I

Social Epistemology and the Reason of "Reason"

2

THE CONSTRUCTION OF SOCIETY AND CONCEPTIONS OF EDUCATION

Comparative Visions in Germany, France, and the United States Around 1900

Daniel Tröhler

In contemporary academic discourses, the notions of "globalization," "standardization," and "unification" have become popular catchwords. They serve two different but interrelated purposes. First, they intend to describe fundamental processes of the social world, and second, they refer (silently) to the apparent legitimation of some of the social sciences to describe such fundamental processes. Against the background of the upswing of economics, sciences, and engineering since the end of World War II, it is perhaps a rather surprising honor for the social sciences to perceive themselves as legitimated to describe contemporary processes that affect the peoples of the world in manifold ways. Not uncommonly, then, the analyses of contemporary processes are tinged with some skepticism toward both, the described process itself and the cultural dominancy of other sciences than the social sciences in the public sphere. We just need to remember how proudly universities list all their Nobel Prize winners—Nobel Prizes are exclusively awarded in physics, chemistry, physiology, medicine, economics, peace, and literature—most of the social sciences and humanities are excluded from its honor.

Together with other academic disciplines such as history or the educational sciences,[1] the social sciences are children of the 19th century, when they were placed in the newly founded research universities. Although academic freedom had been publically assigned to the modern universities,[2] contributions to the process of nation building were culturally expected. Every single one of the leading nation-states of the 19th century—France, Germany, United Kingdom, and the United States—believed in its specific national exceptionalism, and the majority of the intellectuals did, too. It is revealing to have a look at the reactions of the intellectuals in the context of the Great War to understand how nationally biased "academic freedom" turned out to be in reality; in France it was Emile Durkheim, among others, who attacked the Germans; in Germany it was Werner Sombart, for instance, who insulted the whole Western world, whereas John Dewey accused the German philosophy as the foundation of the German aggression, and the British intellectuals—after hesitating for a while—spoke mockingly about the German *Kaiser, Krupp, und Kultur* (Flasch, 2000; Hanna, 1996; Wallace, 1988).

Reading the intellectuals' responses to the Great War makes it clear how "same" events are not same events. What histories tend to narrate about "the Great War" is in reality a unification (or standardization) of multiple experiences and collective interpretations of historical events, often written through the lenses of the victors. The exposure of "path dependencies" in narration has not been unique for military history but has also been discussed in political history under the catchword "whiggism" (Butterfield, 1931), and later—in the context of the social history paradigm of the 1960s—under the catchword the "social construction" of reality (Berger & Luckmann, 1966). Following today's dominant idea of the cultural turn, in this chapter I would like to focus on cultural constructions of realities—and even of cultural constructions of social constructions. In doing so, my notion of the cultural is understood in the broad sense, as we find it in the Anglo-Saxon discussion, and not in the more particular meaning (at least in the tradition) of French or of German. Even the notion of culture is culturally biased.

The social sciences tried and try to make sense of the world that is considered to be social (mostly as opposed to the natural world, for instance). They summarize and aggregate individual phenomena and combine them in social theories or theories of social change(s). Marxism as an economic and historical theory of the social and of social change is only one (but prominent) example of a social science, and it makes particularly clear what it means to summarize individual phenomena in one social theory. As a child of the 19th century, the social sciences were stuck with national—or, as I will argue later—cultural idiosyncrasies that were extrapolated to the whole world. For a French intellectual around 1900, for example, it was just not conceivable how the Germans organized their political life and how they defined the role of the scholars within this political life. The difficult career of the idea of the "intellectual"—a French slogan arising in the Dreyfus Affair—in Germany shows not only the fundamental differences but also the hegemonic aspirations (see, for instance, Bering, 2010) in the same way as the famous distinction made by the German sociologist Sombart (1915) between the heroic people (the Germans) and the mercantile people (the English).

My general concerns in this chapter are generalizations (or standardizations) of nationally, respectively, culturally biased interpretations of phenomena that are or were called "social." In his book *Atlantic Crossings*, Daniel Rodgers (1998) points out that in that time "an entire vocabulary sprang up around the term 'social'—'social economics,' 'social politics,' the 'social problem,' the 'social question'" (p. 51). Rodgers interprets this upspring as "testimony to the growing consciousness of the socially constructed nature of market capitalism" (p. 51). According to Rodgers, this consciousness is transnational and transcultural, for on "both sides of the Atlantic a new world of coal and iron, factory towns and sprawling urban agglomerations, accumulated capital, massed wage labor" (p. 44) arose, and interpretations were accordingly not cultural or national but formulated in "the world between" (p. 5) the United States and the individual European nation-states.

Rodgers (1998) is certainly right that the notion of the "social," as it is more or less understood today, had a boom toward the end of the 19th century in different languages. It was an umbrella term used to make sense of fundamental transformations (or events that are being understood as fundamental) that caused uncertainty and fears. Similar fundamentally threatening events such as the Black Death in the 14th century, the devastating agricultural effects of the Little Ice Age between 1560 and 1700, or the implications of the Thirty Years' War (1618–1648) had not led to interpretations in the name of the "social" as was the case toward the end of the 19th century, although helplessness, despair, and impoverishment had been part of the earlier devastating events, too. The "social" had become intellectually imaginable (distinguishable from the political state, for instance) only toward the end of the 18th century, and it is from the beginning of the 19th century that the "social" has begun to be explored academically. It is no coincidence that most of the histories of sociology identify Auguste Comte (1798–1857), Karl Marx (1818–1883), and Herbert Spencer (1820–1903) as the ancestors of the academic discipline and Lester Frank Ward (1841–1913), William Graham Sumner (1840–1910), Ferdinand Tönnies (1856–1836), Emile Durkheim (1858–1917), Georg Simmel (1858–1918), and Max Weber (1864–1920) as the fathers.

However, the emergence of the "social" as a distinguishable category occurred most prominently in the context and aftermath of American independence and the French Revolution. In this connection, the "social" bore different meanings according to the different revolutionary and counterrevolutionary theories and visions of the political life: The "social" was obviously culturally biased, but it mostly showed up in a generalized or globalized "theory". To the contemporaries and their followers, the French Revolution was not a historical event limited to the borders of France but an event with global consequences. I will demonstrate this cultural construction of the "social" with its temptation to globalization, taking the example of the "social question" and the academic reaction toward the "social question," especially in connection with sociology and the educational sciences. I will do this in four steps. First, I will detect the religious constructions of the "social question" and then I will address the question of its cultural construction. In a third step, I will interpret the emergence of the social sciences and sociology as intellectual reactions toward these cultural constructions in order to identify the different educational responses to these cultural-sociological constructions of the "social question." In the final section, I summarize my thesis on the background of the results of the four first parts.

The Social Question and the Different Denominations

The "social question" is an umbrella term designed to summarize different reactions toward historical events in the 19th century that were identified as very fundamental and unsettling. As a rule, the consequences of the industrialization process, urbanization, the rise of the "proletariat" or "fourth estate," and its living conditions were identified as the "social question," with some emphasis on the consequences of the latter that were interpreted as morally deviant: neglect, alcohol (abuse), gambling, prostitution, teen pregnancy, adultery, and crime. Lay and academic specialists were ready to interpret these conditions, their causes, and the remedies. Often, the difference between the laypersons and the academics was the institutional support by the research universities for the latter, standardizing to a certain degree the way of dealing with social phenomena.[3]

The reactions were manifold, settled on different levels of abstractions—from Christian neighborhood charity to all-encompassing Marxist theories about history and the future—and they of course often disagreed with each other. Looking back at the debates, it seems that the biggest threat to most of the concerned appeared to be Marxism and socialism and not the "social question" itself. Karl Marx and Friedrich Engels had degraded the early Socialists such as Gracchus Babeuf, Pierre-Joseph Proudhon, or Charles Fourier to "Critical Utopian Socialists" by accusing them of rejecting "all political, and especially all revolutionary, action; they wish to attain their ends by peaceful means, and endeavor, by small experiments, necessarily doomed to failure, and by the force of example, to pave the way for the new social Gospel" (Marx & Engels, 1967, p. 255). "Real" socialism was meant to be "scientific" (as opposed to utopian) and thus to be labeled as communism, heading for a political and economical revolution.

Among those who felt obliged to react were the Christian associations and institutions, and they found themselves in an awkward situation. On the one hand, they could not accept the way many of the "proletariat" conducted their lives and recognized that the living conditions were complicit in these lives. On the other hand, they seemed to fear more the anti-Christian doctrine of the Socialists and Communists than the endangered souls of the industrial workers. And at any rate, they recognized in the perceived social crisis a chance to place themselves on the cultural agenda anew. The Catholic Church did this in a very different way than did the Lutherans in Germany and the latter in a different way than did the Calvinist culture in the United States.

The Catholic Church reacted rather late on an official basis. It was Leo XIII (1810–1903) who wrote an encyclical called "Rerum Novarum" ("Of New Things") in 1891 (Pope Leo XIII, 1891). It is no coincidence that in it, the Pope attacked the "new ideas" that had first led to the French Revolution and then to the unbalanced distribution of wealth and consequently to the moral decline of the industrial workers. However, before presenting a solution, Leo XIII attacked socialism[4] by defending private property as legitimate. According to "Rerum Novarum," the solution to the "social question" is not (more) state, but (more) religion, and religion means the Catholic Church: "It is We who are the chief guardian of religion and the chief dispenser of what pertains to the Church" (§ 16). With the words of Saint Thomas, Leo XIII reminds the rich of their religious/moral—not judicial!—duty to share: "Of that which remaineth, give alms," and in addition the poor are reminded: "As for those who possess not the gifts of fortune, they are taught by the Church that in God's sight poverty is no disgrace, and that there is nothing to be ashamed of in earning their bread by labor." The solution to the "social question" is the increased power of the Catholic Church, fostering more solidarity between the classes by influencing the personal dispositions of the individual members of the Holy Mother Church.

In the context of the German evangelical tradition, the reactions to the "social question" were quite different—and earlier than those of the Catholic Church. Especially in the Pietist neorevivalism (after 1810), the general idea was to interpret the changing living conditions as a chance for an *inner* mission of the allegedly endangered. The notion of the "inner" is in analogy to the "outer" mission—the mission of the pagans and Jews—and focuses on the peculiar meaning of the Lutheran understanding of the inward soul as the place of individual salvation. It was meant to summarize the whole program of evangelical salvation—namely, the "total work of the love resulting from the faith in Jesus Christ in order to renew inward and external those masses of Christendom, who are victims of the power and reign of the decay stemming from the sin directly or indirectly" (Wichern, 1849/1979, p. 151, freely translated here). Whereas the Catholic Church headed for more solidarity and thus for some distribution of wealth by means of the church, the Lutheran church emphasized interpersonal love affecting the inward soul. In accordance with Luther's political philosophy, the state had to be protected from upheaval, and the whole society—not only the poor!—had to be evangelized. In parallel with the national church, the "Inner Mission" targeted more dissemination of the Holy Bible, and it founded countless organizations to foster abstinence, to safeguard the children of working poor parents, to care for women in childbed, and to teach the Gospel in Sunday schools.

The Lutherans' inexplicit social theory was rooted in Luther's relatively unpolitical social theory expressed in the dualistic, two-kingdom doctrine, according to which in the one kingdom, Christ rules through word and sacrament, mercy and forgiveness are practiced, and there are no differences among people. In the other kingdom, in contrast, the Emperor reigns with the sword; there is no mercy and no equality. But the worldly kingdom still has a purpose: in that, namely, the prince curbs the evil in men—even if through violence, peace is established, and thus conditions are created for proclaiming the Gospel (Luther, 1523/1983, pp. 41ff.). Logically, ideas like political participation, which are characteristic of the Baptist church and Congregationalism, are foreign to Lutheranism,[5] and therefore a different reaction can be found in the congregational local culture of the United States of America. In a unique microhistorical story, Johnston (1978/2004) described how, after the opening of the Erie Canal in 1821, the economic growth of Rochester started to separate first labor but then also the social spheres of the people involved; this is described as a process of estrangement bemoaned by the middle class initiating this estrangement (pp. 38, 40–42). Subsequently, the moral influence of the proprietors on the employees sank (p. 42), and even more so when employees moved out of the family homes of their employers (p. 45) and when employers started to live in separate quarters (p. 48; see p. 53). This opened the door for separate modes of sociability, a bourgeois sociability and a labor-class sociability. Johnston described how working-class people started to live their own lives in their quitting time (p. 55), whereas the bourgeois middle-class people still felt called upon to control not only the job performance but also the social behavior of their employees (p. 61). Whatever would replace the lost social control, it was not going to come from the city government, for the middle classes were themselves divided into factions favoring social politics (p. 78). According to Johnston, it was this failure of the middle class to moralize the working men, the end of mutual exchange (and one-sided influence), that had drastic consequences, for it created an opening for a fiery preacher named Charles Grandison Finney (1792–1875) to initialize a fundamental evangelization of Rochester, a (Calvinist) cross-denominational process with great impacts on the Second Grand Awakening, leading to a massive increase of church membership at the local Methodist, Baptist, and Congregationalist churches in New England up to the Civil War. The crisis of the social dimension of the congregation was fundamental in Congregationalism. This was the world in which the parent generation of John Dewey, George Herbert Mead, and James Tufts—Mead and Tufts being sons of Protestant ministers—grew up.

The Social Question as Cultural Construction

The denominational patterns of reacting to the "social question" (and foremost in Europe toward socialism, too) did not exist in pure forms but were connected to national ideologies—which, in turn, were of course partly religious as well. In addition to, or maybe better alongside the Christian irritation about individual destinies, the social question was an expression conceptualizing severely disturbed myths about the proper organization of the conditions of living. Whereas Catholic nations were integrated in the imagined and institutional supranational realm of the Catholic Church with its center in Rome—this holds true even for France under the Concordat of 1801, in which Napoleon and the Pope had agreed on the privilege of the state in affairs of the Church[6]—the Protestant national churches, such as the Lutheran church in Germany, were much more interwoven with the national ambitions of the nation-states. The latter applies for Protestant denominations that were not backed up by the states (this is the case in the United States) but by the local community. The differences in the relation of the church to the state and its national identity imposes the use of the notion of "culture" in order to detect the national-religious backgrounds of the construction of the "social question."

An impressive and influential example of the construction of a national myth was written by the Lutheran theologian, German philosopher, and cultural historian Wilhelm Heinrich Riehl in 1854. In his account of the first half of the 19th century in Germany, Riehl (1854) starts with a depiction of the ideal social life in the Middle Ages, when the social classes are described as unequal by nature and having little mutual contact (p. 10). These social classes represented the contrast between the field and the forest, the latter being the true reservoir of the German culture. Whoever sought to destroy the remains of the German Middle Ages, Riehl notes, just had to destroy the forests (p. 29), and the history between the Middle Ages and the present is a history of decay. Riehl accuses technologies of travel like the railroad of having destroyed the organic conditions of social life: The quiet, unmixed idea of social peaceableness in the respective social "classes" as core element of Luther's "political" ideology became endangered through the opportunities of mutual exchange and precarious models of life that had become visible. The advent of the railroad is interpreted as having led to a centralization of the nation, ruining the small cities and accumulating power in the big cities (pp. 44–46). Whereas away from the routes of transportation, there is "dead silence and desolation," the big cities grow and create monetarism, and the proletariat soaks up silly ideas of the natural equity of human beings; the artificial new age generally seduces people to democracy (pp. 56–60). Capitalism, urbanism, natural law theories, the working class, and democracy are seen to be the symptoms of the decay of the German nation that is being understood as rural, selfless, and unequal but united, happy, and just. In the frame of this national ideology of identity, the interpretation of the social question had to turn out different than in other national ideologies, for instance in the French.

In contrast to Germany, in the dominant French ideology of the 19th century, natural right theories, a centralized state, and democracy were not swear words except in part for some monarchists, but not for the socialists or the republicans. Occupied by political upheavals until the creation of the Third Republic in 1871 (after the defeat against the Germans) and "blessed" with a slower industrial growth than England and (later) Germany, questions of (organic) unity never were discussed in the same way as they were in Germany. The questions of the relation between the classes and the destiny of the poorer classes were discussed in the normative horizon of the motto of the French Revolution, liberty, equality, and fraternity,[7] established and institutionalized foremost in the Third Republic after 1871 under the reign of what are called the moderate republicans. Any social phenomenon that disturbed the high ideals of liberty, equality, and fraternity was interpreted as a "social question."

Within this ideological context in France, the "social question" turned out to be very different from in Germany. The 20 novels encompassing the series of the "Rougon-Macquart"[8] by Emile Zola (1840–1902) describe with bitter irony the social corruption on the higher and lower levels of society. The eponymous heroine of the novel *Nana* (1879/1880), for instance, is the daughter of a washerwoman and an alcoholic father. Nana is intellectually and manually talentless but sexually very attractive, so that after some years of prostitution on the street, she exerts tremendous power over ministers, aristocrats, civil servants, and journalists and accepts valuable presents and the like. She seeks acceptance from the higher classes until she recognizes that it was their sexual lusts that led them to descend temporarily to the lower states rather than to accept Nana as equal to their status. An affair with a rich banker allows her to escape her tragic situation until she is confronted with her former lovers. She escapes into a lesbian relationship and ends up where she has started, as a prostitute working on the streets of Paris. All three ideals of the French Revolution—liberty, equality, and fraternity—are violated to a large degree.

If Riehl is suitable to identify the cultural construction of the "social question" for Germany and Emile Zola for France, then William T. Stead (author of *If Christ Came to Chicago,* 1894), son of a Congregational minister, and with him the Social Gospel movement, might be appropriate to identify the cultural construction of the "social question" in the United States. This movement was carried by the Protestant middle class (hardly any Lutherans) and led by Calvinist ministers; it addressed poverty, alcoholism, crime, ethnic conflicts, questions of hygiene, and educational questions. In contrast to the German (Lutheran) model, the Social Gospelists sought a noninstitutional Christianity and accused appearances of having caused the problems. One of the founders of this movement, Congregational minister Josiah Strong, identified the perils of America as "immigration," "Romanism" (Catholicism), "Mormonism," "intemperance," "socialism," and "wealth" (Strong, 1885). All of these factors were seen to endanger the American Protestant dream of democratic local control of affairs. This dream, rooted in the vision of "the city upon the hill" and the "errand in the wilderness," fulfilling the role of New Israel, included the educational idea of John Calvin's perception of "curriculum vitae" as an educational path toward the linking of rationality and morality of the future member of the congregation (Popkewitz, 2008, p. 47).

The Social Gospelists were alarmed. Another Congregational minister and leader of the Social Gospel movement, George Davis Herron, expressed this concern by calling America provocatively undemocratic:

> We Americans are not a democratic people. We do not select the representatives we elect; we do not make our own laws; we do not govern ourselves. Our political parties are controlled by private, close political corporations that exist as parasites upon the body politic, giving us the most corrupting and humiliating despotisms in political history, and tending to destroy all political faith in righteousness.
>
> *(Herron, 1895, p. 76)*

This anticapitalist republican critique finds fertile ground in the ideal of liberal reformed Protestantism, according to which social, religious, and democratic life are fundamentally identical, as an expression of the common interests of men. Through this, institutions become if not superfluous certainly secondary:

> The political realization [of Christianity] will be a pure democracy. Christianity can realize itself in a social order only through democracy, and

democracy can realize itself only through the social forces of Christianity. A pure social democracy is the political fulfillment of Christianity; . . . It is the historical and providential idea that God shall lead the people by his Spirit of right as his sons, governing them inspirationally rather than institutionally.

(p. 74)

Whereas Riehl's "social question" was derived from the national ideology of organic unity and Emile Zola's "social question" from the national ideology of the French Revolution, the "social question" in the United States emerged against the background of the national ideology of a democratic republic. All of them arose from religious ideas of salvation—but from different ones.

The Emergence of Sociology and the Social Sciences as Intellectual Reaction and Construction

It is known that young Emile Durkheim (1858–1917) was impressed by the novels of Emile Zola and Victor Hugo (Korte, 2008, p. 67). In his study of German politics and policies, Durkheim developed a moral doctrine based on sociological investigations, and he sought to implement this moral doctrine in the educational system, foremost in teacher education. This moral doctrine was elaborated in one of his central sociological studies, *The Division of Labor in Society*, published in 1893[9] (Durkheim, 1984), in which Durkheim defined the division of labor and specialization as expressions of modern societies. Durkheim did not assess morally the fact of these modern social conditions but rather asked about their particular "problems." He pointed out that modern societies with their extensive divisions of labor require different processes for the individual personality to acquire social solidarity and common consciousness than primordial societies do. In contrast to his German contemporary colleague in sociology, Ferdinand Tönnies, Durkheim did not assign moral value to the primordial societies (Tönnies, 1991: *Gemeinschaft*) and moral decay to modern societies (Tönnies, 1991: *Gesellschaft*) but understood the rational functioning of the divisions of labor as moral. If modern society with the division of labor lacks morality, it is only because the new "morality we require is only in the process of taking shape" (Durkheim, 1984, p. 340). Solidarity arises and leads to common consciousness when the division is not only distributed but distributed according to the individuals' natural talents (p. 311).

At the time Durkheim published his major theoretical foundations of (his) modern sociology, Ferdinand Tönnies (1855–1936), mentioned earlier, had already published the book *Gemeinschaft und Gesellschaft* (1887).[10] In accordance with the German perceptions dominant at the time, Tönnies assessed the social developments in principle as decay induced by trade, capitalism, and the rise of the metropolis. However—similar to Riehl—he praised the primordial "organic" communities as an associate form of affective proximity of its members, of their close ties and shared values, he criticizes the modern "mechanic" conditions of life as alienated, selfish, and steered by outer events. "Two eras are opposed to each other in the cultural developments," Tönnies wrote in his conclusions, "an era of society follows an era of community. The latter is characterized by the social will as harmony, convention, and religion, the former by the social will as convention, politics, and public opinion" (Tönnies, 1887/1991, p. 215, freely translated here).

Although there are some differences between Tönnies's position and that of other early German sociologists such as Georg Simmel or Max Weber, they all stuck to the normative frame of the German cultural pessimism, according to which modernity—industrialization and its consequences—was something threatening or at least ambivalent for the German Nation. Their American colleagues shared moral concerns about the developments, too, but they were optimistic or, in the words of some of the early sociologists, "melioristic," based on reformed Protestant promises of erecting the city upon the hill. Hinkle and Hinkle (1954) noticed already in the early 1950s that before 1920, almost all of the American sociologists came from rural and devoted Protestant circles; Lester F. Ward's grandfather had been a clergyman, and Franklin H. Giddings's father was a Congregational minister, William I. Thomas's father was a Methodist minister, and George E. Vincent's father was a Methodist bishop; William G. Sumner had himself been an Episcopalian minister, Albion W. Small had graduated in Baptist theology, Edward C. Hayes had been a Baptist minister, James P. Lichtenberger had been minister in the (Congregational) Christian Church of the Disciples of Christ, and John L. Gillin had been a minister with the Church of the Brethren.

This religious dominancy is not surprising, for in contrast to France and Germany, the American research universities did not see a contradiction between religion—that is, reformed Protestantism—and academic research. This becomes clear in the words of the founding president of the model of a modern American university, Daniel Coit Gilman of Johns Hopkins University in Baltimore, who stated in 1886: "American universities should be more than theistic; they may and should be avowedly Christian—not in a narrow or sectarian sense—but in the broad, open and inspiring sense of the Gospels" (Gilman, as cited in Hart, 1992, p. 107). It is a matter of the Gospel, the evangel, that is, the teaching of salvation in Jesus's words on the coming of the kingdom of God, but not with the intention to make the teachings the subject of discussion in theology or the science of religion. The teachings of salvation are seen as the prerequisite to thinking and acting—as the fertile ground, so to speak. Gilman was not singular at all but representative, if we look at the work of William Rainey Harper, a Baptist minister and founding president of the University of Chicago, in which American sociology had its strongest beginnings. Harper (1904) claimed that the United States of America had been assigned a world mission and that this mission had deep educational consequences: "If, now, our faith is sure that there has been committed to us this great mission, shall we not purify ourselves?" (p. 180). Harper's (1904) program of purification involved the fight against both immorality and ignorance:

> The ideal purification is a purification from vice and immorality, from sin of every kind and from impurity; but it is more—it is a purification (I use the word advisedly) from ignorance and prejudice, from narrowness of every kind, and from intellectual dishonesty. What is needed? The gospel and education.
>
> *(p. 180)*

Within this broad cultural and institutional backup, the early sociologists founded the American Sociological Society, and at their first meeting they discussed "Points of Agreement among Sociologists." They agreed on several points: first, that sociology wants to "discover and to formulate the laws of those processes in human association which differ, either in degree or in kind, from processes that occur in antecedent orders in the scale of evolution" (Small, 1907, p. 634). They agreed, second, that social change is to be interpreted as social evolution and thus as progress leading to a better social order. This progress is, third, to be accelerated by specific interferences based on knowledge of the sociological laws, and fourth, social conduct and society are based upon individual conduct and to be deducted from it (Small, 1907, p. 634). American sociology was a cooperative effort devoted to strengthening the social progress that was detected in the process of industrialization, with the aim to prevent unworthy life conditions of the democratic Protestant republic.

Theorizing the Ascertained Need for Action: Educational Theory

Around 1900, sociology and its making sense of the social world and of social change was not the same in France, Germany, and the United States, and the core object of it—industrialization and its consequences, foremost the "social question"—was not the same, either. It is not surprising, then, that the ideas about possible needs for social intervention or social interaction were not the same, either. Certainly, in all of the nation-states mentioned, particular activities emerged—primarily initiated and executed by women—that can be summarized under the notions of "social work," "*travail social*," or "*Sozialarbeit*," and in all of them one finds, for example, more or less successful, local adaptations of the first settlement in London, Toynbee Hall.[11] Whatever the local or cultural adaptations looked like, the question of how these activities were theoretically contextualized and legitimized in relation to education reveals significant cultural differences. In contrast to the practical activities, this work of theorizing was done mostly by men.[12]

In France, "*travail social*" had been a battlefield among socialists, feminists, Catholics, and republicans. Some of the legitimation of social work derived from

Durkheim's idea of solidarity in the context of a society characterized by a high division of labor; other interest groups tried to harmonize the traditional social commitment of the Catholic Church with the idea of the Republic (Rater-Garcette, 1996). Although educational practices were part of the social activities, educational questions regarding the "social question" were discussed in the context of sociology. Durkheim, who had a chair for education and sociology and who was involved in the training of secondary school teachers, developed an educational theory in accordance with his sociology. Whereas his sociological theory of the division of labor had explained the need for a new form of solidarity, Durkheim's educational theory focused on the idea of socialization based on (rational) insights into the modern conditions of life. Accordingly, moral education is not traditional religious education, for in modern societies it is the individual human being that is "the sacred thing par excellence" (Durkheim, 1992, p. 91, freely translated here). In contrast to the German and the American conception in response to the construction of the "social question," Durkheim focuses solely on the institution of the modern school and the proper training of its actors.[13] Since Durkheim does not interpret the modern conditions of life as alienation, moral education is based on the rational understanding of the condition of modern life and the acceptance of its pertinent moral rules. The place for this moral socialization is the laical school with its emphasis on rational artifacts of both the natural sciences and history. It is no coincidence that one of Durkheim's lectures, "The Evolution of Educational Thought," addressed "the formation and development of secondary education in France," as the subtitle states (Durkheim, 1938).[14]

In Germany, the early sociologists hardly addressed any question of social activities such as "*travail social.*" Max Weber stayed with his idea that any academic discipline should be value free, Georg Simmel did not deal with practical questions at all, and Tönnies (1887/1991) was simply skeptical as to whether "more knowledge and education by themselves can make people friendlier, less selfish, and more frugal" (p. 214, freely translated here); according to Tönnies, it would have to be the state to "destroy" society; however, "the success of such attempts would be extremely unlikely" (p. 214). However, Germany stands as much in the Protestant tradition of educationalizing social problems as does the United States (Tröhler, 2011a). Naturally, in the German context of the idealistic (and knowledge-skeptic) *Bildungs* theory, educational solutions had to turn out very different from the knowledge-based and rather optimistic ones of Durkheim. In the middle of the 19th century, a new notion was created, *Sozialpädagogik*, "social education," or "*éducation sociale*," and it was used in the context of the German nation at risk.

From its emergence until the Great War, *Sozialpädagogik* addressed educational questions with regard to the German nation. It was constructed as dualistically opposed to the notion of "individual education," which was blamed as having led to selfishness on the part of Germans. Social and national fragmentation was seen as the consequence of this educational practice, destroying the communitarian foundation of the German nation. According to Tönnies and others, the dualistic opposition between individual and social was a characteristic of modernity and could be fought only by a communitarian education called *Sozialpädagogik*. *Sozialpädagogik* is education both by a community and for a community; however, the aim is not limited to socialization in the values of a particular community but heads instead toward the "idea of community." Paul Natorp, a neo-Kantian philosopher, educationalist, and the son of a Lutheran minister, declared:

> Community exists only in the consciousness of those belonging to the community. But how does it exist in it? Not as consciousness of something that simply exists, but of something that ought to be; not as consciousness of a given fact, but of something that is becoming and is developing; not as simple mechanic result of given forces but as a duty, as an infinite duty.
>
> *(Natorp, 1907, p. 607, freely translated here)*

Naturally, school education and training in modern sciences were not in the middle of this idea of community, and neither was the idea of "consciousness" as expression of rationality; community remained sometimes explicitly, mostly inexplicitly, the (idea of the) German nation (see, for instance, Geppert, 1900, p. 89).[15]

The differences between this and the discussion in the United States could not be any bigger, and after having taken Durkheim for France and Natorp for Germany, John Dewey seems to be equally appropriate to examine the educational implication of the United States's reaction to the "social question." Dewey was well aware of the German critique of democracy: fragmentation on the one hand, dull masses on the other. He suggested something that was inconceivable for the Germans—namely, that "organism" should be combined with "democracy": "If, however, society be truly described as organic [and not as a mere mass], the citizen is a member of the organism, and, just in proportion to the perfection of the organism, has concentrated within himself its intelligence and will" (Dewey, 1888/1969, p. 235). Dewey distances himself from the French solution—according to its natural law theory, sovereignty is natural, that is, "pre-political"—and from the "German theory," that is, giving the idea of the "organic conception . . . a physiological sense" (pp. 235f.). In contrast, the democratic idea of sovereignty in the United States is built on the fact that "every citizen is a sovereign" based on the idea that "every man is a priest of God" (p. 237).

It is obvious that Dewey and most of the other American scholars did not condemn the industrial developments per se. To him, these developments are in the background of a "social progress" that needs—similar to the idea of Durkheim—adaptation in the educational setting (Dewey, 1900/1976, pp. 5f.). To Dewey, it is clear that "industry and division of labor have practically eliminated household and neighborhood occupations—at least for educational purposes" (p. 8). But because it is "useless to bemoan the departure of the good old days," the educational system has to adapt to the new circumstances. The new virtues are "increase in toleration, in breadth of social judgment, the larger acquaintance with human nature, the sharpened alertness in reading signs of character and interpreting social situations, greater accuracy of adaptation to differing personalities, contact with greater commercial activities" (pp. 8f.).

Dewey (1900/1976) goes on to suggest (and this is essentially different from Durkheim)[16] that "object-lessons" could not substitute for actual acquaintance with real things and that (and this is essentially different from Natorp) "household arts—sewing and cooking" (p. 9) should be introduced into the curriculum. To Dewey, these interdisciplinary learning activities are equivalent to the modern social realities because of their "social significance," their enhancement of creativity and cooperation: "Where the school work consists in simply learning lessons, mutual assistance, instead of being the most natural form of cooperation and association, becomes a clandestine effort to relieve one's neighbor of his proper duties" (p. 11). It is in this context that Dewey wanted the modern school—the school intelligently adapted to the requirements of the modern society—to be a "miniature community, an embryonic society" (p. 12), ignoring the well-known difference Tönnies had emphasized between community and society and claiming that only educational practices based on this idea would generate "a spirit of social cooperation and community life" (p. 11) as the basis of (his congregational idea of) democracy (Tröhler, 2011c).

The Temptations of the Social and Educational Sciences

Of course, Durkheim was not the only sociologist in France, and there were differing educational theories. And Natorp was, of course, not undisputed, and during the Weimar Republic new ideas of *Sozialpädagogik*—focusing less on the Nation and more on the *Volk*—arose. And Dewey did not adhere to his manual training idea forever, quite apart from the fact that there were alternative ideas about education and social order (see Tröhler, Schlag, & Osterwalder, 2010). However, they were all dominant thinkers in their places, and scholars trying to define alternatives to these dominant figures had to argue against them.[17] They were dominant in their spheres, and that is one part of the thesis I wanted to highlight, because they represented culturally shared, that is, taken-for-granted assumptions, about the child, the citizen, and ideas of social justice, being denominationally influenced and different in the individual nations with consequences on ideas and the organization of education (Tröhler, Popkewitz, & Labaree, 2011). This part is the comparative part of the thesis, but it has a historical part, too. And this brings me back to the beginning.

The social and educational sciences were part of the national and nationalistic ambitions of their time. They tried to make sense of the social developments, or maybe better of the cultural constructions of the social developments. The obvious congruence among educational theories, sociologies, and popular voices is no coincidence but rather a sign of how little academic research was able to emancipate itself from national ideologies. This holds true even for scholars who were aware of national differences, such as Durkheim or Dewey. Regardless of their comparative competencies, they had little doubt that their respective cultural constructions—their views—were appropriate and generalizable. Durkheim and many other French scholars had little doubt about both the uniqueness and the model function of the French Revolution, the Germans had no doubts about the idea of the German nation as superior to any other, and the Americans felt that their culture should be a model for the whole world. Exceptionalism was everywhere—a paradox situation, indeed, and the social and educational (and the historical) rationalizations (theories) were everywhere, too. Whereas the Germans transformed by the "social question" the "endangered" nation-state to the nation-as-community, Durkheim tried to rationalize the interactions of the free, equal, and fraternal citizen to its cocitizens, and Dewey emphasized the educational community in order to integrate children from immigrant families and different social classes in order to guarantee the development of skills of mutuality and social exchange in order to make the congregational idea survivable. Again, the mutual insults among the intellectuals in the context of the Great War would otherwise not be explainable.

Sociologists have extrapolated their culturally constructed view of the social sphere and of social change to a global level, and against this background it is not surprising that many of today's theories on globalization are written by sociologists.[18] The temptation to make sense of social developments by assembling and clustering events and phenomena in one story or narration implies the acceptance of neglecting cultural differences. Thus, today's popular slogans "globalization," "standardization," and "unification" are at least as much constructions of the social sciences as they are "real" results of a global economy or international organizations such as the World Bank or the OECD. To be part of the generalized and globalized world may improve the cultural acceptance of the social sciences in the short term, but sustainability may not be expected if the major paradigm of intellectual work is still rooted in the ideology of national exceptionalism and global grandeur.

For the social sciences, the proper answer to perceptions of globalization are not theories of globalization and historical accounts that, for instance, try to construct a history of globalization starting at a time around 1500 (see Tröhler, 2011d) but a historical and comparative safeguard reflecting the initial perceptions. Social reality—the object of the social sciences—is much more plural and interesting than the products of academic attempts that are conducted under the pressure of national legitimation and that obviously have not sufficiently managed to become emancipated from them. One way to do so is to question the impact of the sociological paradigms on the construction of reality, and that means accepting the question of the legitimacy of the social sciences and their ideological backgrounds a hundred years after their emergence. The consequences will most probably not be the liquidation of the social sciences but probably better theoretical quality. That this endeavor will have to be historical and international is understood. This present book is, if not the beginning, a good contribution to it.

Notes

1. The question of whether education or history belongs to the social sciences or to other clusters of sciences such as the humanities is of no greater importance for the argument in this article.
2. It is noteworthy that the idea of academic freedom in the Humboldtian sense had already been realized in England before Humboldt but was only realized in the Third Republic of France, that is, after 1871. The Napoleonic model of research and teaching foresaw a central, governmental steering with regard to contents and individual careers. Strictly speaking, France after the French Revolution no longer had universities anymore but instead autonomous faculties and the extremely elitist institutions of the *École normale supérieure*; see Karady (1986a, 1986b).
3. Bledstein (1976) emphasized that the American "professionalism" as social phenomenon in the all-encompassing ideology of equity was the solution to legitimize a meritocratic social order. Professionalism became the mainstay of social stratification, and the instrument of this culture was modern science, including the social sciences. For a less social than political approach, see Ross (1991).
4. "It must be first of all recognized that the condition of things inherent in human affairs must be borne with, for it is impossible to reduce civil society to one dead level. Socialists may in that intent do their utmost, but all striving against nature is in vain."
5. Luther's radical separation of the religious from the worldly dimension led, in the face of the primacy of religiosity, to political indifference. On this background, Luther's rancor against Zwingli—who can be considered one of the political sources of American Protestantism—becomes understandable. Zwingli's intention to work toward worldly—that is, political and social—reform led Luther to make the accusation that Zwingli's republicanism presumed to "scorn everyone, including the princes and potentates." Luther defended the system of state sovereigns and gave republicanism no chances: "It is also said that the Swiss have in the past killed their lords and in this way won their freedom . . . up to now the Swiss have paid in blood for this dearly and are still paying dearly; how this will end is easy to imagine . . . I do not see any type of government to be as enduring as the one in which authorities are esteemed and venerated" (Luther, as cited in Farner, 1931, pp. 18–21, freely translated here). For the whole discussion among Lutheranism, American Calvinism, and Swiss Protestantism, see Tröhler (2011b).
6. This privilege was valid all through the 19th century. In 1905, the new left government of France radicalized this Concordat unilaterally and separated the state and the church fundamentally.
7. Fraternity is a supplement of the 19th century. During the French Revolution, the two other notions, liberty and equality, were often alone or accompanied by a third term such as *friendship, charity, sincerity,* or *union.* In any case, the difficult balance among the three ideals led to different interpretations during the 19th century (Ozouf, 1997, pp. 586ff.).
8. The subtitle of the series is "The Natural and Social History of a Family Under the Second Empire." There is little doubt, however, that the novels, written between 1871 and 1893, address the time of the Third Republic, too.
9. A first English translation was published in 1964 and a first German translation in 1977.
10. A first French translation was published in 1944 and a first English translation in 1955.
11. The founder of the settlement movement (Toynbee Hall, 1884) in London, Samuel Augustus Barnett, was an Anglican minister. The idea was implemented in Paris by the devoted Catholic Mary Gahéry in 1894, who called the settlement a "social house" (*maison sociale*; Guerrand & Rupp, 1978). The most famous of the settlements was Hull House in Chicago, founded in 1889 by the devoted Congregationalist Jane Addams. The affinity of the settlement to the idea of the congregation seems to be one of the reasons for the great success of the settlement in the United States; the "Handbook of

Settlements" published in 1911 came to 413 settlements in the United States (Woods & Kennedy, 1911). In contrast, the idea of the settlement had much more trouble becoming established in Germany; see, for instance, Picht (1913).

12. The abovementioned Jane Addams is an exception (see, for example, Addams, 1909, and, almost forgotten today). Mary Richmond's approach to social work in *Social Diagnosis* (Richmond, 1917) was taken up by the German feminist and social worker Alice Salomon (Salomon, 1926). Salomon focused less on theory than on the training of female social workers (see, for example, Salomon, 1908).

13. Durkheim came from a Jewish family; his father was a rabbi. It might well be that his sympathy with the rational conception of the French Republic was underpinned by the fact that the Jews in Europe had always been more or less excluded from dominant positions within society and thus felt more obliged to ideas of the natural law theory that were in the background of the French Revolution, assuming a presocial individual as the starting point of a social-contract theory.

14. A German and an English translation were first published in 1977.

15. This interconnection between Germany and *Sozialpädagogik* is extremely sustainable. The first (and very sustainable) systematization of *Sozialpädagogik* after World War II based its arguments largely on the descent theory of the abovementioned Riehl (Mollenhauer, 1959). And in one of the recent histories of *Sozialpädagogik*, the author says self-confidently: "Sozialpädagogik—not social work—is a specific German topic," because nowhere else has the dualistic "conceptual couple individual and community" been as dominant in the cultural spheres as in Germany (Reyer, 2002, p. 9, freely translated here).

16. For the reverse side, Durkheim's critique of pragmatism, see Osterwalder (2010).

17. I refer to these actors similarly to Popkewitz, who described them as "conceptional personae" in historical analyses (Popkewitz, 2010, p. 101).

18. There are, of course, exceptions; see Levine (1995).

References

Addams, J. (1909). *The spirit of the youth and the city street.* New York: Macmillan.

Berger, P. L., & Luckmann, T. (1966). *The social construction of reality: A treatise in the sociology of knowledge.* New York: Doubleday.

Bering, D. (2010). *Die Epoche der Intellektuellen 1898—2001; Geburt, Begriff, Grabmal.* Berlin: Berlin University Press.

Bledstein, B. J. (1976). *The culture of professionalism: The middle class and the development of higher education in America.* New York: W. W. Norton and Company.

Butterfield, H. (1931). *The Whig interpretation of history.* London: G. Bell and Sons.

Dewey, J. (1969). The ethics of democracy. In J. A. Boydston (Ed.), *John Dewey: The early works, Vol. 1* (pp. 226–249). Carbondale: Southern Illinois University Press. (Original date of publication 1888)

Dewey, J. (1976). The school and social progress. In J. A. Boydston (Ed.), *John Dewey: The middle works, Vol. 1* (pp. 5–20). Carbondale: Southern Illinois University Press. (Original date of publication 1900)

Durkheim, E. (1938). *Evolution pédagogique en France.* Paris: Alcan.

Durkheim, E. (1984). *The division of labor in society.* New York: Free Press. (Original work published in French 1893)

Durkheim, E. (1992): *L'éducation morale.* P. Fauconnet (Ed.). Paris: PUF. (Original work published 1925, based on lectures held in 1899)

Farner, O. (1931). *Das Zwinglibild Luthers.* Tübingen, Germany: Mohr.

Flasch, K. (2000). *Die geistige Mobilmachung. Die deutschen Intellektuellen und der Erste Weltkrieg.* Berlin: Alexander Fest Verlag.

Geppert, O. R. (1900): Individual- oder Socialpädagogik? (Schluss). *Pädagogische Reform, 24,* 89–91.

Guerrand, R.-H., & Rupp, M.-A. (1978). *Brève histoire du service social en France, 1896–1976.* Toulouse, France: Edouard Privat.

Hanna, M. (1996). *The mobilization of intellect: French scholars and writers during the Great War.* Cambridge, MA: Harvard University Press.

Harper, W. R. (1904). America as a missionary field. In W. R. Harper, *Religion and the higher life: Talks to students* (pp. 173–184). Chicago: University of Chicago Press.

Hart, D. G. (1992). Faith and learning in the age of the university: The academic ministry of Daniel Coit Gilman. In G. M. Marsden & B. J. Longfield (Eds.), *The secularization of the academy* (pp. 107–145). New York: Oxford University Press.

Herron, G. D. (1895). The Christian state: The social realization of democracy. In G. D. Herron, *The Christian state: A political vision of Christ* (pp. 45–72). New York: Thomas Y. Crowell.

Hinkle, R. C., & Hinkle, G. (1954). *The development of modern sociology: Its nature, growth in the United States.* New York: Random House.

Johnston, P. E. (1978). *A shopkeeper's millennium: Society and revivals in Rochester, New York, 1815–1837.* New York: Hill and Wang.

Karady, J. (1986a). De Napoléon à Duruy: les origins et la naissance de l'université contemporaire. In J. Verger (Ed.), *Histoires des Universités en France* (pp. 261–322). Toulouse, France: Bibliothèque historique Privat.

Karady, J. (1986b). Les Universités de la troisième république. In J. Verger (Ed.), *Histoires des Universités en France* (pp. 323–365). Toulouse, France: Bibliothèque historique Privat.

Korte, H. (2008). *Einführung in die Geschichte der Soziologie.* Wiesbaden, Germany: VS Verlag.

Levine, D. (1995). *Visions of the sociological tradition.* Chicago: University of Chicago Press.

Luther, M. (1983). Von weltlicher Oberkeit, wie weit man ihr Gehorsam schuldig sei. In H.-U. Delius (Ed.), *Martin Luther: Studienausgabe. Band 3* (pp. 31–71). Berlin: Evangelische Verlagsanstalt. (Original work published 1523)

Marx, K., & Engels, F. (1967). *The communist manifesto.* London: Penguin Classics. (Original work published in German 1848, first English translation 1888)

Mollenhauer, K. (1959). *Die Ursprünge der Sozialpädagogik in der industriellen Gesellschaft.* Weinheim, Germany: Beltz.

Natorp, P. (1907). Der Streit um den Begriff der Sozialpädagogik. *Die deutsche Schule; Zeitschrift für Erziehungswissenschaft, Bildungspolitik und pädagogische Praxis 11,* 601–622.

Osterwalder, F. (2010). Durkheim's criticism of pragmatism with respect to his educational concepts. In D. Tröhler, T. Schlag, & F. Osterwalder (Eds.), *Pragmatism and modernities* (pp. 123–143). Rotterdam, the Netherlands: Sense Publishers.

Ozouf, M. (1997). Liberté, égalité, fraternité. In P. Nora (Ed.), *Lieux de Mémoire, Tome III* (pp. 4353–5389). Paris: Gallimard.

Picht, W. (1913). *Toynbee Hall und die englische Settlementbewegung. Ein Beitrag zur Geschichte der sozialen Bewegung in England.* Tübingen, Germany: J. C. B. Mohr.

Pope Leo XIII. (1891). Rerum Novarum. Lettre encycliqe de notre très saint père Léon XIII. De la condition des ouvriers. Paris: Ch. Poussielgue. English version: www.vatican.va/holy_father/leo_xiii/encyclicals/documents/hf_l-xiii_enc_15051891_rerum-novarum_en.html

Popkewitz, T. S. (2008). *Cosmopolitanism and the age of school reform: Science, education, and making society by making the child.* New York: Routledge.

Popkewitz, T. S. (2010). The university as prophet, science as its messenger, and democracy as its revelation. John Dewey, University of Chicago President William Rainey Harper, and Colonel Francis Parker. In D. Tröhler, T. Schlag, & F. Osterwalder (Eds.), *Pragmatism and modernities* (pp. 99–121). Rotterdam, the Netherlands: Sense Publishers.

Rater-Carcette, C. (1996). *La professionalisation du travail social: Action sociale, syndicalisme, formation 1880–1920.* Paris: L'Harmattan.

Reyer, J. (2002). *Kleine Geschichte der Sozialpädagogik. Individuum und Gesellschaft in der Pädagogik der Moderne.* Baltmannsweiler, Germany: Schneider Verlag.

Richmond, M. E. (1917). *Social diagnosis.* New York: Free Press.

Riehl, W. H. (1854). *Land und Leute [Country and people].* Stuttgart, Germany: Cotta.

Rodgers, D. T. (1998). *Atlantic crossings: Social politics in a progressive age.* Cambridge, MA: Belknap Press of Harvard University Press.

Ross, D. (1991). *The origins of American social science.* Cambridge: Cambridge University Press.

Salomon, A. (1908). *Soziale Frauenbildung.* Leipzig: Teubner.

Salomon, A. (1926). *Soziale Diagnose.* Berlin: Carl Heymann.

Small, A. W. (1907). Points of agreement among sociologists. *American Journal of Sociology, 12,* 633–655.

Sombart, W. (1915). *Händler und Helden: Patriotische Besinnungen.* Munich: Duncker & Humblot.

Stead, W. T. (1894). *If Christ came to Chicago: A plea for the union of all who love the service of all who suffer.* Chicago: Laird & Lee, Publishers.

Strong, J. (1885). *Our country: Its possible future and its present crisis.* New York: Baker & Taylor.

Tönnies, F. (1991): *Gemeinschaft und Gesellschaft: Grundbegriffe der reinen Soziologie.* Darmstadt, Germany: Wissenschaftliche Buchgesellschaft. (Original work published 1887)

Tröhler, D. (2011a). The educationalization of the modern world: Progress, passion, and the Protestant promise of education. In D. Tröhler, *Languages of education: Protestant legacies, national identities, and global aspirations* (pp. 21–36). New York: Routledge.

Tröhler, D. (2011b). Protestant misunderstandings: Max Weber and the Protestant ethic in America. In D. Tröhler, *Languages of education: Protestant legacies, national identities, and global aspirations* (pp. 37–57). New York: Routledge.

Tröhler, D. (2011c). American culture, pragmatism, and the "Kingdom of God on Earth." In D. Tröhler, *Languages of education: Protestant legacies, national identities, and global aspirations* (pp. 98–112). New York: Routledge.

Tröhler, D. (2011d). Globalizing globalization: The Neo-Institutional concept of a world culture. In D. Tröhler, *Languages of education: Protestant legacies, national identities, and global aspirations* (pp. 181–193). New York: Routledge.

Tröhler, D., Popkewitz, T. S., & Labaree, F. (2011). *Schooling and the making of citizens in the long nineteenth century: Comparative visions.* New York: Routledge.

Tröhler, D., Schlag, T., & Osterwalder, F. (2010). *Pragmatism and modernities.* Rotterdam, the Netherlands: Sense Publishers.

Wallace, S. (1988). *War and the image of Germany: British academics 1914–1918.* Edinburgh, UK: John Donald Publishers.

Wichern, H. (1979). Die innere Mission der deutschen evangelischen Kirche. Eine Denkschrift an die deutsche Nation. In *Johann Hinrich Wichern. Ausgewählte Schriften Band 3. Schriften zur Gefängnisreform. Die Denkschrift* (pp. 132–344). Gütersloh, Germany: Gütersloher Verlagshaus.

Woods, R. A., & Kennedy, A. J. (Eds.). (1911). *Handbook of settlements.* New York: Charities Publication Committee.

3

COLD WAR, HOT PEACE, AND SYSTEMS OF REASONING ABOUT YOUTH

Nancy Lesko

It is not the activity of the subject of knowledge that produces a corpus of knowledge, useful or resistant to power, but power-knowledge, the process and struggles that traverse it and of which it is made up, that determines the forms and possible domains of knowledge.

(Foucault, 1977, p. 28)

Reasoning about youth after World War II focused on quests for autonomy and political freedom, which were imperiled by conformity and authoritarianism. A Cold War imaginary was embodied in Russian collectivism and Nazi authoritarian personalities, in citizens who were followers and unfree, and in the necessity of the arms race. But threats to autonomy and freedom were also present on the home front and figured as mass consumption, mind-warping advertising, and moral, especially sexual, weaknesses. While 1950s America has often been described as homogeneous and quiescent, recent analyses have highlighted the nascent dynamics of dissent and turmoil and the struggles of power-knowledge.

American Rebels in the Cold War

Usually understood as the geopolitics dominated by the competition between the Soviet Union and the United States for superiority during the period 1945 to 1991, new accounts of the Cold War emphasize its global character, or its three worlds, with colonial, semicolonial, and anticolonial regions as the third flank. The United States and the USSR competed for influence in emerging areas, and America touted itself as the proper source of help for young, developing nations by referring to its own revolutionary past and its history as a liberty-seeking people. For example, in 1954, Secretary of State John Foster Dulles declared, "We ourselves are the first colony in modern times to have won independence. . . . We have a natural sympathy with those everywhere who would follow our example." America's association with liberty was presented as a natural bond and a basis of understanding with emerging nations and, fused with the domino theory—if one country fell to communism, adjacent nations would also succumb—animated U.S. intervention in Southeast Asia, the Persian Gulf, and Africa, among other places. Of course, the U.S. version of liberty included freedom of the international capitalist market, and the process of development required equal allegiances to capitalism, democracy, and the United States.

Geopolitical jitters also swirled at home around the figure of the modern teenager. The analogy between young nations and young people offered ways to think about international and domestic sovereignty. According to Medovoi (2005), postwar America was deeply troubled by tensions between the norms of consumer-oriented suburban domesticity and the America idealized in the Cold War imaginary. Popular books such as Whyte's *The Organization Man* (1956) and Riesman, Glazer, and Denney's *The Lonely Crowd* (1971) depicted the toxicity of American corporate conformity, affluence, and peer orientation. While better than totalitarianism, U.S. society also posed threats to freedom.

Erik Erikson's *Childhood and Society* appeared in 1950, and its concept of identity, which merged psychological and political processes, had broad cultural and political utility.

> In Erikson's model, successful identity formation depends upon the legitimate exercise of rebellion. The Eriksonian drama of adolescence, therefore, describes the development of an individual or social character that successfully reconciles "autonomy" and "other-directedness" in Riesman's sense. The patent appeal of the Eriksonian adolescents' "character" is that she enacts the requisite dramas of rebellion *prior* to adulthood. Thus, if an adolescent exhibits a properly rebellious spirit before growing into a conforming suburbanite or an Organization Man, then she has effectively displayed the American self's sovereignty without necessarily sacrificing the eventual conformity of the adult.
>
> *(Medovoi, 2005, p. 23)*

Identity was a unifying object for scientists, policy makers, educators, and parents, as "personality" had been in the early decades of the 20th century. Thus, the rebellious spirit of youth, as a necessary stage in the development of autonomous citizens, became popular. A "rebel metanarrative" (Medovoi, 2005, p. 24) wove together terms such as "identity," "teenager," and "adolescent" with "zoot suits," "rock 'n roll," "gangs," and "juvenile delinquents," the latter terms linked to racialized urban spaces, greater disposable income, less family supervision, and a stronger media and entertainment presence. Calls for "democratic attitudes toward youth," such as a teenage Bill of Rights, fed cultural and political anxieties of both liberal and conservative Cold Warriors yet appeared unstoppable.

> In all of its complexity, the teenager of postwar U.S. culture represented nothing less than a figure of psychopolitical sovereignty, a Cold War instantiation of Erikson's "freeborn American son" as defined against the antithesis, the compliant youth of totalitarian society.
>
> *(Medovoi, 2005, p. 30)*

The teenager, who began as a political citizen-subject bearing his/her own rights, rapidly became an economic consumer-subject as well, bearing a peculiar set of goods, primarily those of the entertainment industry (Medovoi, 2005, p. 36). Burgeoning sectors of books, films, and records targeted teenage consumers. By 1964, teenagers purchased 55% of all soft drinks, 53% of all movie tickets, and 43% of all records sold. Novels, films, and music offered variations on the rebel metanarrative: the critical nonconformist, Holden Caulfield, in the novel *Catcher in the Rye*; the educated young African American in the film *Blackboard Jungle*; and the misfit sons in the films *Rebel Without a Cause* and *King Creole*.

The Catcher in the Rye (1964) embodied the liberal Cold Warrior as a boy who spoke the truth. Like the central character in *Huckleberry Finn*, Holden recapitulated a more principled American past, which could renew hope and self-creation by rejecting the conformist "phonies." The national phoniness (for example, an organizational society, a lonely crowd, a mass culture) is the ground against which his crisis and heroic struggle are narrated. Allegorically, Holden's rebelliousness voiced the "national passion for freedom and sovereignty that America shared with the new nations liberating themselves from colonialism" (Medovoi, 2005, p. 79).

Bad boys, like Holden, became stock figures in Hollywood teenpics and could be read as detestable and/or attractive subjects. The film *Blackboard Jungle* (1955) was a perfect example: condemned as likely to cause riots if the audience members agreed with the film's gang leader, Artie, that crime does pay, the main character, played by Sidney Poitier (African American), is won over to the teacher's (and middle-class White society's) perspective that crime does not pay. Medovoi connects the film's impact with U.S. school desegregation:

> *Blackboard* reveals how the historical moment of *Brown v Board of Education* [U.S. Supreme Court case mandating racial integration of schools] posed the cultural possibility of youth identity being defined against whiteness and in solidarity with racial difference.
>
> *(2005, p. 164)*

Although rebel metanarratives were generally infused with sexism and homophobia, bad boys' identities sometimes drew creatively from minoritized experiences. In the film *Rebel Without a Cause* (1955), Jim Stark's (James Dean) identity crisis is in relation to his father's domesticated masculinity. Jim rebels against school conformity, bullies, and his father's femininity, and he experiments with other models of masculine identity. Psychologist Robert Lindner claimed that conformist pressures force youth into dangerous rebellious acts, which the film portrays as fights, car races, and love.

The Elvis Presley film *King Creole* (1958) narrates the identity crisis of Danny Fisher as that between a White, middle-class, suburban manhood (domesticated and weakened as in *Rebel*) and an urban, not-quite-White working-class masculine agency. It is by taking on certain traits of an "urban Blackness" that Danny can mature into a proper man; those traits include being bad and deferring marriage and suburban life until he can find an alternative map of masculinity. As in *Rebel*, Elvis's bad boy rendered American character as forged from strength and the "inclination to dissent from impending conformities and homogenizations" (Medovoi, 2005, p. 211).

Beyond Cold War Curricula

The previous section's focus on theories of identity and the expectation that youth must rebel against social absurdities and conformities played out within the formal education system, too. Certainly, psychology was ascendant in schools of education during the 1950s, and the 1957 launch of *Sputnik* by the Soviets focused attention on strengthening the curriculum in traditional directions, toward intellectual rigor especially in science and math. *Sputnik* sparked a massive involvement of the U.S. federal government in education, too, as youth's schooling became national defense.

But the psychopolitical identity rebellions described in the previous section also busted open standard curricula and teaching practices. James B. Conant's argument for a "comprehensive" high school model was persuasive; he seemed an impeccable spokesman for the times, having been a chemist, president of Harvard University, a participant in the development of the atomic bomb, and educational commissioner of Germany in the early 1950s, although he had little experience in schools. His 1959 book, *The American High School Today,* funded by the Carnegie Corporation, argued that high school curricula needed to address dual goals: courses of study appropriate for students' various destinations and programs geared toward unifying the diverse groups of students despite their varying backgrounds, abilities, and destinations. Conant's comprehensive high school served many groups of students under one roof and was heralded as "democracy's high school" (Rury, 2002).

Student-centered classrooms, in which students were more active and talkative, grew in popularity. Alternatives to a single course textbook appeared, and students began to read across different kinds of texts. Although the "structure of the discipline" approach to teaching was still strong, interdisciplinary approaches to humanities, alternative schools (often called free schools), and texts such as Postman and Weingartner's (1971) *Teaching as a Subversive Activity* urged teachers to be rebels, too, discarding traditional textbooks and course outlines. Within all of these technologies were ideas of emergent student identities, helping students think for themselves, and educating toward critical-thinking capacities. "Radical" educational reform was acceptable and desirable as students became critical readers, writers, and thinkers who would be less likely to conform to the status quo. Curricula were to be creative enterprises for both students and teachers.

While programs, textbooks, and pedagogies diversified in the 1960s and 1970s, how were such changes related to the pastoral dimension of school life? The pastoral dimension—the moral order of the school—despite program proliferation, movable walls, and flexible seating patterns—still instructed about proper use of leisure, limits to rebellion, and orderliness and power, especially through sexual regulation, dating, going steady, and earlier marriages. While racial integration could be debated in some classrooms, premarital sex could not, with the required subject of "home economics" as close as educators came to the topic.

1950s Youthscapes

This historicizing of the discourses of youth locates them as interdisciplinary constructions with firm ties to national and international politics, economics, psychology, and media. These *youthscapes* were globalized sites of imagined and literal youth with social and political intersections (Maira & Soep, 2005). Cold War–inflected youthscapes included the excesses of manipulated, conforming youth, the vital significance of youth developing into inner-directed, autonomous citizens, and the fascination of bad boys and sexually pure young women. This Cold War system of reasoning prioritized psychological crises through which youth could become autonomous and self-directed, while foreign policy also identified young nations that were similarly struggling. On the international and national levels, "youngness" was imperiled as idealistic and challenged and needing guidance from a "big brother." Because liberty and freedom during these Cold War decades were uniquely claimed by the United States, "democracy's high school" offered a set of technologies to enhance the conduct of conduct in keeping with identities, development, and rebellious youth. Adults—teachers, but also policy makers, psychologists, school architects, textbook authors—were implored to help youth become inner-directed, autonomous citizens. These ideas informed curricula, pedagogies, and textbooks as well as teacher education. However, virulent anticommunists also fostered a hatred of democracy's nuances, dissent, and refusal of one clear truth.

Teen Brains and Risk Taking in the Time of Hot Peace

This section considers the current popularity of neuroscience and specifically research on teen brains and risk taking and its effects on systems of reasoning about youth. Although the previous section looked at the psychopolitical definition of youth identity and some aspects of the system of reasoning marked by the Cold War, other scholarship has examined biologically based developmental schemas and the construction of youth as emotionality, conformity, and hormone-driven behavior. This scholarship may be helpful as we consider the discursive shifts in the making with talk of teen brains. Neuroscience is redefining scholarly fields, and this section interrogates emergent truths about youth by considering neuroscience in current international and domestic contexts.

Catherine Lutz's (2001) study of Fort Bragg, a military base in North Carolina, during its growth and retrenchments across the 20th century frames this section, since she introduces the idea of "hot peace" and its technologies. Lutz notes that with the demise of the USSR in 1991, the "peace dividend" was short lived.

> The U.S. military restructured itself in important ways as the Soviet empire was collapsing. Externally, it applied itself more vigorously to the new forms of what can be called hot peace: training other people's armies and police, drug interdiction, hurricane relief, hostage rescue, the quelling of civil disorder, and what it called nation-building assistance. Internally, it reorganized itself in the manner of American business: It downsized, outsourced, and privatized.
>
> *(p. 217)*

Lutz describes a neoliberal military, the "belief that unregulated markets provide the best way out of social problems and that government attempts to solve them are wasteful, bungling, and/or arrogant" (p. 222). Furthermore, in post–Cold War, hot peace times, the distinction between the civilian and the military has worn down rather than intensified:

> The post–Cold War era has seen the rise of the ideas that the sofa spectator is a linchpin of military success and that soldiers shopping at the mall, teaching Junior ROTC (Reserve Officers Training Corps based in schools) to high school students, and getting educated through Montgomery GI Bill benefits are key to the health and wealth of civil society.
>
> *(p. 252)*

Lutz's study of Fort Bragg might be amended for the post–9/11 world with the centrality of terror and the massive collection of information threats.

Democracy's high school had problems even before the Soviet Union crumbled. "Conant's vision of a uniquely American form of secondary school has grown inherently problematic since the middle of the twentieth century" (Rury, 2002, p. 310) because of racial inequalities, inflexibility, and impersonality. The large comprehensive high school has been divided into smaller schools; small schools are seen as more personalized and thereby more flexible; today's nonpublic charter schools are touted as having greater autonomy, independence, and ability to compete in the market. Inferior teachers are also positioned as threats to excellence and flexibility. Poor teachers threaten economic competitiveness, which is represented by comparative school achievement data, in which the U.S. position has declined, as well as by GDP percentages and the size of weapons arsenals.

Teen Brains

> One of the hottest current topics in adolescent development is brain research, *specifically the role of adolescent brain development in risk taking*. Claims have been made, not just in popular media, but by brain scientists and developmental psychologists, that adolescents are inherently prone to risk behavior due to the immaturity of their brain development. With research on the adolescent brain continuing at a rapid pace, and with adolescent risk behavior a perennially important topic, this is a debate that is likely to continue for some time to come.
>
> *(Arnett, 2010, p. 3; emphasis added)*

Feminist historian of science Donna Haraway argued that the immune system was an elaborate icon for principal systems of symbolic and material difference in capitalism in the 1980s. In her view, myth, laboratory, and clinic were interwoven in their meaningful actions to construct the self and others, the normal and pathological, and capacities and debilities. The brain may be a central symbol of difference today, and the teen brain has appeared on the covers of national news magazines, such as *Time, U.S. News & World Report*, and *The New Yorker*; their reports tell of incompletely developed brains that account for the emotional problems and irresponsible behavior of teenagers. One account of the scientific developments reports:

> Thirty years ago, the brain was understood to be fixed and immutable in its final structure by early childhood. During the last decade, however, brain imaging studies have suggested that cortical development is much more protracted than previously thought, and that beyond childhood the brain manifests significant degrees of malleability, peaking during adolescence and continuing during early adulthood.
>
> *(Choudhury, 2010, p. 160)*

Adolescence is a period of structural and functional plasticity, and studies "point to experience-dependent rewiring" (Choudhury, 2010, p. 160). "The evidence that the most pronounced development are in brain regions associated with 'higher' executive functions and social cognition has inspired numerous studies investigating the cognitive correlates of the anatomical developments" (Choudhury, 2010, p. 160).

The exciting plasticity of adolescents' brains in Choudhury's description becomes biodeterminism in other accounts, with adolescent risk taking during adolescence likely to be normative, biologically driven, and, to some extent, inevitable. The National Research Council held a forum on the emerging science of adolescence in 2006, and special sections of journals have also been devoted to this topic. I want to consider this movement from plasticity to biodeterminism as power-knowledge relays and to highlight some of the effects of what I call actuarial practices around teenage risk taking.

Psychologist Lawrence Steinberg (2007) writes:

> The temporal gap between puberty, which impels adolescents toward thrill-seeking, and the slow maturation of the cognitive control system, which regulates these impulses, makes adolescence a time of heightened vulnerability for risky behavior. . . . *Risk-taking is the product of a competition between the socio-emotional and cognitive control networks* . . . and the former abruptly becomes more assertive at puberty while the latter gains strength only gradually, over a longer period of time.
>
> *(p. 56)*

In the teen brain imaginary, we have a militarized competition between different "control networks" for dominance. Risk is produced by the threat of the competing control networks, since scholarship indicates that cognitive control networks increasingly take over as youth become adults.

Pat O'Malley writes about risk as a form of governmentality and claims that the management of risks, rather than detection and correction, is ascendant whether the risks are health, crime, or accident related. "Prevention and risk-spreading (e.g. insurance) become more central than detection and correction" (O'Malley, 1996, p. 190). O'Malley considers actuarial tables as a method of producing and organizing knowledge to help spread costs and benefits of risks, that is, to manage them. "Actuarial technology" appears to be technical; but it is also moral; the moral banner under which it carries forward this fight is that of the free market—"the free market that reinstates the morally-responsible individual and sets it against the collectivization and social dependency said to be inherent in socialized risk-management techniques" (p. 194). Statistics impose classifications within which people must think of themselves and their possible actions. The insurantial imaginary is informed by a different system of reasoning that relies on a calculus of probabilities. And this type of rationality is capable of transforming the life of individuals and that of a population.

> This shift from moral agent to actuarial subject marks a change in the way power is exercised on individuals by the state and other large organizations. Where power once sought to manipulate the choices of rational actors, it now seeks to predict behavior and situate subjects according to the risk they pose.
>
> *(Simon, 1988, p. 772)*

Simon describes what such transformations involve in his discussion of a 1977 U.S. Supreme Court case, *Los Angeles Water and Power v. Manhart*, which challenged the actuarial use of gender in setting employee benefits. The employer argued that because women live longer than men (calculated as actuarial tables), women employees were required to make a larger contribution to the retirement plan. The plaintiffs charged that requiring a higher contribution by female employees was discriminatory, in that it used their sex as the basis for employment compensation. Although the *Manhart* decision did argue against actuarial reasoning in finding the policy discriminatory, it did nothing to help articulate the basis of membership in an "aggregate," which has no common status identity. The ideological effects of actuarial practices, Simon claims, make more difficult the construction of experiences and status identities that have historically had agency on the streets, in schools, and in the courts. Since "actuarial practices fragment the individual" (p. 786), they also immobilize groups. "Teen brains" aggregate individuals, as do "low test scores," but not in ways that correspond to experience or status groups. The abstract aggregates, such as risk takers or below-grade-level readers, lack subjectivity and thus a certain kind of social substance or "moral density of identity" (Simon, 1988, p. 794).

Simon further distinguishes between disciplinary practices and actuarial practices:

> Disciplinary practices focus on the distribution of a behavior within a limited population (a factory workforce . . . school children, etc.). This distribution is around a norm, and power operates with the goal of closing the gap, narrowing the deviation, and moving subjects toward uniformity. . . . Actuarial practices seek instead to map out the distribution and arrange strategies to maximize the efficiency of the population as it stands. Rather than seeking to change people . . . an actuarial regime seeks to manage them in place. . . . While the disciplinary regime attempts to alter individual behavior and motivation, the actuarial regime alters the physical and social structures within which individuals behave.
>
> *(Simon, 1988, p. 773)*

In the current situation, "it is cheaper to know and plan around people's failings than to normalize them" (Simon, 1988, p. 774).

Simon elaborates on the significance of morally dense identities, such as those discussed during the Cold War decades. "It is the moral density of identity that constitutes both the stigma of stereotypes and the empowerment of consciousness raising" (Simon, 1988, p. 794). Simon's argument relies on the dense "identity" constructed in the Cold War period around rebel youth, which was also used by feminist, queer, and minority groups to challenge discrimination. Medovoi claims that the "age" dimension of identity theories has been forgotten and is thus unavailable for dissenting perspectives on teen brains.

Are Youth Bad Investments?

More restrictive policies toward young people are being proposed and rationalized by claims that "new scientific discoveries" show teenagers and even emerging adults must be custodialized like children rather than afforded adult rights. Scientists cite evidence that although almost all American high school students have had courses in drug, sex, and driver education, large proportions of these youth still have unsafe sex, binge drink, and drive recklessly. It must be their undeveloped brains making them act in this way.

At the same time, education budgets everywhere are being cut because of state budget shortfalls related to the economic downturn, foreclosures, and property taxes as central to local municipalities' revenue. Class sizes are increasing and teachers' salaries and benefits are stagnant or diminished. Also, the rant about accountability and testing continues, with schools unable to measure up to continuous improvement expectations. Curricula and classroom practices are most strongly influenced by the tests and teachers' and administrators' urgent need to demonstrate improvement. The federal law, No Child Left Behind, has pursued a narrow focus on tests, test taking, and textbook knowledge that has largely erased the psychopolitical emphases of democracy's high school.

It is important to acknowledge the demographic context of the focus on the teen brain and risk taking. The racial and ethnic minority component of America's teenage population rose from around 15% in the 1960s to 43% in 2008. As the proportion of non-White-, non-European-origin youth rose, fears about young people have become major institutional and political campaigns. Fears have been directed, for example, toward youth clothed in puffy winter jackets, do-rags, and low-slung pants. However, teen brains and risk taking evidences the actuarial reasoning, in which no individual teen appears, only percentages of risk, such as drinking, driving, drugs, and unprotected sex. MSNBC's Rachel Maddow (Schneider, 2011) reported that states are making it harder for youth, the elderly, and people of color to vote by requiring new forms of voter identification and no longer accepting college-issued IDs. If young people vote more liberally, then such policies narrow the range of ideas and possibilities among voters.

Effects of Risky Teens

Experts propose that the ages for driving, voting, and jobs, such as lifeguards and military service, be raised. The idea of biodetermined teenage incompetence is useful to promote varied agendas, including imposing sweeping curfews on young people, requiring parental consent for adolescents' abortions, abolishing the death penalty for juveniles, and soliciting funding for youth-management industries. O'Malley describes how risk technologies are often connected to reductions in social welfare, and teen risk taking may contribute to the frenzy over schooling as a bad or at least suspect social investment. Neuroscience is also being applied in educational programs that develop students' "executive brain functions" beginning in early childhood. Neuroscience has also been zealously applied to postulated sex-related brain and learning differences; the number of gender-segregated schools and programs has mushroomed, with teachers trained to apply supposed scientifically validated knowledge of masculine-type brains and learning and feminine-type brains and approaches to learning.

This section has described the system of reasoning around neuroscience, teen brains, and risk taking. It has been suggested that actuarial or insurantial technology/ rationality is mobilized, which places an emphasis on risk calculation and risk management rather than on attempts to normalize or correct adolescents who take risks. Although neuroscientists do not necessarily subscribe to biodeterministic interpretations, many scientists have engaged with the inevitability of adolescents' bad thinking and brought popular preconceptions, if not outright stereotypes, to the debates. Biodeterministic views of youth have a long history and can be easily reanimated. This emergent system of reasoning has occurred in the militarized time of hot peace, in which domestic and international threats and risks directly support insurantial technologies. Educators and educational practices are under pressure to make U.S. youth internationally competitive and to not contribute to moral hazard at home by diminishing individual responsibility and freedom.

Discussion

This analysis analyzes the political history of the means of youth making (social technologies and systems of reasoning) in two historical periods to show interactions of theory, social science, international relations, and economics in constructing power-knowledge formations.

Youth identities and the slow developmental progress toward mature identities is the more familiar theory and set of practices about youth. Indeed, it is hard to speak of teenagers (or of gender, race/ethnicity, sexuality, or disability) without using the word "identity." Although the theory and concept of identity have been critiqued as too fixed, as unable to capture multiple, shifting-status categories, identity has also been crucial for movements and social justice actions. It has been able to connect with liberal rationalities established in government, law, and economics and to support a range of curricular approaches.

This analysis of teen brains locates it within different power-knowledge dynamics in which risk and actuarial tables used in various definitions of insurance are ascendant. Neuroscience debates around teen brains have focused on risk taking and the competition between socio-emotional stimulators and executive functions in teenagers' brains. It is intriguing that the preponderance of articles reviewed utilized the term "adolescents," a term that had fallen out of use but has been resurrected along with biodeterministic ideas of young people that emphasize bad thinking, accidents, and crime.

The technologies and systems of reasoning interrogated here suggest challenges for educators committed to identity theories and politics. The languages of developing children and critical youth have an archaic or hollow sound to them now. If nuance and dissent about what can count as youth and about what can count as adequate education for young people is to persist, then some understanding of the actuarial technologies may be useful. Educators and researchers will need to engage with the actuarial imaginary, neuroscientific plasticity, and the political emotional pull of new certainties. Analysis of the power-knowledge constructions and system of reasoning around teen brains and risk-taking behavior can aid in articulating and mounting questions and debate. Certainly, analyses of systems of reasoning can aid in refusing the clarity of one truth about young people.

References

Arnett, J. J. (2010). Editor's note: Special section on the adolescent brain and risk taking. *Journal of Adolescent Research, 25*(1), 3.

Blackboard jungle. (1955). Directed by Richard Brooks. Metro-Goldwyn-Mayer Pictures.

Choudhury, S. (2010). Culturing the adolescent brain: What can neuroscience learn from anthropology? *Social Cognitive and Affective Neuroscience, 5*(2–3), 159–168.

Conant, J. B. (1974). *The American high school today.* New York: Signet.

Erikson, E. (1950). *Childhood and society.* New York and London: W. W. Norton.

Foucault, M. (1977). *Discipline and punish: The birth of the prison* (A. Sheridan, Trans.). New York: Pantheon Books.

King Creole. (1958). Directed by Michael Curtiz. Paramount Pictures.

Lutz, C. (2001). *Homefront: A military city and the American twentieth century.* Boston: Beacon Press.

Maira, S., & Soep, E. (Eds.). (2005). *Youthscapes: The popular, the national, the global.* Philadelphia: University of Pennsylvania Press.

Medovoi, L. (2005). *Rebels: Youth and the Cold War origins of identity.* Durham, NC, and London: Duke University Press.

O'Malley, P. (1996). Risk and responsibility. In A. Barry, T. Osborne, & N. Rose (Eds.), *Foucault and political reason* (pp. 189–207). Chicago: University of Chicago Press.

Postman, N., & Weingartner, C. (1971). *Teaching as a subversive activity.* New York: Dell.

Rebel without a cause. (1955). Directed by Nicholas Ray. Warner Brothers Pictures.

Riesman, D., with Glazer, N., & Denney, R. (1971). *The lonely crowd.* New Haven, CT: Yale University Press.

Rury, J. L. (2002). Democracy's high school? Social change and American secondary education in the post-Conant era. *American Educational Research Journal, 39*(2), 307–336.

Salinger, J. D. (1964). *The catcher in the rye.* New York: Bantam Books.

Schneider, M. (July 16, 2011). Jesse Jackson to Rachel Maddow. Retrieved from www.mediaite.com/tv/jesse-jackson-to-rachel-maddow-anti-obama-mania-sweeping-the-country-and-we-ought-fight-back/

Simon, J. (1988). The ideological effects of actuarial practices. *Law and Society Review, 22,* 772–800.

Steinberg, L. (2007). Risk-taking in adolescence: New perspectives from brain and behavioral science. *Current Directions in Psychological Science, 16,* 55–59.

Whyte, W. H. (1956). *The organization man.* New York: Simon and Schuster.

4

DISCOURSE ON (TEACHING) METHOD

Challenging the Reason of Contemporary Teacher Education

Daniel Friedrich

Examining the top issues being discussed in a specific field tells as much about what is considered to be important for that field at a particular time as it tells about the assumptions that ground all discussions in said field. These assumptions are what make the topics intelligible while at the same time remaining, themselves, mostly unquestioned. If one were to look at the special issues in professional journals, conference programs, and ad hoc meetings, perhaps one of the more pressing issues in the field of teacher education in the United States right now would seem to be the proliferation in the last decades of alternative routes to teacher certification (ARTC) that seem to threaten not only the traditional teacher preparation institutions that have been hegemonic in the last century but the very future of schools themselves. The kind of alternative routes to teacher certification that I am referring to (which could be termed boot camp style; see Friedrich, 2014) boil teacher education down to a minimum, spending a few weeks passing on what they consider to be the basics to prospective teachers before or while assigning them to a classroom as monitored yet full-time instructors. These prospective teachers, usually college graduates or individuals with "significant life experiences," find in these programs a quick way to a profession that provides certain financial stability and in some cases a sense of duty or civic commitment without the costs (both economic and timely) of a university-based program. ARTC are expanding throughout the world at an impressive rate, with a network like Teach For All (www.teachforallnetwork.org) counting 33 international programs under its umbrella by 2014, in locations as distinct as Argentina, China, Latvia, or Pakistan.

Calls for teacher education reform, either supporting or criticizing alternative routes, ground their efforts on the apparently evident differences between traditional and alternative programs. The new programs tend to treat teaching as a set of empirically proven techniques that can be reduced to their core elements and reproduced. These techniques are added to the content knowledge that college graduates bring with them to produce "highly qualified teachers" that are then deployed in urban and rural classrooms, where they are to acquire the feedback from practice that will further refine the techniques. Meanwhile, traditional, university-based teacher certification programs, composed mainly of 4-year colleges but also of postbaccalaureate programs, claim to conceive of teaching as much more than mere techniques. What all of them agree on is the impossibility of producing high-quality teachers by condensing what teaching is about into a few weeks dedicated to mechanized techniques. Educating in schools is a very complex activity, thus requiring a complex understanding of it to achieve success at its goals.

This chapter questions the common sense of teacher education reform that partitions what is there to see, to talk about, and to fight against in terms of where one stands in relation to the ARTC debates by preassigning roles and spaces for the discussions to take place. As will become clear from the argument, the focus on the emergence and proliferation of ARTC leaves the foundational assumptions of teacher education reform unquestioned, inscribing a common sense that determines the outcomes of the discussion. This piece turns its attention instead to the reason of current teacher education reform discourses, focusing on the ways in which certain ideas make particular projects into representations of positions that are at odds, effacing their common grounding.

In this chapter, I will explore some of the discourses that have shaped the common sense of teacher education reformers as a way to reflect on how we have been historically conceiving of teaching and teacher education as a "practice-driven" activity. By delving into the particular ways in which discourses stemming from learning and developmental psychologies have been mobilized in teacher education, how "experience" has been separated from and privileged over "theory," and how diversity has been conceptualized, I will argue that these foundations of traditional teacher education are also at the roots of critical analyses and reform efforts. The goal is to understand the ways in which, by framing teacher education reform in particular ways, the formation of educators has been affected, and so have schools. By making those frameworks visible, possibilities may open up to rethink the conceptions of teaching and teacher education in different paths.

The chapter is organized as follows. Two ideas that are part of the educational common sense—the distinction between teaching methods and content knowledge and the centrality of experiencing diversity—are shown to be pillars of contemporary discourses in the field of teacher education in the United States. It will be argued that these foundations foreclose the kinds of discussions that are made possible by setting limits to the common sense. My goal is twofold: first, I will expose the social, political, and cultural dangers of some of the foundational ways in which teacher education has been thought about in order to, secondly, start imagining what kind of teacher education would be possible once we consider the contingency of said foundations.

Two Foundational Ideas in Teacher Education

Commonsense Idea 1: Teaching Methods Can and Should Be Distinguished From the Content of Teaching

> Two components are critically important in teacher preparation: *teacher knowledge of the subject* to be taught, *and* knowledge and skill in *how to teach* that subject. Research and common sense tell us that subject matter knowledge is necessary for effective teaching. But there is a second part of the equation: knowledge and skill in how to teach is also a must. Effective teachers understand and are able to apply strategies to help students increase achievement. They understand and apply knowledge of child and adolescent development to motivate and engage students. They are able to diagnose individual learning needs. They know how to develop a positive climate in the classroom in order to make it a stimulating learning environment.
>
> *(National Council for Accreditation of Teacher Education [NCATE], n.d.; emphasis in the original)*

Many traditional teacher education institutions, ranging from the most renowned and highly ranked to the mediocre and beyond, have clear demarcations in their course catalogs between content courses and methods courses, while other programs have replaced this distinction with pedagogical content courses that combine these two areas. When the distinction between methods and content is made, curricular content courses are intended—in best-case scenarios—to consolidate and provide new perspectives on the instructional content that future teachers are to teach. In those cases in which students have not had a good schooling experience, these courses aim at compensating for the gaps generated in primary and secondary schooling. Methods courses, on the other hand, are in charge of imparting that knowledge that is unique to education in that they bring together findings from the field of psychology with evidence-based research on the techniques that will make instruction most effective (Shulman, 1987). Pedagogical content courses emerged relatively recently within teacher education as an attempt to bridge the gap between content and methods by providing students with tools that still fundamentally rely on the findings of educational and developmental psychology but are more closely linked to the specificities of each discipline and grade level.

There are several assumptions that ground the distinction between methods and content and that establish the autonomy of the former, following the reasoning exemplified by the quote from NCATE cited earlier:

- First pedagogical assumption: Since children are neither mathematicians nor historians nor biologists, the ordering of knowledge and teaching cannot come from those disciplines. Most people would certainly agree with the first part of this proposition. Children learning the principles of algebra or thinking through the past of particular groups cannot be equated with the adults that produce that knowledge in the first place precisely for that very reason: While pupils might be constructing knowledge, they are not producing it, at least not in the same way experts are. Thus, common sense dictates the need for specialized teaching knowledge.

- Second assumption through which most reforms proceed is: The ordering of curricular knowledge has to be tied to what we know about how children learn, and therefore it has to be provided by psychology. The alchemical process that translates disciplinary knowledge into curricular content reorganizes knowledge under the lens of the psychological sciences, administering content following the rules of what is known about learning and the mind (Popkewitz, 2008). The disciplinary debates that keep each field open (while uncertain) are turned into problems to be solved in a "stimulating learning environment." The solving of these problems functions as ways to inscribe certainty into the uncertain disciplinary knowledge, while the teacher's unique capacity to formulate the problems that are adequate by "diagnosing individual learning needs" and providing the tools to solve those problems at the right time instantiates a differentiation that sets the adult's role as master explicator (Rancière, 1991).

- Third assumption: If content knowledge is organized following principles provided by psychology, then the methods for teaching that knowledge are also to be developed by the "psy" field. The fracture between content and methods that was founded by the two previous assumptions left methods as a domain colonized by learning, behavioral, and developmental psychologies. These sciences, following different psychological models, have been producing the techniques that were to be implemented by teachers, trained by experts, as models of ordering teaching since the turn of the 20th century. The psychological register became thus the dominant discourse in the training of educators in ways that have become so much a part of the pedagogical common sense that are now rarely interrogated. The "facts" that the mind develops in stages, that knowledge has to be structured from lower levels of complexity to higher ones, or that learning has to be supported by positive or negative reinforcements have become what is natural about teaching and learning.

These three assumptions serve as the foundations for thinking about methods and contents as two separate areas of teacher training, supported by knowledge about the student's development. Linda Darling-Hammond (2006, p. 304), one of the leading specialists in teacher education, illustrates this partition in Figure 4.1.

The distinction between methods (or "knowledge of teaching") and content (or "knowledge of subject matter and curriculum goals") appears then not only as natural but as necessary for maintaining teacher professionalism. It is precisely the knowledge of these components and of their distinction that makes teachers into specialists-professionals.

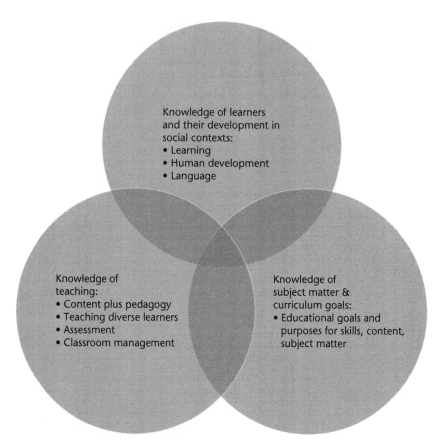

FIGURE 4.1 A framework for understanding teaching and learning. Darling-Hammond & Bransford, 2005, p. 11.

The Problem With Methods

One of the backbones of the idea of professionalizing teaching is by showing that it possesses and produces a set of knowledge that is unique to it. Within that knowledge, teaching methodology assumes a central role. Didactics, or the teaching methodology that is specific to each subject matter, brings together findings in the experimental, social, and developmental psychologies with knowledge gathered from schools and the experiences of teachers and educators in an attempt to devise the best ways to teach in order for students to learn. Yet the very idea of the possibility of discovering the best practices, of being able to compile the techniques that have worked, do work, and will work is certainly problematic.

When knowledge is translated from the different scientific or humanistic disciplines into school subjects, the one element that gets "lost in translation" is the inherent uncertainty of inquiry. Even if many historians, mathematicians, or linguists have particular methodologies that provide tools for them to produce disciplinary knowledge, what they never know in advance is what that knowledge is going to look like. That is the heart of inquiry, and it leads both to failures (probably most of the time) and eventually to groundbreaking moments. And most importantly, the uncertainty I am discussing remains as part of the "established" knowledge; it does not dissipate. Most scientists and academics are constantly aware of the indefinite quality of the knowledge they are dealing with, even when they act *as if* knowledge was certain.

If knowledge produced within disciplines that then feed curricular content has embedded some uncertainty, the ways in which we tend to think about education and, for the sake of this argument, didactics are all about the taming of that uncertainty in order to be able to plan the outcomes of schooling. When disciplinary knowledge is alchemically translated into curricular content, a particular psychological register is deployed to provide the principles to reorder that knowledge and in that process reduce as much as possible the level of uncertainty. Thus, what we know about human development, interactive learning, and communication is mobilized to plan when and how students are going to learn what . . . with certainty. And that seems to be what the curriculum is all about. In the words of Darling-Hammond, "Without knowing deeply how people learn, and how different people learn differently, teachers lack the foundation that can help them figure out what to do when a given technique or text is not effective with all students" (2006, p. 303).

The question now becomes: What if we are eliminating uncertainty? One way of answering this question would be to argue that, since uncertainty is part of disciplinary knowledge, eliminating it would produce an "unfaithful" translation into curricular content. While the idea that there is a missing piece is relevant, what are most significant are the implications of this translation.

When knowledge is taught as if it were certain and unquestionable, without any room for uncertainty, the psychological registers that translate that knowledge into school subjects foreclose what can be seen and acted upon in the world. If knowledge or its foundations are turned into ahistorical and nonepistemological givens that have remained "true" throughout history, these foundations are removed from the field of the perceptible and thus from the field of what can be changed by human action. This is one field of the social that then becomes what is instead of what could be different. The efforts to eliminate uncertainty from teaching and learning through the development of teaching methods that reorganize knowledge by removing uncertainty are therefore inherently conservative, no matter from which end of the ideological spectrum they come.

As long as what we know about the mind is seen as ahistorical facts used to provide principles to order curricular content in such ways that uncertainty is taken out of the equation, the knowledge behind the recipe becomes irrelevant for the people that are supposed to assume it as true and merely carry out the necessary steps for successful teaching. A mere claim for more instruction on ahistoricized *facts* of the mind for student teachers that supports the ways in which said facts inform methods does little to advance the struggle for better schools or teachers and, in fact, facilitates the search for silver bullets that will solve all of our problems based on those established foundations which *everybody knows*. One example lies in current efforts to find that solution not in psychology anymore but in technological advances:

> In the future, teachers will need to go well beyond behavioral or cognitive psychology and the debate between "memorizing the facts" learning versus "constructing your meaning" learning. New technologies can empower well-prepared teachers to synthesize a multitude of internet tools for teaching—co-mingling text, images, audio, video, simulations, and games in ways reflective of how re-wired students develop and use knowledge. Teacher education programs, both traditional and alternative, must fully employ those same tools as they work with New Millennium teaching candidates.
>
> *(Berry, 2010, p. 3)*

The argument presented is not against learning about the mind or interacting with new technologies. It is about the need to consider all findings as contingent, not in terms of knowledge accumulation ("this is the best we have, as the discipline has linearly grown so far, and we will get closer to the truth as time goes by") but in paradigmatic terms ("under this set of contingent assumptions that have changed over time and will most likely continue to change, this is what we believe to be true"), in ways that would work against the tendency to look for easy fix-all solutions. On the other hand, partly because of this contingent nature of knowledge, but also because of the effects of learning and developmental psychologies over disciplinary knowledge, the use of this particular lens to translate disciplinary knowledge into subject matter should be problematized. Mobilizing a psychological register as the privileged lens in the alchemical transformation of disciplinary knowledge into curricular content has become naturalized as part of the educational landscape.

Commonsense Idea 2: Experience With Diversity Is a Central Element in Teacher Education

> When prospective teachers are faced with the challenge of teaching in settings that differ vastly from their own, they experience a dissonance that requires resolution. [Teacher candidates] confront such dissonance when their expectations are challenged, and they must be provided guidance to reconcile their beliefs through self-reflection and critical examination of their own biographies. When they achieve resolution they not only learn more about themselves as teachers but also are better equipped to face head-on the complexities of teaching in diverse settings.
>
> *(Baldwin et al., 2007, p. 325)*

The issue of diversity and multicultural education runs through all ranges of education discourses in the United States. The political and social narratives about America's "exceptional" history continuously bring the diversity in its population to the centerfold of a variety of situations. As a consequence, schools seem to present teachers with challenges that are directly proportionate to the "degree" of diversity of their classrooms. In order to be prepared to face these challenges, teachers need to face diversity during their education, since knowledge about diversity and "diverse learners" can only be acquired through experiences that need to take place in direct contact with diverse learners.

Again, the reasoning behind this commonsensical idea can be disassembled into a set of particular assumptions that ground it:

- First assumption: Experience presents students with a kind of knowledge that cannot be acquired otherwise. The privileging of experience as the quintessential form to acquire particular kinds of knowledge is a central piece of teacher education in the United States. As much as many traditional teacher education programs defend the value of an intellectual focus, it is hard, if not impossible, to find normative accounts of teacher education that do not privilege experiences in "real" classrooms with "real" children as the way to achieve successful teachers, as exemplified by the quote from Baldwin cited previously. Experience is understood by these teacher educators as possessing a higher degree of reality, as being the basis for authentic learning. Experience predates thought and theorizing and appears, in fact, as the origin of knowledge.
- Second assumption: Diversity can only be experienced. Within this commonsense idea, diversity is a component of the fabric of social life that is part of the social experience of living in society. As such, it appears as part of the given of the sensible. The experience of diversity trumps all mere theorizing about it as a way to understand, interact with, and see oneself in relation to diversity. Diversity is conceived then as a category that preexists categories, one that gives meaning to thought, constitutes the pluralist society, and provides the lens through which each individual senses the world and its responsibilities as a citizen of the republic. If this is the case, then diversity is inextricably linked to identity and one's own positioning within society and government.
- Third assumption: A teacher that is able to deal with a diverse population will be able to deal with any population. Within this assumption, "diverse" assumes two interrelated meanings. The first one, which can be easily intuited from any discourse on education, equates diversity with the urban, poor minorities, whereas the second translates diverse into challenging. Diversity, then, serves as a placeholder for difference, that is, for everything that escapes the norm and thus challenges the teacher to encounter that with which s/he is not familiar with. Tying it back to the previous commonsensical idea, these

differences can be breached by an understanding of the normalizing power of the different psychologies of the child that establish relations between the universal (all children) and the particular (*this* kind of children).

The Problem With Experience

Experience could be seen as the most natural encounter with the world and therefore the easiest to naturalize. After all, experience is about the ways in which we sense and perceive what is around us, apparently unmediated by any sort of process. Experience, then, tends to appear as the bedrock of knowing, predating the learning that occurs through the mind. This naïve understanding of experience that creates a temporal-epistemological hierarchy has been contested by the now classic work by Joan Scott (1991), who saw in the treatment of experience as fact a naturalization of difference.

> When experience is taken as the origin of knowledge, the vision of the individual subject (the person who had the experience or the historian who recounts it) becomes the bedrock of evidence on which explanation is built. Questions about the constructed nature of experience, about how subjects are constituted as different in the first place, about how one's vision is structured—about language (or discourse) and history—are left aside. The evidence of experience then becomes evidence for the fact of difference, rather than a way of exploring how difference is established, how it operates, how and in what ways it constitutes subjects who see and act in the world.
>
> (p. 777)

This quote presents two critiques toward the privileging of experience as a way of knowing. The first one is the idea of experience as an effect instead of an origin. Experience cannot but be mediated by the ways in which we are thinking and speaking about the world and ourselves, ways that have been, are, and will be historically constructed. From this understanding of experience as an effect, two main ways of contesting traditional mobilizations of experience within teacher education can be deduced. On the one hand, the hierarchical thinking that attributes a higher level of reality to experience, opposing it to theory, needs to be problematized. While many teacher educators nominally equate all kinds of knowledge, there is a tendency to reinscribe the inequality between the "real experience gained in the trenches" and the knowledge acquired in/by the "ivory tower." For instance: "The enterprise of teacher education must venture out further and further from the university and engage ever more closely with schools in a mutual transformation agenda" (Darling-Hammond, 2006, p. 302). Once the distinction between discourse and experience or theory and practice is problematized and the very act of theorizing is understood as a practice, while experience is seen as an effect of discourses and the intersection of multiple theories, a whole

new perspective opens up for considering what a different kind of teacher education might look like.

On the other hand, but related to the previous point, understanding experience
as an effect of particular discourses and systems of reason instead of as a natural
origin of knowledge adds yet another argument to the extensive discussion against
the distinction between theory and practice. The claim about the need to break
down this distinction has been part of the debates in the social sciences for decades,
if not centuries. In the field of education, this distinction has had an enormous
impact. It has led to a particular kind of anti-intellectualism that has privileged
experience or practice over other kinds of knowledge, as explained earlier. One
example of this tendency can be found in a paper written by Barnett Berry for the
National Council for the Accreditation of Teacher Education (NCATE), in which
the author outlines eight "major issues facing teacher education" (2010, p. 5):
haphazard production of teachers; weak clinical support; skewed faculty priorities
(toward academic research and publishing); a collaboration gap between universities and schools; missed opportunities with universities; isolated and underpub-
licized trailblazers in partnering; hazy conditions on alternate paths to teacher
certification; and residency potential underexploited. Note how, depending on
how one interprets these challenges, at least half relate to "not enough practice."

Returning to the main argument of this chapter, the naturalizing of experience with the consequent fracture between theory and practice/experience and
the privileging of the latter has brought about a common foundation for making possible debates such as the one between traditional and alternative routes
to teacher certification, as this divide becomes inherent in the current reason
of teacher education reform. Even the usual claims about the integration between
theory and practice presuppose the difference between the terms. ARTC take
this to the extreme by focusing on the privileged pole of this dichotomy, that
is, experience. Student teachers that attend ARTC are thrown into the realm of
"experience" counting on the disregard toward "mere theory" by the managers of
those programs. While this attitude toward knowledge production by ARTC has
been decried by many defenders of traditional teacher education programs, what
is rarely acknowledged is that this attitude would not be possible if the distinction
between theory and practice had not been asserted by most people involved in the
first place. When this distinction between theory and practice becomes part of the
given, particular possibilities about what can be seen and acted upon in the world
become foreclosed.

Experiencing Diversity

The second aspect that needs to be analyzed from the quote by Scott is related
to the ways in which diversity is framed by teacher educators, specifically as it
gets linked to experience. Scott (1991) indicates that when experience is taken
as the origin of knowledge, "experience then becomes evidence for the fact of

difference" (p. 777). In other words, all efforts to bring diversity to teacher education through encouraging programs to take their students to populations defined as diverse (i.e., high needs) are mobilizing particular understandings of difference and sameness that end up naturalizing difference at an ontological level. When both traditional and alternative teacher certification programs claim that their students need to face diversity in the classroom, there are a set of assumptions at play: that student teachers—mostly White, middle-class women—do not have (enough) experience with diversity, that said experience in the classroom brings something to the table that is unique and necessary, that diversity implies higher needs, and most importantly—and perhaps at the bottom of all other assumptions—that diversity and difference are interchangeable. Diversity—much like experience—is rarely analyzed or defined, since it is one of those things that *everybody knows.*

Yet equating difference with diversity poses dangers in need of consideration. One of these dangers lies in the predetermination of difference by partitioning subjects into categories that are given in advance. When talking about diversity and the need for student teachers to experience it, the world is divided in advance between those who are the same and those who are different or diverse. Furthermore, the ways in which the diverse are different are prefigured through the categories that are used to set them apart (which are context specific; in the United States, the reigning categories are race, social class, gender, and sexual orientation) and that are utilized to describe lives that can never be of the same order as those led by student teachers. This poses an interesting paradox: While teacher education programs are encouraged to bring their student teachers to the world of diversity, those who inhabit the categories that make them diverse live lives predefined by those categories (that is precisely what makes them diverse under that discursive regime), with experiences and perspectives that are not to be understood but to be lived, following the hierarchy of experience over thought presented previously. In other words, even though student teachers need to experience diversity, diversity is a way of life that cannot be easily transferred. Those who are diverse are different and will always remain so.

Beyond the aforementioned paradox, the equation of diversity with difference forecloses the discussions about how differences are constituted and framed within our (educational) thought and action. Since diversity appears before our eyes as something obvious and unquestionable—in other words, as something from the realm of experience, not from thought—it is treated as a thing in the world that does not merit much debate. Clearly, discussions about what to do about diversity, how to deal with it, and how to benefit from it are abundant, especially as presented by the field of multicultural education. Yet most of these considerations do not question the production of difference per se but assume it as something to act upon, defining it by the categories that were pregiven. This foreclosure of the debates about the production of difference effected by the efforts to improve traditional teacher education by making it relevant implies for all discourses on teacher education reform that practice in urban settings is what is needed in order to "get it," as any questioning of the ways in which we perceive difference becomes superfluous in the face of the evidence of experience.

The argument does not go against experiential learning or practice-teaching in urban settings but forces teacher educators to trouble the ways in which those tools are framed, as well as what is expected as results from those frameworks and experiences. As long as experience is understood as the ultimate origin of knowledge and diversity as a prefigured entity that is there in the world standing in for difference, these experiences do little but advance the reduction of teaching and teacher education to a matter of practice that reigns in our field.

Against the Limits of Teacher Education Reform

One of the first ideas that need to be contested in the exploration for a different kind of teacher education is the idea that there are methods, strategies, or approaches to teaching that work anytime, anywhere. It is not that we have not found them *yet*, but the rationale behind the search itself is what needs to be challenged. Seeking and imparting teaching methods that "work" has embedded in it the assumption of a body of knowledge that is fact and therefore will always be so. Under this assumption, what we know about the mind is the result of an accumulation of progressive discoveries methodically achieved in an unbiased environment. This is why basing didactics on this body of knowledge cannot but guarantee success. Reliance on this particular approach to knowledge (as ahistorical facts) is part of the underlying reason of teacher education reforms, no matter on which end of the political spectrum one focuses one's gaze. All parts are continuously attempting to grasp "what works," that is, sets of universally tested principles that would solve the problems of schooling that are posed to be so urgent and in need of immediate action. The fantasy of a universally good teacher that has been educated to face any challenge well prepared embodies the need by reformers to use solid, unchanging foundations on which to build the scaffold of a certain future. The problem is that such foundations were never solid or fixed to begin with.

The discourse on "what works" has also succeeded in its dominance on current teacher education reforms thanks to the reliance on experimental and developmental psychologies in providing the principles to order subject matter content. Whatever *works* is seen as working because it can be replicated with a minimal level of uncertainty. This reduction is made possible by the translation of disciplinary knowledge into curricular content through the lens of learning and developmental psychologies that offer universal principles without regard to the specificities of each disciplinary field. Yet the logic behind each discipline is unique and, as is the case with the psychologies, constantly in flux. Once again, the need to tame uncertainty is to be found at the core of the reason of teacher education reform.

One of the things that reformers would agree "works" in the sense explained is the privileging of experience over *mere* theory, as this tendency appears throughout the spectrum of reform efforts. Yet, following Foucault: "We've got to avoid the sacralization of the social as the sole instance of the real, and stop treating thought—this essential thing in human life and human relations—lightly" (1982, p. 33). Whereas one would be hard pressed to find arguments against including experience in the classroom as part of any sort of teacher education program, what is not impossible is to think about reformulating the expectations and reasoning behind sending supervised student teachers to schools. What we see, hear, touch, smell, or taste needs to be put under the same critical lens as the theories about human learning and development, since our experience is, as much as those "theories," an effect of multiple frameworks and lenses that made us who we are. Experience does not tell us how the world is but is instead the result of how we understand the world to be. Thus, the role of practice in teacher education programs should be exactly the same as the role of university classrooms: to provide tools to understand the ways in which we are thinking and acting upon schools and students as historical, social, political, and epistemological products.

Finally, a repositioning of experience needs to lead into a different understanding of difference. This shift requires two preconditions. First, as explained, we need to accept that experience is not the origin of knowledge but an effect of it. Second, that diversity is not the same as difference but a negation of difference by prefiguring the categories through which that difference is to be understood. Once those two preconditions are met, then actual difference presents the potential to radically change the ways in which we understand teacher education. A shift in the focus of attention from diversity as something student teachers are to interact with in order to gain a particular kind of knowledge into the ways in which our thought produces difference, both inside and outside the classroom, could potentially force a mobilization of different understandings in the relationship between the self and the Other. If experience is to be questioned and conceived as an effect of knowledge, our relationship to diversity needs to be questioned in the same ways. Categories such as race, gender, age, and class cannot be taken for granted as the ones mapping difference. Difference is precisely that which cannot be mapped. Difference is the encounter with that which is outside our thought, an event that disrupts our categories and thus cannot be planned. The implications of this rationale for teacher education are far reaching and can only be partially explored here, mainly because many of these implications are and need to remain unknown. The goal cannot be to experience difference and recognize it or become aware of it but to provide tools to think about how difference comes to be, and how our thought and action, even with the best of intentions, reinscribe the divisions and inequalities that we are trying to overcome.

Concluding Thoughts

The proliferation of ARTC in the United States is certainly a worrying trend, not only for American educators. ARTC dismiss all efforts to take teaching seriously, boiling it down to basic classroom-management techniques added to content knowledge. The idea behind ARTC seems to be that anyone who knows about something should automatically be able to teach after some practice. If these programs continue expanding throughout the world (as seen in the Teach For All organization), the future of teachers and traditional teacher education programs, which are lengthier and more expensive, seems bleak.

Facing this prospect, scholars have been engaging in debates about the different features that each program offers to teacher candidates either by defending traditional teacher education programs from what they have considered to be the attack from the conservative right that aims at destroying unions, privatizing education, and containing any efforts to change the status quo or by attacking the "old ways" and calling for more funding toward new programs. In this chapter, I have argued that these discussions and the ways in which they force participants to take a stance have been missing an examination of the foundational assumptions that ground these debates. In some aspects, ARTC do not present a different reasoning for educating teachers than traditional programs but merely a reduction of the same ways of thinking. Clearly, boot-camp-style ARTC make experience in the classrooms the be-all/end-all of teacher education, while traditional programs understand practice as the space in which abstract theories get confirmed or refuted. Yet the distinction between theory and practice is still there. In the same vein, both kinds of teacher education programs usually conceive of teaching as the enactment in the classroom of what has been proven to work. Both kinds of programs agree on the need to improve teaching and teacher education following "evidence-based research," finding ways to produce knowledge that are broadly applicable and that can be planned and used for planning.

Questioning the foundations of the debates between the new and the old can contribute to moving the discussion in a different direction. Without guarantees that this will lead to a better teacher education, the goal is to make certain paths visible while engaging in an analysis of the reason of teacher education reform. As teachers and schools become easy scapegoats for a variety of social problems, the restraints that particular ways of thinking put on the reinvention of teacher education need to become the subject of critical analysis without losing sight of the ways in which the same system of thought has produced our own ways of being.

References

Baldwin, S. C., Buchanan, A. M., & Rudisill, M. E. (2007). What teacher candidates learned about diversity, social justice, and themselves from service-learning experiences. *Journal of Teacher Education, 58*(4), 315–327.

Berry, B. (2010, October 7). *Teacher education for tomorrow.* Center for Teaching Quality. Retrieved from www.teachingquality.org/sites/default/files/Teacher%20Education%20 for%20Tomorrow.pdf

Darling-Hammond, L. (2006). Constructing 21st-century teacher education. *Journal of Teacher Education, 57*(3), 300–314.

Darling-Hammond, L., & Bransford, J. (in collaboration with P. LePage, K. Hammerness, & H. Duffy). (2005). *Preparing teachers for a changing world: What teachers should learn and be able to do.* San Francisco: Jossey-Bass.

Foucault, M. (1982). Is it really important to think? *Philosophy and Social Criticism, 9*(1), 29–40.

Friedrich, D. (2014). We brought it upon ourselves: University-based teacher education and the emergence of boot-camp-style routes to teacher certification. *Education Policy Analysis Archives, 22*(2). Retrieved from http://epaa.asu.edu/ojs/article/view/1193

National Council for Accreditation of Teacher Education. (n.d.). *What makes a teacher effective?* Retrieved from www.ncate.org/Public/ResearchReports/TeacherPreparation Research/WhatMakesaTeacherEffective/tabid/361/Default.aspx

Popkewitz, T. S. (2008). *Cosmopolitanism and the age of school reform: Science, education and making society by making the child.* New York: Routledge.

Rancière, J. (1991). *The ignorant schoolmaster: Five lessons in intellectual emancipation* (1st ed.). Stanford, CA: Stanford University Press.

Scott, J. W. (1991). The evidence of experience. *Critical Inquiry, 17*(4), 773–797.

Shulman, L. S. (1987). Knowledge and teaching: Foundations of the new reform. *Harvard Educational Review, 57*(1), 1–23.

5

THE DISASTER THAT FOUNDS PUBLIC EDUCATION

Social Inequity, Race, and Rebuilding the New Orleans School System After Hurricane Katrina

Amy Sloane

Nine years after Hurricane Katrina made landfall and Lake Ponchartrain flooded approximately 80% of New Orleans, Louisiana (NOLA), United States, in a toxic stew, the disaster continues to drag into question the entire founding of education as a social activity, including its purposes, teachers, learners, curricula, and modes of teaching-learning. Rebuilding public education is linked to its history as one of the worst public school systems in the country and also to the unraveling of the social fabric from long-term separation of family members, disproportionate difficulties encountered by low-income residents trying to return to their homes and neighborhoods, and a range of problems related to inadequate relief infrastructure, trauma-related physical and mental health issues, reduced employment, and more.

In NOLA, the question of founding education upon disaster is reasoned and pragmatically lived as a paradigm of the social contract. Before the storm, geographic vulnerability to flooding, race, class, and school quality neatly coincided to map historically deep lines of segregation and disinvestment, foretelling who could evacuate and who couldn't. Likewise, it has been argued that post-Katrina efforts to rebuild public education exhibit a social contract presupposing abandonment of the Black and poor (Brunsma et al., 2007; Troutt, 2006). One argument suggests the newly emergent public school system displays policies and mechanisms that promote criminalization and educational deprivation of children most in need of public schooling.

> The confluence of . . . lack of resources and the failure to provide quality education, combined with overly harsh and punitive discipline policies that criminalize and exclude youth from traditional education settings—has created what many now call the School-to-Prison Pipeline.
>
> *(Tuzzolo & Hewitt, 2007)*

In contrast, Scott Cowen, current president of Tulane University, who has led the city's committee to reform and rebuild NOLA public schools and established Tulane's Cowen Institute for Public Education Initiatives, has stated that

> the day Katrina happened and we closed the system down was probably one of the best days for the future of the children of our city. Because we had a unique opportunity to rebuild, in a new vision, the future of public education. And we did do that. . . . We spent nine months developing that vision and plan for New Orleans. And the first thing we said is, the ultimate goal of any plan . . . is to ensure that every single child has an opportunity regardless of their race, their socioeconomic class . . . to go and get a first class education and go on to college.
>
> *(2010)*

These two statements, while oppositional, nevertheless show that disaster and founding education remain inseparable. The disaster is a past that continues to be present, as marginalization and disinvestment from those most in need of education. And the present reforms and future opportunities of education are accompanied by a constant threat of their passing away. It is not coincidental that "the groups and ideologies battling for dominance over the city's social, economic, and political geographies have expressed their agendas most intensely in the battle over the city's public schools" (Michna, 2009, p. 548).

Holding in focus and analyzing this inseparability of disaster and founding education, I inquire into the way this inseparability functions as a logical activity of reasoning that establishes dimensions of education including opportunity, educability, history, and community with specific possibilities and limits. I make visible this activity of reasoning in order to raise questions regarding its effects and to highlight what it puts at stake. This provides a springboard to examine how exhibiting reasoning in this way might open the possibility of a new understanding of disaster and founding education.

The Reason of Inseparability and Agamben's Paradigmatic Method

The object of analysis is the inseparability of disaster and founding education. I analyze it as an activity of logic with specific pragmatic effects regarding disaster and remaking education. As the hinge of destruction and possibility, this inseparability is worth examining, since on it the entire founding of education has occurred. By founding I mean not only reconstituting the entire system of public education from teachers to students to school buildings and the administration of education but also and primarily setting out the logical structure of the human potential of education, of history, and of community. Holding this object in focus, the guiding question is: How is the event of inseparability grasped as the basis on which to found education, and in what way does it constitute a paradigm of education?

My use of paradigm takes up Agamben's (1999, 2009) paradigmatic method, in which examples are made that illuminate each other and at the same time exhibit the activity of the reasoning they comprise. In my elaboration of this methodological approach, I put oppositional statements regarding Katrina from primarily scholarly sources beside each other, to exhibit the inseparability of disaster and founding education as a specific activity of reasoning. On one side are statements comprising what I will call mainstream educational reforms, implemented through the Bring New Orleans Back Commission and numerous government and nongovernment entities involved in reestablishing the public schools in Orleans parish. On another side are scholarly critiques of these reforms and their principles, emphasizing the continuation of inequities as manifestations of racism in the supposed school reforms.

I present the statements as examples of reason. The examples do not reveal the truth of what happened in the disaster and its aftermath or who is right. They exhibit the activity of reasoning itself. Distinct from the traditional logic of induction and deduction that proceeds by dichotomy, the examples show mainstream and critical statements that appear dichotomous to be paradoxically indistinguishable. Placing this indistinguishability beside other statements illuminates them as further examples of the same logical activity. In this method, what is shared among the examples is analogical, which is to say a resemblance of relation, indistinguishability between the opposing elements in each. In this way, the examples reciprocally illuminate the logical activity of each other, exposing and showing their contingency as groundless presuppositions.

In the next three sections, I examine the inseparability of disaster and founding education with examples of educational disaster and opportunity, student and teacher, and history and community. Each example considers opposing views, exhibiting their logical activity as the same: presupposing this inseparability as a void and the need to divide and abandon from this void to enact education in its possibilities, limits, and stake. The void corresponds to negation and presents itself as lack, absence, or other like expressions. Then I consider the examples together as an index of modern reasoning in which the stake is life and death and raise the question of the reasoning's inevitability. I summarize the analysis, responding to the guiding question and at the same time suspending the current reasoning of disaster and founding education, in order to present a different task of education that can unite a community sharing in what never was.

Educational Disaster and Opportunity

Cowen's statement presupposes Katrina as a natural phenomenon that voided the educational disaster NOLA public schools had become and an opportunity to suspend existing public education and re-vision: "We had a unique opportunity to rebuild, in a new vision, the future of public education." Few dispute the abysmal status of public schooling prior to Katrina, plagued by fiscal mismanagement and political infighting, racial segregation, among the lowest test scores in the nation, violence, decrepit facilities, and more. The void Katrina produced made it possible to suspend the system of public education in its entirety. In this suspension, to re-vision was to grasp public schooling as utterly empty, which must be divided from and abandoned to establish a system of education presenting every child the opportunity "regardless of their race, their socioeconomic class . . . to go and get a first class education and go on to college." This activity of reasoning—establishing public education as an unsalvageable void, suspending it in its entirety, and dividing and abandoning from it to found a reformed system—was the constitutive moment of public education in NOLA.

Critics of this vision characterize it as a monumental instance of "racial marginalization, removal, and state disinvestment" (Buras, 2010, p. 14). In the months after Katrina, Louisiana issued an "emergency suspension of education laws." The State Legislature passed Act 35, allowing 107 of 128 NOLA public schools to be deemed failing, and establishing a state-run Recovery School District (RSD). Shortly thereafter, almost all teachers, principals, and staff were terminated. The Bring New Orleans Back Commission, whose education subcommittee was spearheaded by Cowen, guided the creation of a school system. The system currently has two authorizing entities, the state school board and the Orleans Parish School Board (OPSB). NOLA public schools are operated either by the RSD (56 charters and 12 noncharters), OPSB (12 charters and 6 noncharters), or one of 42 nonprofit charter organizations (Cowen Institute, 2013). As of 2013, New Orleans has more than 40 independent school operators, with more than 70% of students attending charter schools (Cowen Institute, 2013). Throughout the system, the charter schools tend to have selective enrollment criteria restricting, for instance, students with special learning needs. They also tend to have enrollment caps and lower student–teacher ratios and employ experienced teachers. The noncharter schools cannot set such limits; they also have a much greater percentage of new teachers and teachers trained by alternative programs such as Teach for America who are not certified (Buras, 2010; Darling-Hammond, 2007).

This incomplete sketch only alludes to severe inequities and asymmetries recurring in the new NOLA school system. Yet critics use the same reasoning of void and abandonment to recognize a vision of teaching for social justice. Among such critics, the disaster resides with reformers in their ongoing experiment in neoliberal reforms, which, among other things, divide and differentiate schoolchildren through high-stakes testing, track students, enroll selectively, and give differential access to resources (Au, 2009; Giroux, 2006). Au notes how public schools in the United States "serve a dual and even contradictory function: they both reproduce social and economic inequalities and simultaneously create spaces for resistance to those very same inequalities" (in Buras, 2010, p. 138).

Such criticisms bring to light recognized inequities in school reform. Nevertheless, the vision of education for resistance and social justice presupposes public education both as a void or travesty of neoliberal experimentation and as constitutively divided into contradictory functions. The struggle to establish education for social justice thus becomes the necessity to divide and abandon from one of these dual functions. In doing so, "the process of naming our current reality, and . . . its constituent inequalities, automatically creates within us the ability to see the potential for radically new possibilities" (Au, in Buras, 2010, p. 141). Such emancipatory visions present the opportunity for hope, but it is misleading. For while they may produce new possibilities, they project a horizon of social equality that can never be realized, since education is already presupposed internally divided and abandoning itself.

In this way, mainstream reforms and their criticisms share the same reasoning of education's constitutive moment: NOLA public schooling is a void that must be divided from and abandoned. As such they are indistinguishable. The effect is that in both, visions of education expose the disaster—as void, division, and abandonment—only to presuppose it as the basis of opportunity, making any opportunity such as social equity already impossible to achieve. Public education is always already divided against itself, putting at stake the very potential of students and communities it attempts to aid and encourage.

Educability and Teacher Quality

Complementing Cowen's statement, the Bring New Orleans Back Commission's 2006 Education Committee Report states the following guiding principles.

> All children can learn and achieve when provided with the right kind of learning environment.
>
> The entire community: parents, businesses, religious organizations, and community groups all have important roles in supporting our children's education.
>
> Schools have a critical role to play in rebuilding the neighborhoods, culture, and spirit of New Orleans.

These guiding principles are examples that show the inseparability of disaster and founding education as a void that must be abandoned. The first principle emphasizes a good learning environment for all. Yet it entails two presuppositions of this void as the child's educability. For one, the very stating of these principles negates pre-Katrina public school students' learning experiences by alluding to the pre-Katrina system as the wrong kind of learning environment, a disaster fraught with severe deficiencies in educational preparation that must be divided from and abandoned to found the student his/her educability: the potential to learn and achieve and get a first-class education. Second, the learner is presupposed as bearing a void in that his/her potential to learn and achieve is itself indiscernible. Only when the child is provided "the right kind of learning environment" is the child recognizable as having the potential to learn and achieve.

The void is thus both external and internal to the student. The entrenched institutional inequities in pre-Katrina public schools establish students' educability as a function of external factors. And the Cowen Institute's documents acknowledge no potential in the student already there and able to be realized. The Institute's focus on achievement standards and institutional benchmarks to measure success is also silent in regard to the student. This silence and external focus show the student is reasoned first and foremost as a void: uneducable, the very figure of pre-Katrina schooling as the disaster that must be abandoned to found education and give the student his/her potential to learn.

In this reasoning, the experiences of prior learning and also the trauma of moving through disaster are often recognized by school staff as damage that impedes "real" learning or, alternatively, as crisis experiences bearing little or negatively on academic performance. The effect is to presuppose students as unable to meet academic expectations and in need of more ordered and authoritative ways of teaching (Ladson-Billings, 2007). In any case, students are not their own sites for learning. They must recognize, divide, and abandon that part of themselves and their experience that undermines their educability and seek an external knowledge incommensurable with their experience.

That students exhibit their educability through the "right kind of learning environment" reciprocally emphasizes teacher quality. The second principle concerns teachers directly but also extends to the school, family, and entire community. Here I limit analysis to the teacher, and in the next section I focus on community.

In the termination of virtually all NOLA teachers after Katrina, what it was to be a public school teacher was suspended and declared void (Polier, 2006). Existing criteria for recognizing teachers were abandoned—including but not limited to credentials, union representation, professional development—and new ones were established regarding who constitutes a teacher, recruitment and firing procedures, compensation, job requirements, and more. This occurred in the name of a need for quality teachers. Early on, Hill and Hannaway (2006, p. 30) stated the city "cannot afford to be a magnet for weak school providers, teachers, and principals who have failed elsewhere." Yet accountability in the district is so fragmented that teachers are effectively recognized and regulated without reference to a systematic knowledge of what are quality teachers and how to effectively train, recruit, and retain them.

> The state doesn't know what . . . large numbers of students are doing. . . . In public schools it's almost about half now so you . . . don't want half of your student body out of your control. . . . [O]n top of that you have the charter schools who are extremely autonomous in setting their hiring practices and their curriculums.
>
> (Perry & Rowell, 2007, p. 563)

Also, the district operates with no language or plan to direct teacher quality to be in correspondence with student need for support. Further, the district's assessment measures focus primarily on student performance tests, omitting crucial factors such as teacher–student ratios, adequate physical space, textbooks, library books, expenditures per student, and technology (Raynor, 2006).

Thus, while teacher quality articulates the very potential to teach, it has regulated teachers effectively without specific content, accountability, or institutional rules for teaching. Yet it would be misleading to conclude from this that establishing different or better content and rules would solve the problem of teacher quality. For the problem is not in content and rules of teaching but in the reasoning of potential to teach as a void to be abandoned. Every attempt to articulate a content and practice of quality teaching simply repeats this reasoning, negating teaching in the very act of recognizing the teacher's potential to teach.

Critics of these mainstream reforms also presuppose a void in the student and teacher as the problem to be abandoned. Just as mainstream reasoning, the void in the student is his/her miseducation in school. The testimony of Demetria White, who attended a poor-performing high school in Orleans parish, offers an example.

> I am a victim of teachers' neglect to make students think. For the past 13 years, I haven't thought about anything I was taught. I just repeated what the teacher wanted to hear. . . . To tell you the truth, I have no knowledge at all. . . . Everything they said, I recorded, memorized, and repeated in order to get the grade. Now . . . I am being asked to think about calculus. . . . For so long, I've been given the answer, but now I have to find a process, and I just don't know how.
>
> *(Buras, 2010, p. 57)*

Demetria's writing testifies to a range of effects that can occur when the content of performance-based tests comprise a curriculum's core and pedagogy for poor students and students of color emphasizes redemption-remediation through order and compliance (Ladson-Billings, 2007). Yet critics also presuppose Demetria as bearing an inner void that must be transformed by having her tell her story, take control of her voice and representation, and disrupt the dominant pedagogical discourse, creating spaces for students to become agents of their own education. The void is the dominant discourse victimizing the student from which a critical pedagogy becomes possible in the first place.

In critical approaches, the same reasoning makes possible the quality teacher. The inseparability of disaster and founding education appears as the inseparability of teacher and practice. This inseparability is presupposed as a void or negation in the teacher. For instance, the teacher is unable to teach in ways that bridge students' standardized test preparation and their personal experiences (Hursh, 2007). At the same time, the teacher's practice founds the potential of education. For instance, what constitutes exceptional teachers and how they can be trained is

already known but not yet integrated into teachers' training and modes of pedagogy (Robinson & Engel, 2007).

In the name of producing quality teachers, the void in the teacher must be
abandoned. This amounts to abandoning current practices or teachers or both to
improve teaching. At the same time, the division and incommensurability of teacher
and teaching precludes the teacher from actually achieving good educational practice. Thus, the teacher has the potential to struggle "pedagogically and politically
over both ideas and material relations of power as they affect diverse individuals and
groups" (Giroux, 2006, p. 189). Yet in this struggle, it is impossible for the teacher to
achieve good practice, since the division and incommensurability are presupposed.

Mainstream and critical approaches lead to the same effect: Teacher and student can only become agents of educational change through self-negation and
attempts to abandon a void. What it is to be a student and a teacher is radically shifting, uncertain, with no identifiable content or way of achieving quality teaching. In pedagogical practice, the teacher is already self-abandoning. This
self-abandonment is an essential teaching to the student, passed on as the potential
to learn that is reflected in Demetria's experience. At stake is what pedagogy and
learning reach and pass on, in this common condition in which neither teacher
nor student confronts the ongoing educational disaster.

History and Community

The following is a critique of mainstream reforms to NOLA public schools.

> New Orleans has a new time line. A new zero point. However, a natural
> event is by no means the sole cause for our new era. To understand post-
> Katrina, you have to understand pre-Katrina. Many folks in post-Katrina
> New Orleans, particularly in terms of public education . . . are salivating to
> start from scratch, to establish a new day and a new order, with nothing but
> disdain for the prezero.
>
> *(Randels & Salaam, 2010, p. 15)*

This critique exhibits a reasoning not just of historical events but of time itself as "a
new zero point." Cowen's statement of "the day Katrina happened and we closed
the system down" presents the notion of a zero point in mainstream reforms. In this
section, I show mainstream and critical reforms to share the same reasoning of this
zero point as division from and abandonment of the past as a void.

Mainstream reforms attempt to abandon the past, defining it as a failure in
order to establish "a new day and a new order." To state, as Cowen did, that the day
Katrina hit was "one of the best days for the future of the children of our city" was
to establish the present as the need to literally forget the past system, to "start from
scratch." To forget was thus to presuppose the past as a void from which to divide
and abandon "as if the *histories* of families, students, teachers and communities

could be wiped away by a flood, never to return to complicate a rebuilding effort" (Dingerson, 2007, p. 5, italics original).

In this forgetting, the students and communities in which education took place are abandoned. This is exemplified in numerous dimensions of reform for rebuilding. For instance, pre-Katrina, many New Orleanians lived near family and extended family among a strong network of neighbors and in the same neighborhood for generations. Now, in most parts of the parish, the school–neighborhood connection remains broken, with no plan to prioritize reestablishing it. In fact, numerous efforts have combined to maintain this separation. Planned closing of public housing projects or their transformation into less affordable mixed-income housing has meant fewer poor people, who were concentrated in specific neighborhoods, returning to the city. The return of students at different times and rates, along with charter schools' enrollment caps and the phenomenon of students being unchosen by charters for behavioral or other specialized needs, has meant that students go to schools wherever there is room and where they are not formally or informally pushed out (Frazier et al., 2007; Perry, 2007). Forgetting as abandonment of community also occurs as poorer communities are recognized only as detrimental to students' educability: sites of intergenerational trauma, disinterest in academics, and more. The student must abandon his/her community in order to succeed in school (Ladson-Billings, 2007).

The forgetting enacted by mainstream reforms has produced an educational "future of the children of our city" in which more students than before the "zero point" have access to academically achieving schools. Alongside is an "educational dumping ground" composed of certain noncharter schools whose physical space, curriculum, teaching-learning modes, and students are remnants of the past: disinvestment and being abandoned as uneducable. These remnants appear as a continuous generalized threat to securing the goals of mainstream reform.

Critics of the mainstream reforms function in the same way, producing the past as a void and forgetting. The past is presupposed as the act of forgetting one's ancestry and cultural history. The struggle to reclaim it thus becomes a positive potential to found critical education. To reclaim the past is to reclaim and develop students' voices as part of a greater historical struggle to articulate the truths of their lives, understand inequality, and see themselves as able to challenge existing dynamics of power and oppression.

Some of the educational work at Students at the Center, a writing-based program founded in part on the notion that "education is for community development in addition to individual student development," aims at reclaiming the past as a positive foundation (Frazier et al., 2007, p. 30). For instance, past and present are brought together to be mutually interrogated. Students are asked to bring questions in their present lives to inquire into and tell about the past; reciprocally, they reflect on how particular events of the past might have impacted them and how they might have responded (Michna, 2009). In this work, students recognize and identify with past oppression; simultaneously they refuse it in the present by seeking value and truth in themselves and their communities to overturn exactly what reformers condemn as negative. Education is experiencing the potential of struggle toward social justice, an ancestral past that is passed as a birthright to the present generation, a zero point from which to initiate a new future.

But this work of seeking to reclaim the past does not simply critique mainstream histories and reclaim a marginalized historical content of positive traditions and struggles to ground students and communities. For in this difficult work, the first thing learned is struggle itself, which is presupposed in order to be able to bring the present into relation with the past as one of abandonment. Further, the difficulty and intensity of examining the original forgetting or void is realized by Kalamu ya Salaam, an educator with Students at the Center, acknowledging that the experiences students write and speak of show great suffering and intergenerational trauma in which what is self-inflicted and inflicted by racism are not clearly distinguishable. As Salaam candidly expresses, examining this void opens both to the realization that an unproblematic history and set of traditions is mythical and to the potential of new voids or zero points (e.g., as shame) within oneself and one's community from which to divide and abandon (in Buras, 2010). The presupposition of original forgetting and struggle to remember and reclaim thus destines the student and community to be divided in themselves and from each other, belonging to a community dislocated in time: not yet present because learning to resist and already present from which a certain division and distance is sought.

Thus, the reasoning of both mainstream reforms and their critics places students at a present zero point presupposed as a void. This void is forgetting as wiping away the past or as losing one's ancestry and traditions. Forgetting must be divided from and abandoned to constitute history and community in the present. Yet the effect of this critical reasoning is that its gesture opens only to a freedom to participate or not in the presupposed and therefore interminable struggle, while the mainstream gesture opens only to a freedom of improving education as broadening who is responsible for it. At stake in both is what is forgotten every time, silently accompanying the classroom and neighborhood communities as the measure of disaster that education incessantly tries to but cannot put to rest.

Critiquing the Philosophical-Historical Existence of Presupposition

This analysis presents the inseparability of disaster and founding education as a reasoning of presupposition whose logic is declaring a void and dividing and abandoning from it. While ideas and criticisms on both mainstream and critical sides may expose problems and limits of education, the concern of my analysis is that they exhibit the same logic; their opposition is a consequence of differences in localizing the void. Drawing on the work of Agamben and Foucault, I now show this presuppositional logic as an index of modern reasoning. I consider the reasoning's historical existence, what is at stake in it, and its inevitability. I also point to implications of this reasoning for the case of NOLA schooling as regards the concept of racism through which the experience of inequity is represented.

In his inquiries into human potentiality, Agamben has shown how in Western reasoning, presupposition as producing a void to be divided from and abandoned has been the logical activity of human language as early as Aristotle. He has also shown how it has founded sovereign power (Agamben, 1998, 1999). But only in the latter half of the 18th century was this presuppositional power interiorized into humans, founding their existence as speaking, knowing, historical, and sovereign beings. One example illustrating this shift in reasoning to interiorize presuppositional power is found in Kant's faculty of judgment, through which human experience is formulated into systematic laws of nature. With judgment, Kant established human knowing nature as presupposing a void to be divided from and abandoned. Kant first presupposed the potential of human knowing as the constitutive impossibility for man to know nature (of which humans are nevertheless a part). This impossibility is a void. Then Kant presupposed nature as determined by universal laws of human understanding and as intelligible to the human mind. With this presupposition, the impossibility to know nature is divided out and abandoned, establishing human existence in the potential to know. At the threshold of modernity, Kant exemplifies this presuppositional reasoning of human potentiality that characterizes modern inquiry into experience and nature.

Foucault's work on modern biopower both corroborates this modern presuppositional reasoning of human potential and shows an effect is to put life and death at stake. The modern concept of biological life emerged as the presupposition of a void that both abandons itself to bring living beings into existence and paradoxically remains as the death that constantly threatens and reduces living beings to nothing (Foucault, 1994). He also showed a characteristic effect of modern biopower is the state's ability to make live and let die, one manifestation of which is racism. Racism appears inscribed in modern governing to identify within the state's population an internal figure of death incessantly threatening survival, which must be divided from and abandoned to make the population and state live and self-preserve (Foucault, 2003).

This confluence of Agamben's work on modern presuppositional logic and Foucault's work on modern biopower and racism shows an analogy of functioning through void, dividing, and abandoning. The present case of NOLA schooling permits a further analogy of functioning. Establishing public education and struggling to resist it, setting out future opportunity, and recognizing a historical legacy entail a reasoning of disaster and founding education that functions the same as the reasoning of human and nature exhibited in Kant's judgment and Foucault's characterization of racism.

Andre Perry, a leader in NOLA's charter movement and scholar of equity in education, stated Katrina exposed that the system of public education in New Orleans produced people who could not "get out of harm's way."

And we know that if you do not have a good education you are more likely to go to prison, you don't have adequate health care . . . but we learned . . . that you can't get out of harm's way.

(Perry, 2010)

Figures of the inability to get out of harm's way include the bloated Black body floating by in the toxic floodwaters and the survivor stranded on the rooftop ignored for rescue. These figures of desperate life seen yet overlooked accompany educational reformers and their critics, undercutting all illusion of new opportunities and critical struggles as actual ways out and demonstrating that the goal of education is now mere biological survival in a world of making live and letting die.

What distinguishes mainstream and critical reasoning is, first of all, which group is localized and isolated as the figure of letting die: Are poor Black people authors of their own plight? Are racism and capitalism and the oppressed existence within oneself? Are we all implicated because we first degraded nature that creates consequences that haunt us all? And second, who gets to divide and abandon from it? Whatever the internal figure of death, it remains threatening biological survival as the very inseparability of disaster and founding education.

The reasoning itself, founded on the logic of void, dividing, and abandoning, is not registered as a problem even as it attempts to address asymmetries of equity in education and social life. Perry exemplifies this predicament. He suggests the sign of educational innovation will be that the very people trapped and neglected after the storm are those sustaining public education. Yet the goal remains, "We have got to build an educational system in the very least to get out of the way of a storm." At stake is biological life divided out and abandoned in public education; simultaneously, biological survival is the criterion above all of education; that is, "in the very least . . ." Innovation is conceived as "having the same educational opportunity" such that those currently on the margins who suffer from social-political-economic inequities are brought into education as the element to identify education as a success or failure (Perry, 2010). Rather than removing those suffering from abandonment, they are localized at the center of education to found it, again, as the same precarious internal-exterior void through which education is to rebuild.

This not only leaves the reasoning intact but also presupposes its logic as the goal and solution. As such, the reasoning—including its concepts of racism and educational reform—appears inevitable. It is inconceivable, in this reasoning, to guarantee life and education for those who find themselves at its center and foundation. Thus it remains haunted by those figures of death that constantly open it to its own repeating disaster.

Responding to the Question

At this point, I offer a provisional response to the guiding question. The inseparability of disaster and founding education is not only a phenomenon that exposed broad, profound social inequities in public schooling. It is a historical paradigm of that through which reasoning presupposes, at the level of ontology, human potential of education and the social. The response is further summarized in the following comments.

- The reasoning of reestablishing public schooling in NOLA exhibits a logical activity of declaring a void and necessity to divide from and abandon it.
- The disaster identified in this analysis is not an objective state of events, whether natural and/or human induced. It is the presupposition of this reasoning, the reasoning as presupposition.
- This presupposing functions to set out the ontological existence of entities including public schooling, racism, community, and human potential.
- The reasoning of mainstream educational reforms and that of its critics shares this ontological activity. Their objects of concern, possibilities, and limits appear oppositional but only repeat the same reasoning. This situation ensures that rebuilding public education, history, and community share the common condition of dividing, abandoning, and being abandoned.
- A philosophical-historical analysis of the reasoning indicates analogies of functioning across different ways human being is enacted in different spheres of life.
- One of these analogies relevant to NOLA schooling is racism. In light of this analysis, racism, while recognized as a problem, nevertheless corresponds in mainstream educational reform and its critics to the same reasoning of presupposing a void from which to divide and abandon.

A Different Task, Uniting in What Never Was

The analysis has presented in practice and scholarship the tendency to negate and abandon what is lost by erasing it as a blank slate, filling it with a historical ancestry or future opportunity, inquiring into it as becoming educated. This double gesture of negation and turning away from what is lost, the dead, forgotten, without potential as such, is repeated beyond NOLA schooling in every sphere of life education touches.

The analysis and provisional response open upon a new question: what would it be to present an experience of education without repeating this double gesture? Without abolishing current reasoning of education, allow for innovation with the very element abolished in this reasoning: the void itself. To present such an experience would entail, first of all, noticing that the void abandoned is not simply an absence or nothing, that is, strictly a form of being-negativity. It is rather the experience of being-void, -death, -privation as experiencing education, participating in a community, having a history and identity. This experience is active within and among schoolchildren, including Demetria and countless others, precisely as being negated and forgotten. It indicates something remains of being-void that is irreducible to negation even if intangible, ungraspable, and not recognizable as an attribute.

What would it be to present an experience of education with this sense of being-void? To not betray it would correspond to bringing the disaster, which is to say the reasoning, to a stop without negating and abandoning it, to hold the reasoning as that in which is a chance to welcome being-void as a positive experience of what was never seen, realized, or remembered. With this innovation, being-void remains as firm and sure. In the inability to learn what should or must be learned, one is now simply being true. In the inability to belong to history or community, one now shares in an experience of being separate together, realizing what never was. Such a community is separated from the reasoning of mainstream educational reform and its critics yet inseparable from current conceptions of education and race as embodying their limit and end. Being and community are, poised, the weight of educability itself.

References

Agamben, G. (1998). *Homo sacer: Sovereign power and bare life.* Stanford, CA: Stanford University Press.

Agamben, G. (1999). *Potentialities: Collected essays in philosophy.* Stanford, CA: Stanford University Press.

Agamben, G. (2009). *The signature of all things: On method.* Cambridge, MA: Zone Books.

Au, W. (2009). *Unequal by design: High-stakes testing and the standardization of inequality.* New York: Routledge.

Bring New Orleans Back Commission—Education Committee. (2006). *Rebuilding and transforming: A plan for improving public education in New Orleans.* Retrieved from www.coweninstitute.com/our-work/applied-research/education-archive/education-transformation-archive/rebuilding-and-transforming/

Brunsma, D., Overfelt, D., & Picou, S. (2007). *The sociology of Katrina: Perspectives on a modern catastrophe.* New York: Rowman and Littlefield.

Buras, K. (2010). *Pedagogy, policy and the privatized city: Stories of dispossession and defiance from New Orleans.* New York: Teachers College Press.

Cowen Institute for Public Education Initiatives. (2010). *2010 state of public education in New Orleans.* New Orleans, LA: Tulane University.

Cowen Institute for Public Education Initiatives. (2013). *2013 state of public education in New Orleans.* New Orleans, LA: Tulane University.

Cowen, S. (2010). *Our children are the future.* Retrieved from www.youtube.com/watch?v=nDfrvYGhvTc

Darling-Hammond, L. (2007). Countering aggressive neglect: Creating a transformative educational agenda in the wake of Katrina. In S. Robinson & M. Christopher Brown II (Eds.), *The children Hurricane Katrina left behind: Schooling context, professional preparation, and community politics* (pp. xi–1). New York: Peter Lang.

Dingerson, L. (2007). *Unlovely: How a market-based education system is failing New Orleans children.* Retrieved from http://theneworleansimperative.files.wordpress.com/2011/02/n-o-_charters_dingerson_20071.doc

Foucault, M. (1994). *The order of things: An archaeology of the human sciences.* New York: Vintage.

Foucault, M. (2003). *Society must be defended: Lectures at the Collège de France, 1975–76.* New York: Picador.

Frazier, A., Hernandez, M., Barconey, J., Mayfield, C., Jones, A., Carr, C., Kelly, A., & Randels, J. (2007). Narratives from 'Students at the Center.' *High School Journal, 90*(2), 30–50.

Giroux, H. (2006). Reading Hurricane Katrina: Race, class, and the biopolitics of disposability. *College Literature, 33*(3), 171–196.

Hill, P., & Hannaway, J. (2006). *After Katrina: Rebuilding opportunity and equity into the* new *New Orleans.* Washington, DC: Urban Institute.

Hursh, D. (2007). 'No Child Left Behind' and the rise of neoliberal education policies. *American Educational Research Journal, 44*(3), 493–518.

Ladson-Billings, G. (2007). Pushing past the achievement gap: An essay on the language of deficit. *Journal of Negro Education, 76*(3), 316–323.

Michna, C. (2009). Stories at the Center: Story circles, educational organizing, and fate of neighborhood public schools in New Orleans. *American Quarterly, 61*(3), 529–555.

Perry, A., & Rowell, C. H. (2007). An interview with Andre Perry. *Callaloo, 31*(2), 556–563.

Perry, A. (2010). *Education reform.* Retrieved from www.youtube.com/watch?v=CL-YZy QduLw&feature=related

Polier, N. (2006). After Katrina: Tales from a chartered school classroom. *Radical Teacher, 76,* 20–23.

Randels, J., & Salaam, K. (2010). Introduction: Scorching the earth isn't the way: New Orleans before and after. In Buras, K. *Pedagogy, policy and the privatized city: Stories of dispossession and defiance from New Orleans* (pp. 15–16). New York: Teachers College Press.

Raynor, A. (2006). Save the last chance for me: Quality education in high schools for the young people who need it most. *High School Journal, 90*(2), 51–58.

Robinson, S., & Engel, P. (2007). Creating world-class teachers: Prospects for Katrina recovery and beyond. In S. Robinson & M. Christopher Brown II (Eds.), *The children Hurricane Katrina left behind: Schooling context, professional preparation, and community politics* (pp. xi–1). New York: Peter Lang.

Troutt, D. (2006). *After the storm: Black intellectuals explore the meaning of Hurricane Katrina.* New York: New Press.

Tuzzolo, E., & Hewitt, D. (2007). Rebuilding inequity: The re-emergence of the school-to-prison pipeline in New Orleans. *High School Journal, 90*(2), 59–68.

6

VOLUNTARY SERVITUDE AS A NEW FORM OF GOVERNING

Reinstating Kneeling-Bowing Rites in Modern Chinese Education

Weili Zhao

Confucian Kneeling-Bowing Rites Creeping Back Into Contemporary Chinese Schools

Since the 1912 Sun Yat-sen administration constitutionally banned and replaced the kneeling-bowing rite with (standing)-bowing rite in daily and social life, movies and TV plays, like *The Last Emperor* produced by Bernardo Bertolucci in 1986, seem to be one of the only few remaining venues for visually refreshing this historical memory about imperial China. However, in the past few years, a similar theatrical scene finds its stage once in a while in China's real-life schooling milieu when hundreds or thousands of students are called upon to kneel-bow to their teachers/parents as an expression of gratitude.

In his lecture at the Inner Mongolia high school, Li Yang, an English teacher famous for promoting his own Crazy English pedagogy at Chinese schools, called upon more than 3,500 students to kneel-bow toward the few teachers on the stage to show their gratitude right before the 2007 Teacher's Day (Wang, 2007). On June 6, 2010, more than 900 high school seniors in Wuhan City were asked to kneel-bow to their teachers to show gratitude in their commencement ceremony. The school leader said they would develop this kneeling-bowing rite into school commencement culture (Chongqing Morning News, June 6, 2011). On May 4, 2011, the well-known Guangdong Experimental Middle School held a Passage Rite for the eighth graders in the school sports field, where they were called to kneel down to receive a family letter from their parents. This youth Passage Rite was claimed to commemorate the 1919 May 4th spirit, that is, science, freedom, democracy, and progress. The principal said this nice Passage Rite idea, actually from a student, would be continued in the future because they believe this kneeling-bowing rite, as a highest

Confucian ritual format, would remain profoundly impressive to the students in their whole life (Xin Kuai Bao, 2011).

These kneeling-bowing events happened at a time when China's current educational reforms claim to be "human-based and morality-education-prioritized" (Middle and Long Educational Reform, 2010) and its morality education policy has witnessed a "care-of-life turn" from its earlier state-ideology focus (China Ministry of Education, 2003; Lu & Gao, 2004). Both reforms aim to train and produce virtuous, wise, strong-bodied, and aesthetically beautiful students. Along with this kneeling-bowing rite is the reintroduction of some Confucian value primers like *Three Character Classics* (三字經) and *Filial Piety Classics* (孝經) into the K–12 school morality education curriculum. With China's market economy prospering, overall moral quality deteriorating, and nationalistic Confucianism rising, that nationwide morality education is highly needed seems to be a unanimous consensus. However, every time when students physically kneel-bow as in the abovementioned events to show gratitude to teachers and parents, willingly and/or unwillingly, it immediately incurs a nationwide outcry that such kneeling-bowing performance is a huge pain and shame to China's current (morality) education. They argue that education is supposed to train *upright* students, so how can students kneel down like slaves?

The pain-shame plays out in an incessantly entangled discursive battle mediated through numerous online media and weblogs (blogs). Two apparently oppositional modes of reasoning are schematically discernible from these discursive debates, which frame the kneeling-bowing performance within a value pendulum— highest (Confucian) versus servile feudal ritual. Meanwhile, this commonsensical and reductive binary reasoning almost violently drowns out an intermittent, barely audible, but provocative sensitivity voiced by some students, teachers, and parents, saying that in performing or receiving the kneeling-bowing rite, they experienced an ethical new form of understanding and being of themselves and others.

The highest-ritual reasoning, not a popular viewpoint and mainly based upon some claimed traditional Confucian cultural principles, argues (a) since it is traditionally said that "it is parents who give children the bodies but teachers who cultivate (illuminate) the bodies" (生身者父母/明身者師長), it is surely appropriate for students to kneel-bow to their parents and teachers to show respect and gratitude; and (b) that the reinstatement of this kneeling-bowing rite in China's schooling symbolizes a "Chinese Renaissance" (Wang, 2007), would produce virtuous students, and would revive China's boasted old civilization of respecting teachers and prioritizing education (see, e.g., Chou Yu Ni Mo, 2010; Topic Today at QQ.com 2011).

The feudal-ritual reasoning is overwhelmingly predominant and historically mainly derived from the 1919 May 4th New Cultural Movement thought, a cultural milestone highlighting the introduction of modern Western notions such as science, freedom, democracy, and progress into modern China. This reasoning argues that (a) the kneeling-bowing act, as a most humiliating demeanor signaling an absolute servile submission to power domination, humiliates whoever performs it and should be sent to tombs for good; (b) its reappearance in schooling has set China's current education in downgraded pain and shame as it distorts the students' soul and personality into abject servants rather than the sought-after independent, free, and modern citizens; and (c) its reappearance in the current democratic, modern, and rational China marks a humiliation to the Chinese people, who finally and just recently stood up in 1949 when Chairman Mao claimed sonorously in the Tiananmen Square that "Chinese people finally stood up" (see, e.g., Chou Yu Ni Mou, 2010; Feng, 2007; Wang, 2011; Zhu Feng Hou Niao, 2007).

Media reports on the Guangzhou Middle School Passage Rite said that most parents were deeply moved into tears by this kneeling ceremony. One father said in tears in the interview that he found his daughter had already grown up and he felt deeply moved but also guilty, as he didn't care enough about his daughter at other times. The daughter said with tears in her eyes that she was very surprised to hear such words from her father, and although most fellow classmates hesitated a bit about kneeling down at first, afterwards they felt really touched (Xin Kuai Bao, 2011). For the Chongqing High School Commencement Ceremony, one 12th-grade Chinese teacher said that he was deeply touched on the stage when students knelt-bowed to teachers and saw it as an expected expression of the school's persistent morality education. One 12th-grade student said that "teachers work really hard and sacrifice a lot for us at other times and our kneeling-bowing is just a more formal way to show gratitude." One parent said, "China has a historical tradition of respecting teachers and prioritizing teaching, but kneeling-bowing doesn't have to become a necessary form to show gratitude" (Chongqing Morning News, 2010).

It is not hard to see from these discursive fragments that these controversial educational kneeling-bowing events actually implicate a whole ensemble of social and cultural issues related to tradition–modernity, body–self, governing, embodied (ritual) education, teacher–student (parent–child) governing, and their intersubjectivity. The complexity makes the events significant to scholars, though intellectually unpacking their complex contour becomes extremely complicated, too. This chapter makes one tentative, far from exhaustive attempt to untangle the convoluted contour of the kneeling-bowing controversy.

Specifically, this chapter examines the convoluted reasoning on the contentious governing rationality between teachers/parents and students/children embedded within the kneeling-bowing events. Methodologically, Foucault's governing logic guides my historicizing and problematizing those traditional Confucian and modern (associated with the reform May 4th movement) epistemological and cultural principles that ground and enable the dominant binary reasoning. I approach this binary by examining intersected domains of body–self conflation, teacher–student power relation, and subjectivity. This examination entails the discursive analysis of online media and weblogs about kneeling-bowing events and their intersection with other indexed classical and modern texts.

Governing Dynamics Rethought: Should-Be to Can-Be Intersubjectivity

Focusing on the teacher–student governing rationality shifts my focus from institutional (say, schools) pragmatics of enforcing the kneeling-bowing practices or teachers' psychological will to govern students to unpacking the various cultural principles that have legitimatized the various kneeling-bowing ways of reasoning. It sets the teacher–student intersubjectivity into a broader social and historical context and conceives the pragmatic objectives and psychological will (if there is any) as effects of historical power relation dynamics, embodied through the subjects' conducting of conduct in the Foucauldian sense.

Foucault's governing logic helps to discern that the value-laden predominant debate about bowing/kneeling placed in the "highest versus servile ritual" binary is actually limited to an identity struggle—that is, what teachers and students are or should be vis-à-vis themselves and relationally in order to gain more power along the culturally inscribed hierarchical or egalitarian teacher–student intersubjectivity. This should-be identity contention reductively couches the kneeling-bowing performance within a schema of involuntary servitude and violently precludes the ethical and harmonious understanding as a possible but provocative affect sensed in the kneeling-bowing events.

Therefore I argue this binary governing logic is not sufficient to understand the rationality of the new ethical principles of governing voiced by some kneeling-bowing performers. I reframe this governing dynamic in a way that brings together and rearticulates Foucault's ethical sense of caring for self and others and Confucius's narrative on ritual performance in *Analects* as a what-teachers-students-can-be logic. This governing is imagined as voluntary servitude, not in the sense of voluntarily seeking to be slaves that Foucault jokes about in his retort (how can we seek to be slaves?) but in the sense of voluntarily and actively serving and caring for self and others toward a harmonious teacher–student mutual understanding. To be more specific, this voluntary serving and caring is a governing through an opened emanation of the inner dispositions after the imposed epistemological common sense is bracketed or exploded. This recalibrating Foucauldian thought within classical Chinese thought is to provide a way of studying the new ethical form of intersubjectivity as a new cultural and social space to rethink the controversial kneeling-bowing events in China's current (morality) education reform in a manner that is not merely adding one analytic onto another.

What Should Teachers and Students Be? Historicizing Body–Self Ambiguity, Embodied Education, and the Kneeling-Bowing Rite

The cited statements—"parents give children bodies but teachers cultivate (illuminate) their bodies" and "the kneeling-bowing practice distorts the soul of the students and personality and marks a humiliation to the Chinese people who finally and just recently stood up in 1949"—underlie an intricate body–self separation and conflation. The visible bodily (knees') up-down distance is superimposed upon and gets conflated into an invisible social differentiation, that is, bodily categories get socialized. In this section, I historicize this body–self separation–conflation in relation to embodied education and the historical kneeling-bowing rite.

Historically, the Chinese cultural notion body points toward a "psychosomatic" self (Ames, 1993, p. 165), that is, a whole person with heart as a unified counterpart for the Western modern divisions of body-mind-soul self. This Chinese body is not a mere given or owned object as some essential locus or container of universal claims such as individual, nor merely a source of representations (Hevia, 2005) that can, for example, be transposed into and give meanings to Chinese arts and literature. In a perpetual making or cultivating process, the Chinese body is to be lived and done, mediated in as well as mediating and naturalizing the patterns, roles, and relations of power in Chinese social communication. Interpersonal understanding is hence to be bodily performed and heartily felt toward each other (Sun, 1991). There is a strong ambiguity between a physical body and a psychological self in (especially pre-modern) Chinese thought.

Learning in the Confucian sense is learning to make an exemplary person through the lifelong stonecutting process of body cultivating or body beautification through the cultivation of six arts or techniques including ritual, poetry, and music. By body beautification, it means that

> an exemplary person's learning (is supposed to) enter into his ear, reach his heart, permeate through the limbs and embody itself fully in a person's every single movement and posture, spanning a whole body of 7 feet, while a petty person's learning enters into his ear and exits from his mouth, spanning only four inches.
>
> *(Xunzi: Quanxue, n.d.)*

An ideal body beautification is a harmonious cultivation and expression of psychosomatic dispositions including both a nonformalized humane person (self) and a formalized structure with comportment of bodily behaviors (Ames, 1993).

The kneeling-bowing rite, "as the head touches down to the ground and henceforth the highest format of showing respect" (*Banggu: Baihutong* cited in Yan, 1999), functions as such an embodied educational ritual in Confucian teacher–student relation. In ancient China, with no chairs or tables, people all kneel-sit on the floor mattress with their hands laid on their laps. When receiving honorable guests who also kneel-sit on the floor, people simply conveniently straighten them up into a kneeling posture and lay their hands on the floor, which is later appropriated and developed into the kneeling-bowing ritual practice (Wang, K.X., 2004; Yan, 1999). Within the psychosomatic body–self framework, performing this highest respectful format doesn't entail a body–self conflation; that is, the physical kneeling down is not interlocked with social/mental submission.

Ironically, after Chinese body and self are separated into two domains, this same psychosomatic body–self ambiguity surreptitiously reunites and conflates the bodily with the social and political. Actually, the conflation of the physical genu-flection with mental and spiritual submission reaches an extent unimaginable in the past. In the imperial Qing Dynasty, this kneeling-bowing rite was structured into nine extreme formats and reached its heyday ordering the then hierarchical society. Its canonical status started to be challenged through the few historical cross-cultural events in which the 1783 McCartney Mission Group and the 1873 Foreign Mission Groups refused to perform the full kneeling-bowing guest rites to the then Qing Emperors (see Hevia, 2005; Wang, K. X., 2004). New cultural movement forerunners Tan Citong and Liang Qichao claimed that traditional kneeling-bowing rites, mobilized by rulers as a mean mechanism to enslave mass people's minds, could only develop people's slavelike blind loyalty and filial piety at the cost of their independent personality and sense of democracy. Therefore, they argue revolution should first of all start with the debasement of the superior and the cancellation of kneeling-bowing ritual practices (Wang, K. X., 2004). Finally, the standing-bowing rite constitutionally replaced it in 1912; however, the body–self conflation remains.

When Chairman Mao claimed sonorously in the Tiananmen Square that "Chinese people finally stood up," what is made clear too is a paradoxical body–self separation–conflation: Physical standing up symbolizes a mental standing up and independence from imperial colonialism and feudal lords. What is meanwhile explicitly implied is that Chinese people's knees can't be genuflected again, as in modern China, kneeling down is already symbolically transformed into an essen-tial feature of the traditional Chinese world order as feudal servile dross in relation to total power submission and distortion of one's dignity. Put succinctly, it should be sent to tombs for good.

Historicizing Teacher–Student (Parent–Child) Identity Contention

The kneeling-bowing events also foreground an identity contention on who teachers and students should be in their power relation. The contention plays out through these questions implied in the cited statements: Would the performing of this kneeling-bowing rite in China's schooling help to revive China's boasted old civilization of respecting teachers and prioritizing education—in other words, to put teachers back in their ideal authoritative social positions as historically assumed? Would the performing of this kneeling-bowing rite help to imbue a sense of gratitude in students toward teachers/parents, that is, to produce virtuous students? Or would it instead distort the students' soul and personality into abject servants submissive to teachers' power domination?

The cultural principles through which the identities of teacher–student relations are being made contentious also saliently strike China's current debates on curriculum reforms, basically, a Soviet Union Kaiipob's knowledge-based curriculum versus a constructionist student-based curriculum (Wang, C. S., 2004; Zhong & You, 2004). Since 2001, the student-centered pedagogy reform, coupled with the over-spoiled, ego-centered, only-child generation, is often cited as jeopardizing the authoritative social status that Chinese teachers used to assume. One expression is that teachers' scolding rights, which used to be thought as a taken-for-granted necessity (to note: not in the sense of good or bad) in Chinese teacher–student power relations, had to be legally stipulated by the Ministry of Education in 2009 as a "protection of teachers' rights" (Popkewitz, Khurshid, & Zhao, in press). This regulation was claimed to have empowered teachers in their conducting and managing the conduct of students in schooling (Shanghai Oriental TV News Report, 2009). And the current kneeling-bowing events are claimed to have set China's modern education in shame and pain, as kneeling jeopardizes modern students into becoming abject servants rather than who they should be—independent, free, and modern citizens.

So the kneeling-bowing event should be further historicized through the teacher–student power relation in Chinese society that claims to have a past civilization of respecting teachers and prioritizing education. That is, teachers or masters in their broadest sense historically enjoy a very high social status ordered right after heaven, earth, emperors, and parents (天地君親師). Other cultural expressions include: It is parents who give children bodies but teachers who illuminate/cultivate their bodies; teachers for one day should be treated by their students as "fathers" for a whole life (一日為師一生為父); teaching is expected to be very authoritative and teachers very strict with students (师道尊严). The Confucian value primer *Three Character Classics* that is being reintroduced to K–12 schools as part of their morality education curriculum says, "lack of the strictness symbolizes the laziness of the teachers" (教不嚴師之惰). These cultural principles make it possible to reason about the kneeling-bowing events as cited in the introduction of this chapter: It is surely appropriate for students to kneel-bow to their parents and teachers to show respect and gratitude; the reinstatement of this kneeling-bowing rite (not only) in China's schooling symbolizes a Chinese renaissance and would produce virtuous students, as well as revive China's boasted old civilization of respecting teachers and prioritizing education. In other words, students should be virtuous and respectful and teachers/parents should be authoritative and respectable.

Apart from showing respect and gratitude to their authoritative or egalitarian parents, the Guangdong school principal claims that performing the educational kneeling Passage Rite is also to commemorate the 1919 May 4th spirit: science, freedom, democracy, and progress. Ironically, the critics say the very kneeling-bowing rite goes right against the May 4th spirit (see, e.g., Topic Today at QQ.com 2011; Wang, 2011) and would, to their dismay and anger, train students into becoming abject servile subjects instead of the free, democratic, progressive citizens sought after by the May 4th spirit. The kneeling-bowing rite, they claim, has set China's current education in pain and shame, and three cultural statements or theses strike out supporting their arguments.

First thesis: "There is no gratitude between fathers (parents) and sons (children)," a claim by Lu Xun, a cultural movement forerunner, which adamantly challenges the Chinese hierarchical ordering between parent/teacher and student. In his *How Do We Make Parents for the Present?* (1919), Lu Xun argues that the Chinese hierarchical parent–child way of thinking entails parents' total psychosomatic determination of children. That is, parents' giving bodies to children entails parents' owning children's bodies (and selves) and children's paying the gratitude-debt for a whole lifetime. This mode of thought, Lu Xun further argues, works against the natural law such as Darwinism and eugenics and has caused Chinese society to retrogress. He wishes that "the then fathers would shoulder the dark inheritance burden and liberate their children to bright places for living a happy life as rational humans" (cited in Wang, 2011).

Second thesis: "To fight for your individual freedom and integrity is to fight for freedom and integrity for your nation and free and equal society can't be built by a group of servile subjects," a claim by Hu Shi, another cultural movement forefather, which is quoted by the critics as "admonition to be given to every current educational worker" (cited in Wang, 2011). As current educational workers, the critics continue, "they should regard it as their obligation to clear away the servile factors in the students, help students establish ideals of democracy and equality, and train students to become modern citizens with independent integrity" (Wang, 2011).

Third thesis: *(Teachers) Can't Teach With Knees Down,* the title of an anthology by Wu Fei (2004), a current well-known high school Chinese teacher, who argues that "teachers can't teach kneeling down if they want their students to become a standing-up person" because "kneeling down is a symbol of servile submission to power dominance and a constraint of free and independent thinking." Therefore he asks, "If teachers can't think independently, what kind of people would their students be?" (cited in Chou Yu Ni Mo, 2007). His way of reasoning is an expression of the highlighted May 4th thinking that symbolically conflates physical genuflection with mental submission.

The endless critiques on the kneeling-bowing events are heavily confined to this hierarchical or egalitarian and virtuous or abject teacher–student (parents–children) identity debate. Seen this way, the kneeling-bowing rite becomes a decontextualized cultural symbol (virtuous or abject) that should be gladly reinstated or sent to tombs for good in current China.

This reductive logic violently dismisses the possible opening up of performers' agentive or authentic pure being and precludes the possible emergence of an ethical and transformative understanding between the teachers/parents and students as voiced by some kneeling-bowing performers. Then how can it be possible to theoretically reframe and practically render visible the authentic, pure teacher–student being and the ethical teacher–student governing sensibility?

What Teachers and Students Can Be: Voluntary Servitude as a New Lens to Rethink Teacher–Student Intersubjectivity

This ethical understanding between teachers and students (parents and children) implies that Foucault's governing rationale can be brought into a conversation with elements of classical Chinese thought. I pick up Foucault's understanding of the ethical sense of being imagined in the case of homosexuality and reframe it into my understanding of the Confucian narrative on ritual performance in *Analects*. In so doing, I argue this transformative, ethical teacher–student understanding evidenced in the kneeling-bowing events can be understood historically as a relational mode of thought embodied in the lens of voluntary servitude. This voluntary servitude has two mutually informing layers of meaning for this chapter. First, it means a system of reason whose logic of governing is one of actively and voluntarily serving and caring for self and others; and second, it means a bracketing of the imposed epistemological framings through which an authentic being of self and others, that is, the Confucian sense of humane dispositions, is given a chance to emanate voluntarily.

Foucault argues that "at the very heart of the power relationship and constantly provoking it are the recalcitrance of the will and the intransigence of freedom," which entails not to "discover what we are" but to "refuse what we are" and, more important, to "imagine and build up an ethical sense of freedom," a new what-we-could-be mode of being of self and others (Foucault, 2003). Foucault illustrates this new form of subjectivity as a being of care for self and others toward a new form of friendship in his homosexuality argument. To some extent, this gesture of Foucault overlaps with my hermeneutical interpretation of the Confucian narratives in *Analects* about ritual performance (*li* 禮) in relation to inner dispositions (*ren* 仁) and an expectant harmonious affect (*he* 和). My hermeneutical textual rendering aims to expose this Confucian sensibility in order to better understand contemporary Chinese subjectivities: Performing the embodied rituals is justified by Confucius as an invaluable technique or art through which an authentic, pure sense of being can be happily and directly opened up, experienced, understood, and rendered visible bodily. This cultural sensibility is largely obscured or covered up in the later prevalent and reductive treatment of (largely canonical) Confucian rites as merely external norms for the rulers to top-down govern the subjects (see, e.g., Hall & Ames, 1987; Qian, 2005; Zhang, 1996).

In the *Analects*, Confucius maps out the ordering between *ren* (humane dispositions), *li* (embodied ritual performing), and *he* (harmonious affect) like this: Actively and joyfully performing the socially established, say, kneeling-bowing ritual is first conditioned upon a person's inner humane disposition and meanwhile best embodies a voluntary emanation of those humane dispositions. Performing rituals this way is to hopefully achieve a valuable, contingent, harmonious intra-/interpersonal understanding that is heartily felt by and toward each other. However, this valuable harmonious understanding can't be achieved for the sake of harmony itself; it is only made possible as an emergent felt with the inner humane dispositions as its source and the appropriate ritual performance as its embodied and ordered expression. Confucius says, "If a person is not humane in the first place, how can he perform the rites appropriately and how can he enjoy performing the appropriate rituals?" (Analects 3:3), and the achieved harmonious state or affect is the "most beautiful in the Way of the Former Kings, and manifest in all things great and small" (Analects 1:12). (*A note is here about the Confucian notion he understood as a harmonious state in which the ritual performers dwell in a joyful togetherness yet remain in separateness rather than a unified, stable state in the Western sense of harmony.*) Confucius would still perform the complicated kneeling-bowing rite even though most people at his time prefer the easy standing-greeting rite (*Lunyu: Zihan*) as, to him, the voluntary and active performing best experiences and embodies a humane (virtuous and authentic pure) subjective being.

This Confucian *ren* (仁), just as Ames rightly argues, "as a homophone of person (*ren* 人) denoting achieved personhood, is the whole human process: body and mind" (Ames, 1993, p. 164). Furthermore, Confucian *ren* and *li* are both psychosomatic dispositions in that they differ qualitatively in degree (not in kind) within an ordering of a whole being, with *ren* being nonformalized while *li* is a formalized and refined structure with a comportment of bodily behaviors. The fullest realization of the human being is as an active and creative participant in experiencing the ongoing shaping of a harmonious (aesthetic, moral, physical, psychical) order with a person and among humans. This harmonizing interpersonal relationship is to be achieved through the actors' productive and active embodiment and expression as well as the receptive experience of their heart through bodily performances toward each other (Ames, 1993; Hevia, 2005; Qian, 2005).

Seen this way, it is possible that students are called upon to kneel-bow without a voluntary will and heartfelt gratitude to teachers, and accordingly they don't feel anything in their performances. If so, their involuntary performing can be turned into a forced physical submission or servility, that is, involuntary servitude. It is still possible that students' kneeling-bowing performance (voluntary or not) can be institutionally and psychologically appropriated as a political strategy to, say, empower teachers indirectly or directly and gain dominance (physical or mental) over students. It is also possible that this unwilling kneeling-bowing performativity gestures toward a situational understanding and care of self and others. More important, though maybe less likely, it is possible that performing the kneeling-bowing rite *become* a gesture of voluntary servitude as a newly exposed form of being to serve and care for self and others, the productive force of which can give the inner human dispositions, say, heartfelt gratitude, a possibility to flow out voluntarily and meaningfully.

Inverting Body–Self Conflation, Identity Contention, and Symbolic Representation

The productive force of this ethical care of self and others also lies in the extent to which the lens of voluntary servitude can bracket and subvert the current predominant epistemological binary logic enveloping the principles of interrelated body–self conflation, identity contention, and symbolic representation. (*This subversion of the binary logic also gestures toward a possible, not necessary, dynamic movement experienced by the kneeling-bowing performers in their bodily performance, embodying the making and unmaking of what they can be vis-à-vis themselves or relationally.*)

First, this voluntary-servitude lens can loosen up the normalized separation–conflation complex between bodily genuflection and social submission toward experiencing a new movement between one's physical body and a holistic mode of being. That is, an attitude of voluntarily and actively serving or caring for self and teacher/students can temporarily subordinate the physical kneeling body to a harmonious affect of dwelling in togetherness. That is, the visible kneeling act is deferred to the background and forgotten and the heartfelt deep feelings voluntarily flow out and get accented. With a serving heart, what is bodily rendered visible in the embodied teacher–student kneeling-bowing performance is no longer the physical kneeling down but a humane emanation of inner virtuous dispositions, the heartfelt respect and gratitude and care in this case.

Second, this voluntary-servitude lens, marking a paradigm shift from a teacher–student should-be identity to a can-be possibility, calls for an alternative understanding of the teacher–student differentiation. Socially and culturally inscribed differentiation in teacher–student social positions is bracketed for a moment toward a harmonious belonging. This doesn't mean that performing the kneeling-bowing ritual from a voluntary servitude perspective precludes or dissolves the social differentiation of the teacher–student identities. Rather, the socially imagined differentiated identities are not politically or psychologically interlocked with winning a power struggle in this fluid space. Instead, the differentiated identities of teachers and students give way to a mutually informing experience of understanding and enjoyment. Borrowing Foucault's idea of ethical freedom, teachers and students can now build up a new form of intersubjectivity through a refusal of both the claimed hierarchical and egalitarian power relations that have been imposed on them historically and culturally.

Third, this voluntary-servitude lens disrupts the value inscription of the symbolic representation of the kneeling-bowing rite as the highest Confucian ritual or servile feudalistic dross that should be either welcomed or sent to tombs for good in current China. It contextualizes the specific kneeling-bowing performances and sets its possible social and educational value in the extent to which the subjects are "opened" to an ethical mode of being of self and others through the performing experience. One graduate from the Guangdong Experimental Middle School comments on their schooling Passage Rite in his blog: "During the Passage Rite, when you look up, you may see strings of grey hair or watery eyes of your parents and a sudden feeling of gratitude may emanate from your heart. Isn't that enough for the gratitude education?" (Wang Le De Kong Jian, 2011). In other words, this possible and situational feeling and understanding is an opening for a transformed ethical form of intersubjectivity, and this kind of transformative opening is, I argue, what education in its broadest sense hopes to get at.

Opening Up Education as a Self-Transformative Technique Toward an Ethical Freedom

This chapter is not to argue for or against the reinstatement of the traditional and controversial kneeling-bowing performance, collective or individual, in modern China's schooling or other social milieu. Rather, it maps out, problematizes, and inverts the historical cultural principles along the three intersected dimensions—body–self conflation, teacher–student identity tension, and symbolic representational logic—that have enabled and legitimized the predominant discursive battle along the "highest Confucian versus servile feudal ritual" value pendulum. This binary logic, I argue, is heavily confined to an identity struggle on what teachers and students should be (hierarchical or egalitarian), that is, an identity imposed upon them both culturally and historically. Furthermore, it has marred the authentic and ethical being of self and others from rendering itself visible.

Foucault's ethical care of self and others shares with Confucius's reasoning about ritual performance a gesture toward opening up a harmonious interpersonal understanding. By reframing the lens of voluntary servitude within this conceptual overlapping, this chapter theoretically provides a social and cultural space to rethink about the controversial kneeling-bowing events. Through subverting and inverting the epistemological principles that ground the predominant binary reasoning, voluntary servitude paves a way toward exposing the authentic, pure, ethical being of teacher–student (or parent–child) intersubjectivity—what teachers and students can be—which is actually evidenced, though barely audible by some kneeling-bowing agents.

Therefore, I hope the controversial kneeling-bowing events have mapped out a glimpse of the entangled assemblage or disassemblage among the various social and cultural principles (Confucian or modern) in current Chinese society. This should-be to can-be paradigm shift through the voluntary lens renders explicit the educational and social value that the controversial kneeling-bowing events can bear upon China's current educational reform. This paradigm shift, I hope, also enriches Foucault's governing dynamics and offers a new perspective to rethink about governing in the making of subjectivity in sociological and educational research.

References

Ames, R. (1993). The meaning of body in classical Chinese thought. In T. P. Kasulis, R. Ames, & W. Dissanayake (Eds.), *Self as body in Asian theory and practice* (pp. 39–54). Albany: State University of New York Press.

China Ministry of Education. (2003). *Guideline for moral character and life in full-time compulsory education in China* (experimental draft). Retrieved on September 30, 2011, from www.moe.edu.cn

China Ministry of Education. (2010). *2010–2020 middle and long term educational reforms and development planning guidelines.* Retrieved on October 30, 2011, from http://baike.baidu.com/view/2801453.htm

Chongqing Morning News. (2010, June 6). Chongqing 900 duo ming gaozhongsheng biyedianlishang guibai laoshi 重庆900名高中生毕业典礼上跪拜谢老师 [Over 900 high school seniors kneel-bow to teachers to show gratitude at the commencement ceremony]. Retrieved on October 30, 2011, from http://news.163.com/10/0606/09/68G2957 U00014AEE.html

Chou Yu Ni Mo. (2010, June 7). Jin qianren jiti xiagui shi chiru shi meide? 近千学生集体下跪是耻辱是美德? [Is it shame or virtue for thousand students to kneel down?] Retrieved on October 30, 2011, from http://blog.sina.com.cn/s/blog_44491d9d0 100iaey.html

Feng, G. C. (2007, November 20). Xiagui pinxian, zhongguo jiaoyu yijing zouxiang tuifei 下跪频现,中国教育已经走向颓废 [Kneeling down often has led Chinese education to an end]. Retrieved on October 20, 2011, from http://hi.baidu.com/%B0%CD% C0%E8%D6%AE%C3%CE/blog/item/4410ca0a9624093db0351df5.html

Foucault, M. (2003). The subject and power. In P. Rabinow & N. Rose (Eds.), *The essential Foucault: Selections from essential works of Foucault, 1954–1984* (pp. 126–144). New York: The New Press.

Hall, D. L., & Ames, R. T. (1987). *Thinking through Confucius.* Albany: State University of New York Press.

Hevia, J. L. (2005). *Cherishing men from afar: Qing guest ritual and the Macartney embassy of 1793.* Durham, NC: Duke University Press.

Lu, J., & Gao, D. S. (2004). New directions in the moral education curriculum in Chinese primary schools. *Journal of Moral Education, 33*(4), 495–510.

Lu, X. (1919). How do we make parents for the present? *Xin Qing Nian* 6(6). Retrieved on October 20, 2011, from www.southcn.com/news/community/shzt/youth/forerunner/ 200404280880.htm

Popkewitz, T. S., Khurshid, A., & Zhao, W. L. (In press). Comparative studies and the reasons of reason: Historicizing differences and "seeing" reforms in multiple modernities. In L. Vega (Ed.), *Empires, post-coloniality, and interculturality. New challenges for comparative education.* Rotterdam, the Netherlands: Sense Publishers.

Qian, M. (2005). *Lun yu xin shi* [New interpretation on Analects]. Shenghuo, Dushu, Xinzhi: San Lian Shu Dian.

Shang Oriental TV News Report. (2009, August 24). Retrieved on October 10, 2010, from http://video.sina.com.cn/p/news/c/v/2009–08–24/193360383302.html

Sun, L. K. (1991). Contemporary Chinese culture: Structure and emotionality. *The Australian Journal of Chinese Affairs, 26,* 1–41.

Topic Today at QQ.Com. (2011, May 6). Guibaili bufuhe wusi jingsheng 跪拜礼不符合五四精神 [Kneeling-bowing rite goes against May 4th spirit]. Retrieved on June 6, 2011, from http://view.news.qq.com/zt2011/guifumu/index.htm

Wang, C. S. (2004). A critical reflection on the thought of "despising knowledge" in Chinese basic education. *Beijing University Education Review, 8*(4), 5–23.

Wang, K. X. (2004). Shi lun zhong guo guibai liyi de feichu [On the abolition of the Chinese kneeling-bowing rite]. *Collected Papers of History Studies, 2,* 18–21.

Wang Le De Kong Jian. (2011, May 15). Xiaguili qima cong xingshishang rangni zhidao gan en下跪礼,起码从形式上让你知道感恩 [Kneeling-bowing rite at least formally lets you know gratitude]. Retrieved on October 20, 2011, from http://hi.baidu.com

Wang, X. J. (2011, May 5). Guifumu de qingnianli yu wusi jingsheng gege buru 跪父母的青年礼与五四精神格格不入 [Kneeling-to-parents Passage Rite goes against the May 4th spirit]. Retrieved on October 30, 2011, from http://blog.qq.com

Wang, Y. (2007, September 11). 对老师行"跪拜礼",是中国的文艺复兴!—支持疯狂英语李阳设计的"拜师礼" [Performing the kneeling-bowing rite to teachers symbolizes the Chinese Renaissance—supporting Li Yang's Kneeling-bowing rite]. Retrieved on October 30, 2011, from www.boraid.com/darticle3/list.asp?id=80178

Wu, F. (2004). *Can't teach with knees down*. Shanghai: Huadong Shifang Daxue Chubanshe.

Xin Kuan Bao. (2011, May 5). 广东一中学组织全体学生给父母下跪 [Guangdong Middle School organizes all students to kneel to parents]. Retrieved on October 10, 2011, from http://news.sohu.com/20110505/n306793006.shtml

Xunzi: Quanxue. (n.d.) Retrieved October 30, 2012 from http://cn.netor.com/know/hist/book21.htm

Yan, C. F. (1999). Gudai guibaili zhishu [On ancient kneeling-bowing rite]. *Jiangxi Guangbo Dianshi Daxue Xuebao, 4,* 50–51.

Zhang, X. L. (1996). *Heidegger sixiang yu zhongguo tiandao: Zhongji shiyu de kaiqi he jiaorong [Heidegger and Chinese Taoism]*. Beijing: Shenghuo-Dushu-Xinzhi Sanlian Shudian.

Zhong, Q. Q., & You, B. H. (2004). Moldy cheese—reading reflection on a critical reflection on the thought of "despising knowledge" in Chinese basic education. *Global Education, 33*(10), 3–7.

Zhu Feng Hou Niao. (2007, October 5). 三次'下跪',现代中国教育的最大耻辱 [Three "kneeling" events are the greatest humiliation to modern China's education]. Retrieved on October 30, 2011, from http://hi.baidu.com

PART II

"Reason," Science, and Making Kinds of People

7

GENIUS AS A HISTORICAL EVENT

Its Making as a Statistical Object and Instrument for Governing Schooling

Catarina Silva Martins

It was in the context of a vocational setting of artistic activity that, in the second half of the 19th century, a literary series emerged around the problem of genius and its relations with pathology or abnormality, as well as with the idea of a hereditary talent. Names like Francis Galton or Cesare Lombroso are unavoidable references in the theory of genius and the development of eugenic theories during the last half of the 19th and first half of the 20th centuries. These discourses, though coming from science, took different social actors as their object of inquiry. The great geniuses were artists, politicians, or scientists.

The modern artist would appear as a social actor above the common people. His place, not different from the place of saints in hagiography or from God as a creator (in a premodern system of thought), would establish what we can call a vocational regime for the arts. As stated by the Austrian psychoanalyst Otto Rank, "the religious category of God (looking to the glory of God) being thus transferred to man himself. Sociologically, it meant the creation and recognition of 'genius' as a type, as a culture-factor of highest value to the community, since it takes over on earth the role of the divine hero" (Rank, 1968 [1932], p. 24). There is the commonsense belief that for artistic creation, certain traits and dispositions are required. The vocational scheme was based on the idea of the precocity of talent as a symbol of an innate gift or a natural aptitude, sometimes seen as dependent on the internal dispositions of the subject and sometimes as the result of divine inspiration (Heinich, 1996). A few formulas were developed to portray the lives of geniuses, such as the early striving for expression in childhood.

Since then, the artistic competence begins to be seen not in the transmission and learning of a set of techniques but through the individuality and the knowledge of each subject. Within artistic learning environments, the notion of natural aptitude quickly would serve as justification to support different inequalities (Bisseret,

1979, p. 31). It was believed that if people performed differently, it was because of their biological characteristics and not any social constraints. Within the school arena, the notion of aptitude would function as a means of comparison and differentiation, referring to what in particular was contained in what exceeded the norm.

This chapter is divided into five parts. The first part signals the emergence of a new literary interest on genius, trying to understand the system of exception that would become proper of the artist. Transformed into exception, the artist as genius is seen as a technology of government, from both a political and a social point of view, and at the level of artistic learning through the impossibility of learning itself. In the second and third sections, I assist in the shaping of a gallery of notables, representing the top of the race and the nation but also constructed as the site of eccentricity and abnormality. From this perspective, the genius as a technology of government, in a biopolitical perspective, allowed for the definition and government of the normal citizen. But it was also this incursion of science on the subject of genius—turning it into a materiality visible and measurable in the body—that allowed the transformation of the concept of genius, making it also a field of government.

The fourth and fifth parts of the chapter have a different scope, attempting to read how in the pedagogical arena the idea of genius becomes natural. I discuss how the concept of genius was taken and, close to the concept of natural aptitude, seen as no more than an instrument of government, of selection and exclusion of certain types of persons. Deepening this analysis, I address how the individual aptitude was imagined to be measured through drawing.

The Genius and the Impossibility of Learning

Western modernity was marked, within the visual arts, by the multiplication of art academies. But at the same time, it lived around the ambiguous and contradictory idea that art could not be taught. From a system of learning based on the workshop under the guidance of a master and a system of patronage that determined the visual discourse of painting and sculpture according also to a visual literacy of the audiences, the artistic learning within art academies made the separation between arts and crafts a meaningful principle for the coming into being of the modern artist.

The vocational regime of the arts, heir from the Protestant notion of vocation (Weber, 2001), was understood as a calling that was then articulated with the choice of a professional destination. Like a priest that "is more than a man among men" (Corish, 1970, p. 289), also the artist from modernity is set apart among men. In fact, his importance does not arise from the discipline and work in his task but from predestination. At the center of this idea was the romantic notion of genius as one who, as formulated by Kant (1998 [1790]), dictated the rules of nature. I seek to understand how this contradiction started from the degree of exceptionality and state of exception in which the place of the artist in modernity was drawn, as opposed to the need of a set of rules based on technical exercises, copy, and invention from specific grids of thought that formed the visual repertoire of the schooled artist. The devaluation of school learning as a process of formation of artistic competence is due to the appreciation of freedom and individualism of the genius, or, in other words, owing to the inner vision and inspiration of the artist. These ideas underline the notion that art is an area in which only individuals whose exceptional works and singular talent could unfold. Then, the state of exception of the artist is here understood as the limit of the indetermination of the being, not exactly in the sense developed by Agamben (2007) but as the suspension of rules that determined the simple and unquestionable existence of geniuses as those that differentiated from the common people.

In 1720 appeared one of the first texts directed to the explanation of genius. "Of Genius," by an anonymous author, began by trying to explain genius as a variability of human nature. The causes of individual differences were not easy to determine:

> Whether this be from the Constitution of the Mind itself, the Soils some are more apt to produce some Plants and Herbs than others, or from the Laws of Union between the Body and Mind the Climates are more particular to kindly nurse Vegetables than some others, or from the immediate Impulse of Power Which governs the World, is not so easy to determine.
>
> *(Hill, 1720)*

Such as in the biological world, in the case of genius, specific behaviors were due to different attributes among men or women. The genius of the person was something that regulated action.

The Athenians had a notion of genius. It was believed that from birth, each individual was led by an invisible being. Shaping the mind, government, and the conduction of life were tasks directly attributed to this genius, who in Greek would be called "Daimon" or "Daimonion" and, in Latin, "genius." It was to this last notion, joining it with "ingenium," that the author attributed the more precise meaning of genius in the 18th century. The genius then passed through a mutation: from something that was outside the individual but intrinsic to his/her actions, guiding and inspiring them, starts to be inscribed in the subject itself, turning into an internalized quality. Geniality became a field of government as it was inscribed as a property of the subject that would have signals to be read and identified in the material body. The "ingenium" would be the strength and power that each individual would have, and that, in conjunction with a particular mind and through a business activity, study, or a way of life, would result in what would then be genius. But it seemed clear that a genius in the maximum power of the term, "a finished genius," existed only when a strong inclination was accompanied by a force and strength of mind to achieve it (Hill, 1720).

What, asked the English poet Edward Young (1918 [1759]) a half century after, was meant by genius? The answer allocated genius in the limbo of the inexplicable: "A genius differs from a good understanding, as a magician from a good architect; that raises his structure by means invisible; this by the skillful use of common tools." And, he continued, "learning inveighs against natural unstudied graces, and small harmless inaccuracies, and sets rigid bounds to that liberty, to which genius often owes its supreme glory" (p. 13).

Invisible and difficult to articulate in words, it was clear that the process of learning would kill the possibility of genius and conduct to ruin. It was this freedom that was also part of the French painter Roger de Piles's discourse (1707). He stated that "genius is the first thing that one must assume in a painter. It is a part that cannot be acquired nor by study or by work" (p. 3). The artist was becoming honored as a divine being with divine thoughts as formulated by Vasari (1965 [1568]), who inaugurated the biographical writing of the lives of artists. Even if there was no description of how to be a genius, the category was becoming stronger in defining the great man. The genius is a kind of person, borrowing from Hacking (2006), that exists only in a particular historical and social setting. As a classification, it interacted with those that were called genius but also served as a barometer for all those that were not classified as such.

This divine ecstasy gives us a framework that allows us to think about how the problem of freedom and autonomy of the artist addresses the problem of learning. The birth of the social sciences and humanities and the new system of thought according to which each subject is thought of as autonomous strengthened this desire of the artist to assert his own autonomy from the rules and codes of art. For the French painter Théodore Géricault, in the first half of the 19th century, the greatness of artists like Jacques-Louis David was to be due solely to his genius and not to any college or school. Rather, "the influence of the school might have been extremely detrimental to his talent in his own taste, at an early stage" (Géricault, 1998 [1842], p. 24). The idea of school was seen as dangerous. "How can one hope," asked Géricault (1998 [1842]) "after this that they might conserve some spark of originality?" (p. 26). The same concern occupied the author of *The Painter of Modern Life*. It was not the study of Rubens or Verone that gave the modern artist a sense of his own contemporaneity. "It is doubtless an excellent thing to study the old masters in order to learn how to paint," stated Baudelaire (1993 [1863]), "but it can be no more than a waste of labor if your aim is to understand the special nature of present-day beauty" (p. 22).

Within the academies, the discourse on genius and learning occupied a different position. The genius as a technology had to govern what had to be said and made, in terms of codes of correspondence of theories of visual representation. Here, the genius as a technology of government, through a Foucaultian (1988) lens, means that the ways in which power operated within the epistemology of the arts were dependent upon techniques that determined and made desirable certain ways of saying, seeing, and making that had the genius as a model. Joshua Reynolds was a striking figure, positioning himself against the discourse of inspiration and a kind of magic out of the scope of the rules of art. Reynolds, president of the Royal Academy in London, justified the need of a learning process for those that were becoming (not born) artists. For him, the main advantage of an academy was, in addition to skillful men to direct the student, that it was a repository of great examples of art: "[T]hese are materials on which genius is to work, and without which the strongest intellect may be fruitlessly or deviously employed" (Reynolds, 1891, p. 55). He recommended a strict obedience to the rules of art, according to the practice of the great masters. Within these mechanisms of academic learning, the genius as a technology of government also activates a set of techniques of the self in which the subject desired and transformed himself in order "to attain a certain state of happiness, purity, wisdom, perfection, or immortality" (Foucault, 1988, p. 18). The great masters were the true geniuses, and they should be considered perfect guides and infallible objects of imitation, not to be considered in a critical way.

These were the rules that had opposed the supporters of the artist as a genius. Rousseau walked in these paths. Emilio would not have as a teacher of drawing someone who would force him to draw from drawings or imitate by imitations. Genius was linked to a language of invention. How? There was no explanation. This idea stemmed from the connections among genius, originality, and predestination. The vocational system developed around the notion that, for example, the artist child would achieve future greatness, and this was just an inevitable consequence of his genius.

In the various treatises about genius that were emerging was drawn up a common sense that has become fixed as a new way to a truth: "It must have occurred to everyone who has surveyed, with an ordinary degree of attention, the unequal distribution of natural talents among mankind" (Duff, 1767, p. 3).

This common sense, which would be the basis of the scientific discourse of Lombroso or Galton, was based on the evidence of a universal observation. The gallery of geniuses that began to form in the Renaissance and also included those of antiquity seemed to be proof of the inequality of talents among men. This inequality was seen in relation to the gifts with which each one was born and, while defining who was a genius, it also foreclosed those who were not. The genius as a regulatory element in fine arts, poetry, and science began to take its power over those who would devote themselves to these arts but also all those who should recognize this exceptionality of a few. Functioning as an example, the genius was to ensure differentiation among different types of person (Hacking, 2006):

> Illustrious *examples engross, prejudice, and intimidate.* They *engross* our attention, and so prevent a due inspection of ourselves; they prejudice our judgment in favor of their abilities, and so lessen the sense of our own; and they intimidate us with the splendor of their renown, and thus under diffidence bury our strength.
>
> *(Young, 1918 [1759], p. 9)*

William Duff (1767), in *Essay on Original Genius*, was the first to analyze the nature of genius as part of human psychology. Three basic ingredients were necessary to the genius: imagination, judgment, and taste. In this composition, imagination was essential to the taste and taste also influenced the ability of imagination.

The latter was the most easily identifiable by all those who looked to a genius.

The French psychologist Théodore Ribot (1900) put the problem also from the point of creative imagination. He stated that creative imagination was different from reproductive imagination. The creative imagination would require the totally new and original. The transition from reproduction to production, from repetition to creation, would be due to the qualities found in only a privileged few. The study allowed the psychologist to show, with method and strictness, what was vague before and simply attributed to a power of imagination. It was now possible to analyze examples in which tingling or pains in various parts of the body were due to the effects of the imagination. The genius began to cause symptoms that were thought to be measured in the body. To confirm this subjective capacity of a sensory field, Ribot explained that certain persons could accelerate or delay the movement of their heartbeat by the effect of persistent and intense representations in the mind. Genius was turning into a materiality of the body and thus becoming a field of government.

We saw how genius as a category of making up people was a technology of government. It transmitted and distributed particular features and ways of thinking and being that made possible certain ways of seeing. I did, thus, not an essentialist reading of genius as a property of human nature but rather a cultural and historical inscription that made this coming into being an event within the Enlightenment thought. As we will see in the next section, the studies on genius that were developed from the second half of the 19th century onward do not deny its existence. Quite the contrary; genius becomes inscribed in the body of the subject, aiming to provide a cause and an explanation for this event that was visible in both body and behavior.

The Inscription of Genius Within the Body: Some Atlas of Species

The second half of the 19th century joins to the romantic vision of genius another view intended to be more scientific. All symptoms of genius, from suffering and pleasure of creation to inspiration, emotion, or originality, were based on the personalization of the author but also on his physical and psychological conditions. We will now focus on the relationship between genius and madness. The issue was raised by Cesare Lombroso: "[H]ow, in fact, can one suppress a feeling of horror at the thought of associating with idiots and criminals those individuals who represent the highest manifestations of the human spirit?" (Lombroso, 1891, p. 5). These exceptional capabilities were believed by Galton to be based in inheritance and were seen by Lombroso as marks of degeneration, which approached, by the excess compared to the norm, the genius of the insane. What was being fabricated was, borrowing from Ian Hacking (1992), a new style of reasoning about genius that was constructed in the connection of truth, meaning, and verification.

The giants of thought, as they were called by Lombroso, tended to degeneration and psychosis. Degenerative signs were manifested more in geniuses than in the insane. He did not deny that among geniuses, there were not those with a balance of intellectual faculties, but he was certain that their affection and feelings manifested some imbalances. Even if it were not possible to find scientific records, in fact, history was full of cases. The genius was an object of study and was emerging as a whole set of techniques for extraction and accumulation of knowledge, which had no longer basis in the work of the genius or their capacity for originality but rather in his or her own body.[1] For Lombroso, the behavior appeared as the derivation of any demonstration that was inscribed in the materiality of the subject's body. Napoleon was reported as having a moral insanity, Carlyle had tortured his wife, Richelieu was epileptic, Cavour attempted suicide. These particular cases were only the expression and effect of a law that allowed scholars to state with accuracy the probability of similar events in other elements of the same group: "The fact, now unquestioned, that certain great men of genius have been insane, permits us to presume the existence of a lesser degree of psychosis in other men of genius" (Lombroso, 1891, p. vii).

Cesare Lombroso considered genius and talent distinct things, but like addiction and crime, they were unlikely to be accurately determined. Traces of morbidity would be patent in both. The talent, like the genius, was accompanied by a cortical excitement, though in a lesser degree and in a little smaller brain. The abnormality was detected in the genius by a multiple and contradictory personality. This multiplicity is important, and somehow it appears unfolding the romantic genius. Denis Diderot, the author of the French Encyclopédie, had already noted this approximation of exceptional men to madness, and Lombroso rescued him to prove his theory:

> These men of sombre and melancholy temperament only owed that extraordinary and almost Divine penetration which they possessed at intervals, and which led them to ideas, sometimes so mad and sometimes so sublime, to a periodical derangement of the organism. They then believed themselves inspired, and were insane. Their attacks were preceded by a kind of brutish apathy, which they regarded as the natural condition of fallen man. Lifted out of this lethargy but the tumult within them, they imagined that it was Divinity, which came down to visit and exercise them . . . Oh! How near are genius and madness!
>
> (quoted in Lombroso, 1891, p. 3)

The doctor of criminal anthropology was bringing the physical characteristics of geniuses to be considered. The examination of the insane productions allowed for new elements of analysis and criticism in the study of genius, both in art and in literature. Above all, from this knowledge, an infinite number of criminal questions could finally achieve a solution. Madness was not just a weird psychiatric singularity but rather a form of insanity that hides dangerous impulses.

The botanical garden of the species took shape. The identification of the disease in the exceptionality of the great men was dependent on an accurate observation of signs of degeneration. In either of the following elements, it would be possible to extract symptoms of geniality that governed the figure of genius. Usually, geniuses were short, of lean stature, many suffered from rickets, and their pallor was seen as the color of the great men, and was also one of the most common signs among those suffering from moral insanity. Socrates, Skoda, Rembrandt, Dostoyevsky, Magliabecchi, Pope, Carlyle, and Darwin were geniuses with idiots' physiognomy. Head and brain injuries were also frequent in geniuses. Kant, Romagnosi, Bichat, Chenevix, and Dante had had abnormal development of the left parietal bone and two osteomatas at the frontal bone. The genius appeared as an organization of individual properties and as an excess over the normal.

The montage of the argument of different kinds of person followed a policy of visibilities, an atlas of human types and cultural theses about modes of life. In the late 19th century, there were four main groups of people: geniuses, idiots, insane, and normal. Identification of the normal would be possible due to the possibility of comparison with the extreme cases of insanity, idiots, and genius. The connection of these categories responded to a policing of the body and of behavior that would lead to an entire system of visual presentation of these "figures." Within the catalogues of the human species, they were photographed as crazy, hysterical, criminals, and geniuses.

As we observe from the foregoing, the genius as a discursive construction begins to articulate itself as a technology of power in the general government of life. It opens the possibility of controlling one's life based on the biological history of each individual subject. Thus, the scientific research on genius and its relationship with a potentiation of the qualities of a population, race, or nation and the eradication of degeneracy fall within a biopolitical perspective (Foucault, 2002 [1976]). Biopolitics, in a Foucaultian sense, is the government of life through a statistical reasoning that takes not the body of man but the living man as a species as its object. What follows is the construction of genius as an event of biological inscription that could be read as a statistical object.

The Construction of Genius as a Statistical Object

Hereditary Genius, written by Francis Galton, was a study published in 1869, although in 1865 the author had already published about the subject in the *Macmillan's Magazine*'s journal. His interest in the study of hereditary genius arose from an ethnological incursion around the mental peculiarities of different races.

Galton positioned himself as the first to address the issue of heredity and genius in a statistical way. That meant that it was a scientific reality with a small percentage of error and inaccuracy. It was, therefore, to achieve numerical results and introduce the law of the deviation from the average. This statistical reasoning implied the creation of these statistical objects and, as we shall see, these objects came from a general observation and acceptance of the exceptionality of the great men.

Galton used the word "genius" not in a technical sense but merely as the expression of an ability that was exceptionally high and innate in certain individuals. There was, in his opinion, a large uncertainty when it came to objectifying the genius. Genius was not something supernatural or even a sense of inspiration. On the contrary, to become an area of government, genius would emerge as being located within the individual:

> If genius means a sense of inspiration, or of rushes of ideas from apparently supernatural sources, or of an inordinate and burning desire to accomplish any particular end, it is perilously near to the voices heard by the insane, to their delirious tendencies, or to their monomanias.
>
> *(Galton, 1869, p. x)*

Defined as such, genius was not a desirable trait to be perpetuated in subsequent generations. This idea was the skeleton of eugenic theories that began to emerge precisely with Galton, carrying in them the principle of the well born as being those whose physical, mental, and moral heritage were positioned in the top of a social hierarchy that should be preserved. In order to ensure the continuity of those who were deemed to belong to the group of good heirs, the required natural selection was policed through a rational selection by the state. It was in 1883 that Galton first used the word "eugenics" in a work titled *Inquiries Into Human Faculty and Its Development*. For eugenics, he understood the demand for indications of caste or superior races to be multiplied and gradually replacing those that were not of the same type. In a footnote, he explained the rationality of a whole program of modernity:

> That is, with questions bearing on what is termed in Greek, eugenes namely, good in stock, hereditarily endowed with noble qualities. This, and the allied words, eugeneia, etc., are equally applicable to men, brutes, and plants. We greatly want a brief word to express the science of improving stock, which is by no means confined to questions of judicious mating, but which, especially in the case of man, takes cognisance of all influences that tend in however remote a degree to give to the more suitable races or strains of blood a better chance of prevailing speedily over the less suitable than they otherwise would have had.
>
> *(Galton, 2001 [1883], p. 17)*

Twenty years later, the author of *Hereditary Genius* would explain, in more detail, the systematic nature of his work. Eugenics pursued quantitative results. For him, words like "more" or "less" were not sufficient. The bank of data gathered from reality would appear accurate and true: He wanted to know exactly "how much." The first part of his treatise *Hereditary Genius* pursued the aim to show to what extent and degree a natural ability was transmitted hereditarily. The question of heredity and the maintenance of exceptional qualities transformed into a field of government asked for the possibility of observation, description, collection of data, and classification in order to control the ghost of deviation and produce the desire for the norm.

> There can be no doubt that a thorough investigation of the kind described, even if confined to a single grade and to a single form of degeneracy, would be a serious undertaking. Masses of trustworthy material must be collected, usually with great difficulty, and be afterwards treated with skill and labor by methods that few at present are competent to employ. An extended investigation into the good or evil done to the state by the offspring of many different classes of persons, some of civic value, others the reverse, implies a huge volume of work sufficient to occupy Eugenics laboratories for an indefinite time.
>
> *(Galton, 1907, p. 14)*

As noted by Nikolas Rose (2007), biopolitics took various forms: "from the management of cities, space, and sociality in the name of minimization of disease, to attempts to maximize the quality of the race through the administration of birth and death" (p. 54). Each person could be measured on a common scale that unfolded later in various spaces: spaces of norm and of deviation. With respect to the notion of genius, the focus was directed to both sides of the question. The downside was the finding of degeneration among the population and, therefore, the need to control their proliferation. "The tables of deviancy," as stated by Hacking (1992), "seemed to show that averages [. . .] were pretty constant" (p. 147). Gathering information required time and technical and competent experts. But the positive is outweighed by the possibility of what the simple distinction between good and evil could bring to the development of the social body. The description of the new object of statistical reasoning or of a new phenomenon embedded the prediction and the possibility of governing the deviancy. The impetus to detect the movements that seem more random in the functioning of the body responded not to the development of each subject but to the need to control and predict the collective. The individual was only the focus of observation as a passage for the population as a whole.

Classifications define, thus, kinds of person (Hacking, 2006). And among musicians, painters, or poets, there was no doubt, to Galton, that talent was hereditary:

> The question is rather, whether its distribution in families, together with the adjuncts necessary to form an eminent painter, follows much the same law

as that which obtains in respect to other kinds of ability. It would be easy to collect a large number of modern names to show how frequently artistic eminence is shared by kinsmen.

(Galton, 1869, p. 239)

A gallery of geniuses took shape in the discourse of science, but again from a common sense. Galton chose 42 painters from the Italian, Spanish, and German schools that were ranked by an apparent common consent that defined them as illustrious. Among them, he sought to trace the lines of inheritance that allowed him to assert that the genius was something innate. And so he blended blood relations with relations of talent, but in fact he did much more. The statistical style created the possibility of new meanings and the making of new ways of saying, seeing, and thinking through the possibility of measuring how someone was close or distant from the exceptional. In the next section, I seek to explore how the idea of genius was taken in proximity with the idea of natural aptitude and how it allowed for a distribution that determined the place of those who had the ability or the inability to take part in the common sense of exceptionality.

The Search for Geniuses: Natural Aptitude in School

Here I start another history. This history exists as a sequence of the previous two histories, but acquires different meanings in the school arena. The concepts of natural aptitude, genius, and vocation are connected. Although they undergo some changes over time, in the 19th century, their conceptualization in psychology, criminal anthropology, sociology, and anthropometry allows what Jacques Rancière (2007) defines as a policed distribution of the sensible. Each subject occupied a specific place in society, and this assignment, seemingly inevitable, was, however, arbitrary.

As theorized in the 15th century, the word "aptitude" meant only the capacity to receive an education in a given area. Subsequent connections with the natural and divine forces, though active during the old regime, had not yet provided any superiority of class. The power was held by birth and not by individual capabilities, although these were determined by the will of God (Bisseret, 1979). By the second half of the 18th century, a theocentric vision gave place to an emphasis on aptitude as a fully human, innate, and measurable element and, thus, as able to serve as a barometer of differentiation. Aptitude then emerges as the instrument to divide society from which would be the professional destiny of each one, and becoming scientific argued to prove the force of nature as an interior, immanent, and essential necessity.

New arrangements, such as aptitudes, talents, geniality, way of walking, and intelligence, among many other characteristics, were made evident as the result of heredity. Inequalities that manifest themselves among men find themselves explained from a schema whose starting point would be equality, but they continued to operate by the agency of an arbitrary gift. The whole program of Galton had been to show that natural abilities were derived by inheritance just like any other physical feature was.

Biology would only confirm what became clear in the eyes of those who saw the arts as a form of human completeness. Henceforth appeared as evident what a century and a half before had just begun to be fabricated. The idea was tautological and self-evident. Artists were born artists, geniuses were born geniuses, and these were determined by the laws of heredity, to prove that the inequalities between men came from birth and determined what each might be in the future. There was no way to refute the theories of Galton, who wanted to show that mental and creative capacities of men depended, like their physiognomy, on heredity. Proving his theory, there was the huge gallery of illustrious men of arts, sciences, and politics. The geniuses were mobilized to explain, in a natural way, their own difference and superiority. The argument of this common sense was the recognition of the exceptionality and uniqueness of the works of great men.

Faria de Vasconcelos (2010b [1934]), a Portuguese pedagogue, talked about the natural aptitude of the student under the lenses of classification. Natural aptitude, as well as any psychic phenomena, would always be studied for each individual case and compared within the group. It was in the mutant line of variations that the specificities, regularities, and deviations were found. Whether in the height, weight, or strength, whether in mental balance, intelligence, emotion, or morality, there was no physical or spiritual characteristic that did not differ, and these differences were not qualitative but quantitative. The procedures of individualization to mark exclusion were operated regularly by disciplinary institutions as a way of control and separation of dangerous relations (Foucault, 1995, p. 198).

The place, according to Foucault (1995), that the individual occupies within a series governs, in a single gaze, a multiplicity. The possibility of calculating exactly "how much" corresponded to a new political anatomy of the body and new technologies of power. Natural aptitude produced new types of person. Under this large instrument of selection, examples unfolded:

> There are capabilities that are revealed almost immediately at the beginning of the activity of the individual: the case of genius. Example: Mozart. There are aptitudes that only appear after some time and effort: Example: Edison, Franklin, Milton. There are finally latent skills that are slow to appear, where it takes time and effort.
>
> *(Vasconcelos, 2010d [1935], p. 961)*

Genius and natural aptitudes were connected. It was now the moment to show that the subjects would hardly be able, by themselves, to realize their own abilities. Like diamonds, genius would be detected immediately in the surface layer of the earth, but the precious metal would be more hidden. "The latent aptitudes" would be like "gold mines located in the bowels of the earth. The aptitudes, the gifts that are hidden are like rough diamonds that need to be cut, filed, polished and displayed in the light before its rays can shine" (Vasconcelos, 2010d [1935], p. 962).

Mapping and Making Natural Aptitudes
Objective Realities Through Drawing

I will continue to follow the argument of Faria de Vasconcelos in the making of drawing a way of determining the natural aptitudes of each child. From his study come a polyphony of features, in terms of aptitudes, that each child would manifest as compared to any another, and her social position as due solely to the manifestation of the natural aptitudes. Natural aptitudes are not only theories based on a differential psychology of the child but systems of practices that govern who the child is and what she should be, as well as the matrix through which cultural theses emerge about modes of living (Popkewitz, 2008). Psycho-pedagogical interventions were "design projects to plan society and individuality" (Popkewitz, 2008, p. 67). The guiding principle was that of statistics, by obtaining numerous drawing collections of children, "then sorting these drawings according to age, environment, race, etc. . . . , and study the drawings in accordance with certain views and objectives" (Vasconcelos, 2010a [1934], p. 218).

The relations established for the observation of drawings were tight and resulted from the observation of a spiral of perceptual, sensory, and motor skills of the child: "ability to perceive differences and similarities," "discrimination sizes," "proportions and directions [. . .] of lines, surfaces, volumes and movements," "capacity to see colors, shades, gradations of light," "capabilities of speed, dexterity and accuracy," "fatigue capabilities," "capabilities to control and coordinate the oculomotor functions," "visual memory of shapes," "muscle memory of executed movements and coordinations established," "capabilities of comparison, abstraction, generalization and reasoning," "ability to adapt and driving the visual new forms, movements and coordination," "ability to creative imagination," "ability to mental representation" (Vasconcelos, 2010a [1934], pp. 217, 218). In addition to these different guiding principles, the taste, the beauty, and the direction of the line would help in determining the degree of exceptionality of aptitude.

The methods for obtaining data were varied. The collections of drawings that would be placed under critical scrutiny would be obtained either from spontaneous sketches or drawings produced after a prescribed issue or through the biographical method consisting of the gaze cast upon a set of drawings of a child at different stages of the childhood. And so the reader of the present chapter can have a vision of the making of reality through a mass of data through, for example, the collections of drawings analyzed by the German pedagogue Kerschenteiner, consisting of 500,000 drawings. From these archives emerged classifications from which the reality of childhood would be read, or, put in another words, the interior world of the self was being objectified.

The evolution in drawing and the different stages of development of the child are the result of these processes. The diversity of each child would arise only from the standardizing of all her possibilities of action. From the 1930s on, children would go through six stages of development in drawing. From the summary description of each stage stands a cross between features seen as natural and psychological discourses. In the fourth stage, for example, the "logical realism," the 7- or 8-year-old child would be capable of "a realism that was more descriptive than representative, more logical than visual." It was made a generic type: "at six years 70% of the drawings are made from the front, at 8 years 70% are made from profile." The face was the first element to undergo this rotation. The drawings were filled with details, and the child's performance was given a scientifically measurable and explainable cause. All reality was likely to be made intelligible: "[B]y virtue of their logical realism the child seeks to highlight all elements of the drawn object, it is natural that this concern results in the juxtaposition of details and not its true synthesis" (Vasconcelos, 2010a [1934], p. 221).

The data taken as the object of observation turned up in universal. The grids that would define the different stages of development contributed to a government of childhood. The fundamental belief in the sciences of individualization was linked to a normalized view of childhood, and within this field of government, the notion of development was one that fulfilled a more powerful effect.

Given the knowledge of these different stages, the teaching of drawing would be organized to be adapted not by reference to drawing as a form of artistic knowledge but rather to the fabrication of a given idea of children or adolescents. Conceived as "a powerful tool" that allowed observers "to appreciate the development of children and adolescents in drawing and their dispositions, their aptitudes and disabilities," these scales made drawing a device of measurement (Vasconcelos, 2010a [1934], p. 224).

It was in this framework of the registration of individual differences and their milimetric placement in the social map that the concept of "orientation" was invented. The right man in the right place becomes the expression of a whole generation of pedagogues that took differential psychology as their territory of intervention. Vocational guidance would refer to the individual psychology, the aptitudes and capacities of individuals. There was a science, wrote Faria de Vasconcelos, "which teaches us to orient the individual to careers that suit their aptitudes, a delicate and difficult science, which draws heavily on psychology but will seek to physiology, medicine, economics, technical crafts of the elements needed to fulfill its purpose" (Vasconcelos, 2010c [1934]), p. 923).

Conclusions

It seems now less strange to affirm that natural aptitudes were technologies of power that allowed for the differentiation of types of person. Even if what was in question was the choice of a career, the scientific expertise showed that it should not be left to the individual free will, but rather it needed to be determined through clinical, anthropometric, physiological, and mental examination. From the poles of exceptionality, abnormality, and the heredity of genius, we saw how a whole movement around normalization was sketched. However, the scientific movement that formed from authors as Lombroso and Galton started from a common sense that is still present today. The great geniuses of the past remain celebrated and socially reproduced as representative of an exception and of a knowledge ("the already known") always in the urgency of being reproduced. The inscription of genius in the body would create the genius as a statistical object. The proximity among the artist, the criminal, and the insane but also of genius as something innate and read in the sphere of natural aptitudes was a way of reasoning that, in terms of its rationality, was part of a biopolitical thought that ended, as the history of the last century taught us, in the concentration camps. Probably it is difficult for us, historians of education and educators, to look to ourselves and try to understand the historicity of our own ways of reasoning. What a history of the present allows us to think is that school lives through ways of constructing a truth and a totality of a world that orders and classifies what is possible to think, know, and act on.

Note

1. Even if I am using the plural and also both genders, the fact is that in the 19th century, there was no possibility of considering a woman as a genius. In his book *The Man of Genius*, Cesare Lombroso stated that:

   In the history of genius women have but a small place. Women of genius are rare exceptions in the world. It is an old observation that while thousands of women apply themselves to music for every hundred men, there has not been a single great woman composer. [. . .] There are no women of genius; the women of genius are men.

   (Lombroso, 1891, pp. 137–138)

References

Agamben, G. (2007 [2003]). *Estado de exceção*. São Paulo: Boitempo.
Baudelaire, C. (1993 [1863]). *O pintor da vida moderna*. Lisboa: Vega.
Bisseret, N. (1979). A ideologia das aptidões naturais. In J. Durand (ed.), *Educação e hegemonia de classes* (pp. 33–67). Rio de Janeiro: Editora Zahar.
Corish, P. (1970). Vocation: Its historical forms. *The Furrow, 21*(5), 287–291.
Duff, W. (1767). *An essay on original genius, and its various modes of exertion in philosophy and the fine arts particularly in poetry*. London: In the Poultry, near the Mansion-House.
Foucault, M. (1988). *Technologies of the self. A seminar with Michel Foucault*. Amherst: University of Massachusetts Press.
Foucault, M. (1995). *Discipline and punish. The birth of the prison*. New York: Vintage Books.

Foucault, M. (2002 [1976]). *Em defesa da sociedade*. São Paulo: Martins Fontes.

Galton, F. (1869). *Hereditary genius: An inquiry into its laws and consequences*. London: Macmillan and Co.

Galton, F. (1907). *Probability, the foundation of eugenics*. The Herbert Spencer Lecture, delivered on June 5, 1907. Oxford: At the Clarendon Press.

Galton, F. (2001 [1883]). Inquiries into human faculty and its development (electronic edition from the Galton Archive, available at: http://galton.org/books/human-faculty/text/galton-1883-human-faculty-v4.pdf).

Géricault, T. (1998 [1842]). On genius and academies. In C. Harrison & P. Wood (Eds.), *Art in theory, 1815–1900* (pp. 23–26). Malden, Oxford: Blackwell Publishing.

Hacking, I. (1992). Statistical language, statistical truth and statistical reason: The self-authentification of a style of scientific reasoning. In M. Ernan (Ed.), *The social dimensions of science* (pp. 130–157). Notre Dame, IN: University of Notre Dame Press.

Hacking, I. (2006). *Kinds of people: Moving targets*. British Academy Lecture, 11 April 2006 (web version).

Heinich, N. (1996). *Être artiste*. Paris: Klincksieck.

Hill, A. (1720). Of genius. In *The occasional paper and preface to the creation*. (Project Gutenberg ebook, available at: https://archive.org/details/ofgeniusintheocc15870gut).

Kant, I. (1998 [1790]). *Crítica da Faculdade de Juízo*. Lousã: Imprensa Nacional Casa da Moeda.

Lombroso, C. (1891). *The man of genius*. London: Walter Scott.

Piles, R. (1707). *L'idée du peintre parfait, pour servir de régle aux jugemens que l'on doit porter sur les ouvrages des peintres*. Londres: Chez David Mortier.

Popkewitz, T. (2008). *Cosmopolitanism and the age of school reform: Science, education, and making society by making the child*. New York, London: Routledge.

Rancière, J. (2007). *The politics of aesthetics*. London: Continuum.

Rank, O. (1968 [1932]). *Art and artist. Creative urge and personality development*. New York: Agathon Press.

Reynolds, J. (1891). *Discourses*. Chicago: A. C. McClurg and Company.

Ribot, T. (1900). *Essai sur l'imagination créatrice*. Paris: Félix Alcan.

Rose, N. (2007).*The politics of life itself. Biomedicine, power, and subjectivity in the twenty-first century*. Princeton, NJ, and Oxford: Princeton University Press.

Vasari, G. (1965 [1568]). *Lives of the artists*. London: Penguin Books.

Vasconcelos, F. (2010a [1934]). Problemas escolares. In *Obras completas de Faria de Vasconcelos V, 1933–1935* (pp. 1–271). Lisboa: Fundação Calouste Gulbenkian.

Vasconcelos, F. (2010b [1934]). Une écolle nouvelle en Belgique. In *Obras completas de Faria de Vasconcelos II, 1915–1920* (pp. 3–144). Lisboa: Fundação Calouste Gulbenkian.

Vasconcelos, F. (2010c [1934]). Os cursos para a formação de peritos orientadores. In *Obras completas de Faria de Vasconcelos V, 1933–1935* (pp. 921–924). Lisboa: Fundação Calouste Gulbenkian.

Vasconcelos, F. (2010d [1935]). A orientação profissional e os estudos no liceu. In *Obras completas de Faria de Vasconcelos V, 1933–1935* (pp. 945-966). Lisboa: Fundação Calouste Gulbenkian.

Weber, M. (2001). *A ética protestante e o espírito do capitalismo*. Lisboa: Editorial Presença.

Young, E. (1918 [1759]). *Conjectures on original composition*. Manchester: At the University Press.

8

"CATHOLIC" SECULARISM AND THE JEWISH GAUCHO SCHOOL

Salvation Themes of the 19th-Century Argentinean Citizen

Ezequiel Gomez Caride

The Anti-Argentinean Schools Controversy

> I would like to believe that . . . on the second centennial of Argentine independence, my children's children will hear praises of Jewish pioneers sung under the cathedral's sacred arches, after the Catholic Te Deum.
>
> *(Gerchunoff, 1910, p. 132)*

In 1908, a passionate controversy pervaded the titles of Argentinean newspapers. The "Anti-Argentinean Schools" was the name editors selected to describe it. The Jewish and Russian schools were being attacked by the mainstream media and national educational authorities. The criticisms were based on the fact that such schools were being partially funded by the state and did not teach even a minimum of Argentinean instruction—Spanish language, history, geography. In the midst of this controversy, the well-known Argentinean nationalist Ricardo Rojas stated, "The danger in Jewish schools comes with their fanaticism which implies the Anti-Semitic matter that happily wasn't present here [Argentina] but will emerge as soon as the immigrant's Semitic son would prefer to be a Jew instead of an Argentinean" (Rojas, 1909, p. 341). The quotation explains the extent to which Rojas attributed the whole responsibility of the anti-Semitic matter to Jews' religious fanaticism. Throughout the chapter, I argue that although at an institutional level, Jewish religious heritage was perceived as a threat to Argentinean "pureness," a deeper historical analysis shows how Jewish narratives shaped the grids of discourses that forged the seemingly "secular" Argentinean citizen. In this chapter, first, I provide a brief historical context of the Argentinean social and political events related to immigration at the beginning of the 20th century. Second, I describe how the Jewish schools acted as the kaleidoscope space through which identity tensions emerged. Later, in order to explore how these tensions were perceived by Jewish immigrants, I analyze the book *Los gauchos judíos* (1910) by the Jewish-Argentinean writer Alberto Gerchunoff. The book was a bestseller, with 10 editions, and it has been translated to English and Hebrew.[1]

The chapter shows how opposite the roles attributed to Jewish religion were in shaping notions of citizenship in the beginning of the 20th century. The national educational authorities and their educational journal, *El Monitor*, do not hesitate in describing the Jews as fanatics, incapable of being assimilated. On the other hand, Gerchunoff's book aimed to depict the everyday life of Jewish colonists and portrayed a completely different picture. Following Gerchunoff's stories, Jewish religious heritage helped to shape the Argentinean citizen. The aim of this piece is to explore how Jewish religious notions play out in the seemingly secular construction of the Argentinean citizen. Educational authorities claimed that Jewish narratives were incompatible with the "secular" Argentinean citizen. Throughout the chapter, I problematize such assertions by arguing that the transformation of religion into secular notions of the citizen is a constant changing process. The notion of the Argentinean citizen has been changing since its emergence at the beginning of the 19th century. Within this, different religious narratives have been playing diverse roles shaping the "secular" citizen in different historical moments. Central in this formation of the Argentinean citizen were Catholic salvation narratives that move into the civic realm in the making of the citizen (Gomez Caride, 2014). In this chapter, I describe how religious particularities—Jewish religious discourses—were connected with but gave a particular nuance in the making of the Argentinean citizen.

Immigration as a National Policy: To Govern Is to Populate

The Argentinean constitution (1853) highly encouraged European immigration. The liberal policies of the end of the 20th century focused on fostering European immigration. During almost four decades, the yearly number of immigrants who arrived to Argentinean shores was a sign of political success and national pride. Behind this process was an economic rationality. The exportation of crops and cattle would only be possible at a massive scale if the infinite landscape of the Argentinean pampa was able to produce it. Hence, to fulfill this national strategy, a vast increase in manpower was necessary. Between 1889 and 1914, more than 2.5 million immigrants arrived in Argentina (Faulk, 2008, p. 53).

A relevant layer of this national policy was the focus on schooling. These vast populations who came from the most distant places of the earth would become Argentinean citizens through public education. Therefore, the role of the school in the forging of national identity was crucial. In a country in which immigrants were constantly arriving without any knowledge of the country, its language, or its law, the school was the space to shape an Argentinean citizen.

The dream of these liberal policies was to construct a White, European, civilized Argentina. However, for several reasons, at the beginning of the 20th century, immigration's landscape drastically changed. For instance, the immigrants were not the expected and hoped-for civilized Europeans but the lower, illiterate classes, mostly from Italy and Spain. The utopian dream of the melting pot lost its ground. In fact, in the beginning of the 20th century, national authorities were beginning to evaluate the negative social outcome of the massive immigration policies (Avni, 1991a, p. 42). In this complex environment, the whole wave of Jewish immigration surpassed 100,000 Jews.

Throughout the chapter, I focus on the province of Entre Rios, since it was the main province the Jewish Colonization Association (ICA) acted upon. Entre Rios is a central province located in the Mesopotamia region. Entre Rios's subtropical weather and its almost completely flat land make the region a worthy place for agricultural developments. In the first decade of the 20th century, of a population of 435,000, about 100,000 were foreigners. In some regions of the province, the foreigners were a clear majority, such as in Villaguay, Genacito, Molino, and the like. From those 100,000, about 10,000 were Jewish from Eastern Europe, mostly from Russia. The whole immigration process of Jewish colonies was sponsored by the ICA, which in 1913 had bought about 1,432,394 acres of land (Avni, 1991a, p. 60).

The ICA was founded by Baron Hirsch in 1891. After the death of his only son, he devoted his energy and fortune to improving the quality of life of the Jewry that was under attack. His aim was to create "a sort of autonomous Jewish state where our coreligionists would be protected from anti-Semitic attacks once and for all" (Avni, 1991a, p. 35). Baron Hirsh quickly realized that "the Jews of the United States, England, France, and Germany feared that the arrival of large numbers of impoverished and strange-looking Russian immigrants would endanger their own emancipation" (Avni, 1991a, p. 37). In addition, in 1891, Turks banned Jewish immigration to Palestine. Therefore, Argentina, a country with large extensions of land and a pro-immigration policy, appeared as the perfect choice.

The Anti-Argentinean Schools and Ernesto Bavio's Report

In 1908, the Argentinean daily newspaper *La Prensa* titled a column "Anti-Argentinean Schools." A whole controversy emerged in the public opinion. The mainstream media spread the term, arguing that such schools were receiving funding from the state, and not even a minimum of Spanish language was being taught. The educational magazine *El Monitor*, which was edited by national educational authorities, dedicated two articles to the topic. The first, titled "The Foreign Schools in Entre Rios," affirmed that a "national political issue" was at stake. The article referred to the lack of fundamental principles of Argentinean national identity in the Jewish and Russian schools under examination. The second article (1909) had the same title but was a longer one, with more than 40 pages that tackled notions of cosmopolitanism, the role of the state, the Jewish colonization in Entre Rios, and the work of Jewish schools. The documents and reports of such articles included voices from different actors: the national educational

authorities, the educational superintendents from the province and from the nation, Jewish colonists, the ICA, and its educational superintendents.

In the region the ICA had in Entre Rios,[2] the Jewish Colonial Association had 23 private schools, while the province only had 3. From the 3,400 kids in ICA's region, only 180 students went to province's schools and 1,450 students to Jewish schools. In these Jewish schools, the majority of the students were Jewish, but occasionally some sons of the Argentinean agricultural workers attended. These private schools were sponsored by the ICA, which provided the building, furniture, didactic materials, teachers, and even superintendents. However, the province also gave funding to those schools, and this point raised the heated controversies because the Jewish schools had specific features that did not foster, in their words, a "teaching with national character" (Bavio, 1908).

In the second article, Juan Nissen, the general superintendent, argued that Jewish schools should be closed for several reasons. First, Jewish schools devoted the majority of their school days to teaching Hebrew (Bavio, 1909, p. 20). Following the report of Juan J. Nissen, in the whole school year the students had 7 hours of Argentinean history instead of the 55 required by the educational regulations. In a similar vein, students received only 14 hours of Spanish-language instead of the 90 required. Additionally, the Jewish academic calendar barely amounted to 100 days of instruction with all the Jewish holidays—around 53. Finally, the school week running from Sunday morning to Friday noon because of the Sabbath clashed with the National Academic Calendar, which states that on Sunday schools were supposed to be closed. In sum, officials stated that Jewish schools gave priority to Hebrew education instead of the secular or laic education fostered by the state. The Jewish schools favored the teaching of Hebrew, its religiosity, and the ancient and contemporary history of the Israelites (Bavio, 1909, p. 25). Therefore, officials stated that both the Jewish and the Argentinean students attending those schools shaped a "soul totally Hebrew and mystical without any Argentinean feelings or generous instincts common in people who grow in this land of freedom [Argentina]" (Bavio, 1909, p. 26). In fact, the superintendent mentioned that students preferred the Hebrew language to Spanish. In the Jewish schools, the majority of the instruction was in Hebrew, leaving behind the instruction in Spanish. Therefore, the results in Spanish language were insufficient. Following Bavio, the instruction could never be successful (1909, p. 31) with foreign teachers that have a weak knowledge of Spanish.

In addition, the report says that memorization was the most common method used by teachers, without encouraging in students habits of observation, critical thinking, or rhetoric. Besides, the rote learning approach was against the educational law that forbade teaching based exclusively in memorization (Bavio, 1909, p. 32). The priority of Hebrew was justified by the ICA, saying that the Russian colonists were extremely conservative. In Argentina, the Spanish language was the mandatory language and followed the national educational policies all the schools in Argentina should use Spanish for instruction. Within the latest pro-Hispanic

Las escuelas extranjeras de Entre Rios

ESCUELA DE 3 MAESTROS. — EMPLEO DEL TIEMPO 1908. — 3.ª CLASE

	MAÑANA					TARDE				
	ESPAÑOL		RECREO	HEBREO		ESPAÑOL		RECREO	HEBREO	
VERANO...	8.30—9.10	9.10—9.50	9.50 — 10.10	10.10—10.50	10.50—11.30	1—1.40	1.40—2.20	2.20 — 2.40	2.40—3.20	3.20—4
INVIERNO.	9—9.35	9.35—10.10	10.10 — 10.20	10.20—10.55	10.55—11.30	12.30—1.5	1.5—1.40	1.40 — 1.50	1.50-2.25	2.25—3
Domingo.......	Lectura	L. nacional	—	Lectura	Escritura	H. nacional	Escritura	—	Biblia	Escritura
Lunes..........	Cálculo	Geografía	—	Biblia (gr.)	Idioma	Agricultura	Costura	—	Lectura	H. sagrada
Martes...	Lectura	L. nacional	—	»	Inst. religiosa	Lec. s/objetos	H. pos bíblica	—	»	Idioma
Miércoles......	H. nacional	Lec. s/objetos	—	»	Idioma	Geometría	Cálculo	—	»	H. sagrada
Jueves...... ..	L. cívica	Cálculo	—	»	Inst. religiosa	Agricultura	Costura	—	Gramática	Escritura
Viernes........	Lectura	Escritura	—	»	Raschi	—	—	—	—	—

FIGURE 8.1 The school's schedule was printed by national educational authorities and shows the activities ranging from Sunday to Friday and the bilingual approach of Hebrew and Spanish.

El Monitor de la Educación Común, Journal (Bavio, 1909, p. 11)

nationalistic trends, educational authorities believed that the appropriate medium to foster national identity was the Spanish language, and without it any national education was fruitless. In this regard, Ernesto Bavio asserted, "the first duty of the Argentinean elementary schools whatever the citizenship of its teachers, is to teach the country's language that it is the most powerful bond of nationality" (Bavio, 1909, p. 599). Therefore, the instruction in Hebrew was something totally unacceptable for educational authorities. In fact, it was perceived as a threat to Argentinean nation building.

Some of the subjects of the national curriculum were not being taught in Jewish schools. Specifically, civic education, Argentinean geography, and Argentinean history were not taught at all in Jewish schools. Regarding the teaching of Spanish language, the report said that students learned more Spanish in their interactions with gauchos than in their schools. For example, different actors pointed out that the majority of the students in Jewish schools did not know the Argentinean national anthem.

The *Monitor* article that quoted the report from Angel F. Schenone, the educational provincial superintendent (1908), claimed that Jews were "indolent by idiosyncrasy," "religious fanatics" "bounded to their language"; hence he considered Jewish colonists inassimilable to the Argentinean environment (Bavio, 1909, p. 11). In a similar vein, Superintendent Juan Nissen states, "[Jews] are adverse elements to Argentina, very different from immigrants from other countries that contribute to our stables developments" (Bavio, 1909, p. 13). In the same article, the province inspector insisted that the Jewish population was incapable of being assimilated and noncompliant to the Argentinean way of life and mores (Bavio, 1909, p. 35). In sum, from all the criticisms that Jewish schools received, their religious identity was the principal reason for which educational authorities attacked them.

In the last section of the 1909 article, educational authorities propose several recommendations to ameliorate the situation. In fact, one superintendent recommended the closing of all Jewish schools (Bavio, 1909, p. 20). However, a milder solution was adopted. In order to shape "Argentinean feelings" (Bavio, p. 39), the authorities recommended (a) Jewish religious instruction should be outside the school building; (b) compulsory celebration with the singing of the national anthem in national memorials; (c) flag-raising ceremony every day; (d) diffusion of patriotic readings such as "Argentinean Soul" or "National Events"; and (e) the use of an Argentinean badge during national ceremonies. In the next section, I will return to the topic of the Argentinean national anthem.

The two articles issued by the *Educational National* journal describe how, from an institutional perspective, educational authorities were opposed to all that could be considered Jewish religious culture. The governmental approach aspired to eliminate all the singularities of the Jewish culture in favor of a homogenization that aimed to erase all kind of singularities. However, this perspective ignores the extent to which Jewish religious narratives were effectively merging within the grids of discourses that shaped Argentinean "secular" citizens. Gerchunoff's account shows how Jewish religious narrative got assembled into "secular" notions of the Argentinean republic and the Argentinean citizen.

Ricardo Rojas's book *La Restauracion Nacionalista* (1909) is a clear example of the Argentinean nationalistic discourses that were arising in the first decade of the 20th century. In his book, sponsored by the secretary of education, Rojas tackled themes of national identity, and specifically he criticized the role of foreign ideas and foreign schools in Argentinean character. Regarding the Jewish schools, Ricardo Rojas writes, "one of the disadvantages of the Jewish School is that creating the Jewish family and its religious culture prevent the Jewish families to melt with the rest of the families of the country" (Rojas & Rojas, 1922, p. 180). The idea of Rojas was that education was useless with such "elements." Jewish religious practice was seen as the reason for such stubbornness.

Los gauchos judíos

Alberto Gerchunoff was born in Proskurov, Ukraine, in 1884. At the age of 5, he immigrated to Argentina with his family. His family settled in the city called Moisesville, one of the colonies sponsored by the Jewish Colonial Association (ICA). After the tragic murder of his father, the impoverished family moved to Buenos Aires, where Alberto Gerchunoff rapidly excelled as a journalist and writer. His most famous book, *Los gauchos judíos*, describes through several short stories the everyday life of those first Jewish colonists with long white beards that lived in the midst of the Argentinean pampas. Gerchunoff's book reflects the enthusiasm that these Jewish settlers had and their interactions with an entirely new environment full of challenges and opportunities.

At this point, in order to describe the extent to which religious salvific narratives silently shaped the Argentinean citizen, I change from an argument about agency and voice represented by the school authorities to one of discourse analysis. Gerchunoff is considered the founder of Jewish Latin American writing and the founder and first president of the Argentine Writers' Association. The discourse his "voice" expresses is helpful to describe how Jewish religious narratives finely merged with "secular" discourses of the Argentinean citizen, producing a different quality and nuance in the assembly of who the Argentinean citizen was. In the previous section, I described how the national educational authorities perceived the Jewish colonists and specifically their religious background as an impediment to shaping citizens able to respect and love Argentina. However, Gerchunoff's stories show a rather different perspective regarding the role of Jewish religion in the assembly of the Argentinean citizen.

The Argentine's Passover or Zion

The first line of the *Los gauchos judíos* starts with a sentence from a reading from the Passover Haggadah: "With an outreached arm the Lord delivered us from Pharaoh, in Egypt" (Gerchunoff, 1910, p. 39). The pogroms that Jewish colonists had recently suffered in Russia were the "Egypt" that Jewish immigrants have experienced. Immediately after, Gerchunoff says, "Remember how, back in Russia, ye set tables to celebrate the ritual of the Passover? This [the travel to Argentina] is a greater Passover" (Gerchunoff, 1910, p. 38). Once and again the writer chooses the Passover to exemplify the situation of the Jews in Argentina. The religious Passover becomes the narrative that Gerchunoff selects to understand the colonists' journey from Russia to Argentina. Therefore, since the Passover was the journey from Russia to Argentina, a whole range of expectations—later considered utopic—and feelings would arise in the subjectivity of those colonists. If Passover was their travel from Russia, Argentina became their new Promised Land, the Zion that would nurture them with care and love.

> Generous is the [Argentinean] flag that succors the ancient hurts of our race, that binds its wounds with maternal care. Wandering Jews, tortured and torn, redeemed captives, let us bend the knee beneath the unfurled banner; in unison, beside choirs bejeweled by light, let us intone the song of songs that begins thus: "Hear Oh ye mortals . . ." [Argentinean National Anthem].
> *(Gerchunoff, 1910, p. 38)*

Jewish religious discourses about the Egypt's Passover triggered in the Jewish immigrants a metamorphosis that transformed Argentina into Zion. Embedded in the stories are images that portrayed the gratitude of Jewish immigrants toward Argentina, the Zion that gave them a land of milk and honey. Along the same lines, in 1910, Juan Alsina, the Argentinean immigration chief, ended his post at the Immigration Office. As a way to thank Alsina for his work, the Jewish community in Argentina gave him a gold medallion and an album with thousands of congratulatory messages. The cover of the album shows a wandering Jew offering up his offspring to the Republic.

In Figure 8.2, Argentina is portrayed as Zion, the fertile land that with its inspiring sun was receiving the laborious Jewish immigrants. The sacred figure—an

FIGURE 8.2 The Jewish Hope
(Avni, 1991, p. 50)

angel representing the Republic—is at the same time comforting the elder and showing the route to the new Zion. The image resembles, from the book of Genesis, the sacrifice of Isaac, with the angel comforting Abraham. Argentina is represented through Jewish religious images as the new Zion that would nurture the Jews with its fertile lands.

In another story called "The New Immigrants," Gerchunoff describes how the old Jewish colonists were in the train station of the city awaiting the arrival of the new colonists.

Everyone in the crowd relived the morning of departure from the czar's cruel empire and the day of arrival in the Promised Land, in the Jerusalem extolled in sermons and acclaimed in leaflets whose Russian verses, printed under the portrait of Baron Hirsch, praised the excellence of the soil:

> To Palestine and to the Argentine,
> We'll go, to sow,
> We'll go, brothers and friends,
> To live and be free . . .
> *(Gerchunoff, 1910, p. 58)*

Suddenly, Argentina was coupled with Palestine as the Holy Land of Hebrew history. Its soil and freedom made it the new Zion, the announced Jerusalem in the rabbinic preaching. Argentina acquiring features of the Promised Land is a theme that was already present through Catholic narratives. In the nascent Argentinean republic (1810–1830), the Promised Land shaped the grids of discourses (Carranza, 1907). Hence, the theme of Argentina as a salvific space was already incorporated in the narratives of the "secular" republic. However, in this case, the Jewish "sacralization" of Argentina has a new nuance. In the Jewish tradition, Zion is at the same time a holy place and a real city. On the contrary, in the Catholic tradition, the Promised Land is a supernatural space beyond earthly life—Heaven. Hence, from a Catholic perspective, the Promised Land is always a future project—an eschatological reality never fully achieved on Earth.

By pointing out Argentina as the new Zion, the Jewish tradition shaped an even bolder sacralization of the Argentinean republic. Argentina was the *actual* Zion for Jewish colonists. The Jewish religious tradition of Zion helped to give even more gleam to the Argentinean exceptionalism that, although already secularized, ironically came from Catholic narratives.[3]

The Archetypical Jewish Farmer

During the early 20th century, the Zionist movement fostered all around the world the stereotype of the Jewish farmer and his virtuosity. In the chapter in which Gerchunoff describes the genesis of the Jewish immigration to Argentina, he claims,

In Spain, Jews stopped tilling the earth and shepherding their flocks. Do not forget, my dear rabbi, what it says in Zeroim, the first book of the Mischnais, about life on the land: It alone is wholesome and worthy of God's grace. That's why, when Rabbi Zadock Kahn informed me about immigration to Argentina, I forgot the return to Zion in the midst of my joy, and remembered the words of Yehudah Halevi: Zion is wherever peace and happiness reign.

(Gerchunoff, 1910, p. 43)

During thousands of years, Jewish religious tradition praised the austere and graceful life of those who live off their flocks and harvest. The quotation describes that the reason for the Jewish expulsion from Spain was that Jews stopped their farming activities. One of the ICA goals was to "accomplish the moral and physical regeneration of the Jews through agricultural labor" (Elkin, 1980, p. 127). In fact, for Baron Maurice de Hirsch, international migration provided the means to foster the Jewish regeneration. Argentina provided an atmosphere of infinite pampas and religious tolerance that allowed the fulfillment of such dreams. Gerchunoff's narratives about the sacredness of the pastoral life intersected perfectly with the narratives about the ideal of pastoral life that the emerging Hispanic nationalistic movement was looking for, a peaceful and laborious immigrant eager to cultivate the sacred soil and pace the cattle. The "good" immigrant—a docile, austere, and hardworking farmer that loved the sowing of the earth and the shepherding of the cattle—was portrayed in the pampas. Interestingly, the religious virtues of the archetypal Jew corresponded with the ideal virtues of the secular "good" citizen that should be austere, laborious, and politically meek.

Gerchunoff assembled rabbinic religious narratives about the hardworking farmer with the now utopian space of the Argentinean pampas that was starting to be described as the core of the Argentinean identity.[4] In the establishing of a national imaginary, Sarmiento, president of Argentina (1868–1874), had a relevant role through his famous book *Civilización y Barbarie* (1845), in which he established a dichotomy between the civilized European ideals represented by the metropolitan Buenos Aires and the barbarian archetype caudillo: Facundo Quiroga. In the first decades of the 20th century, Sarmiento's barbarian theme moved from the pampas to the urban technical space. In such a transition, the pampas was considered by the nationalistic movement as the true Argentina, while the modern Buenos Aires, the urban city, was the savage space. Buenos Aires's cosmopolitanism threatened "Argentinean" pureness (Sarlo, 1988, p. 34). The true republic would be the Hispanic colonial provinces, not the modern Buenos Aires.

From the 20th century, nationalistic narratives started a call for a return to "golden ages" represented in the value of the pampas and the figure of the native gaucho. As Antony Smith explained in *Chosen Peoples* (2003), the "golden age" rhetoric has religious roots. Through the narratives that proclaim the return to the golden ages of Argentina, the citizen, a "secular" kind of person, was shaped by religious salvific themes that transmogrify those of Catholicism into seemingly ones of the "true" republic. Catholic images such as the Garden of Eden, the Promised Land, and the early primitive church lent their salvific connotations to the nascent republic. The republic got transformed into a salvific space, giving intelligibility to the republican project.

The moment when the Jewish identity is given as a citizen, these religious salvific themes were so naturalized so as to go unnoticed but were crucial to matching the secular Argentinean citizen with the Jewish religious stereotype of the Jewish farmer that admired the Argentinean gaucho (Gerchunoff, 1910, p. 113).

The National Anthem and Argentine Independence Day

In the last chapter, Gerchunoff describes how the settlers found out about the Argentinean independence day. In one trip to the city, they saw that the main street of the city called Gualeguay was decorated with Argentinean flags and arches. So, after a meeting of the elders, they decided to hold the celebration and prepared their first national celebration. Gerchunoff describes the scene and the rationality Jews used to celebrate the Argentinean civic celebration:

> The colony realized that 25th was Argentine Independence day. The day was approaching and the elders gathered to decide if they will hold a celebration. They decided to celebrate. The dialogue between two colonists says: "I remember" he said, "how after the massacre of Jews in the city of Elizabetgrad, we closed the synagogue because we didn't want to bless the czar. Here, no one is forcing us to bless the republic and its president; we do so gladly, of our own free will." No one knew who the president was, but that did not matter very much.
>
> *(Gerchunoff, 1910, p. 168)*

The almost comic description reflects another feature of the Jewish religious experience, their immemorial sufferings and oppressions. The Russian pogroms were still very fresh in the memories of the colonists. The fact that Argentina was, so far, a safe place moves the colony to celebrate and adhere to the civic ceremony. After the words of Jacobo representing the Jewish colony, the civic authority answers:

> In response, Don Benito [the colony's police chief] recited several stanzas of the national anthem. The Jews did not understand what he was saying, but the sound of the word "liberty" rekindled bitter memories of centuries of suffering. With their hearts and their mouths, just as they did in the synagogue, they responded with a resounding "Amen!"
>
> *(Gerchunoff, 1910, p. 169)*

The civic dimension represented by the national anthem and the religious one characterized in the "amen" get completely intertwined. The Jewish colonists expressed a religious obedience to the civic republican hymn. The republican adherence of Jews was a religious one because their religious language was the bridge that helped them to become republican citizens. In the cited scene, the borders between the secular civic realm and the religious one that educational authorities proclaimed disappeared. In that moment, the religious heritage of the Jewish immigrants made possible their acceptance of the Argentinean republican dogma. The national anthem and the "amen" of the Jewish immigrants merged, and the term "liberty" had a crucial significance.

Liberty, a word that in the Argentinean anthem repeats several times, becomes the impossible space, the space of encounter between persecuted Jews and the Argentinean civic authorities. Liberty raised and kindled the spirits of persecuted Jews that were eager to sing and celebrate the civic national ceremony while liberty was granted for them. In that sense, liberty became the new language for both. While liberty was granted for Jews, it did not matter who the Argentinean president was. A new civic and somehow religious contract based on liberty was established between Jews and Argentina.

The "amen" of Jewish immigrants shows how the republic was treated as a deity. In a similar vein as with the Promised Land, at the beginning of the May Revolution (1810), Catholic narratives also helped to shape the republic as a salvific space. The Jewish religious narratives merged with such salvific narratives toward the republic but with a somehow different horizon. During the colonial domination, liberty was a prevalent theme of republicans against Spain. However, once the threat of Spain was superseded, liberty lost its momentum in the public debate. The notion of liberty brought by Jews was broader, and hence their understanding of liberty incorporated a new nuance into the narratives about the Argentinean citizen. Jews' acceptance of the Argentinean republic was dependent on the freedom from religious persecution they experienced. In the Argentinization of Jews, the Jewish narratives brought to the table a dimension of religious liberty that was somehow new in the Argentinean scenario in which Christians—Catholics and Evangelicals—were the clear majority. It is interesting to compare the critiques that educational authorities made about Jews that did not know the Argentinean national anthem. Gerchunoff's description shows the extent to which Jewish colonists were eager to comply with their civic duties.

The Argentinization of Jews: The Hispanic Heritage

Jewish narratives infused the narratives about the Argentinean citizen. Jewish narratives about the austere, hardworking farmer or the perception of Argentina as the new Zion were relevant ingredients assembled with the seemingly secular Argentinean citizen. Within the assemblage, the Jewish Hispanic heritage also helped to merge Jewish narratives within the secular Argentinean citizen.

The Jewish revival of their Hispanic past is another layer of this cultural intermingling. In those years, within the anxieties that massive immigration raised, an emerging Argentinian nationalism linked to the Hispanic heritage was starting to be considered as the core of the Argentinean nationality. As I introduced earlier, the liberal cosmopolitanism of previous years was diminishing, while Spain and Hispanic tradition were starting to gain momentum in narratives about the Argentinean national identity. The Hispanic heritage, the Spanish language, and native elements such as the pampas or the brave gaucho started to be considered as essential ingredients of the Argentinean identity. Hence, the challenge for Jews was to somehow merge with the emerging Hispanic nationalistic trends.

In the complex Jewish immigration history, a milestone was the expulsion of Jews from Spain by the Catholic kings in 1492. Interestingly, the Argentinization of Jews intersected with the linkage of the immigrant Jews with their Hispanic heritage. Jewish narratives started to highlight the Hispanic roots of Jews to merge with this emerging pro-Hispanic Argentinean nationalism. In a laudatory description of the old Jewish colonist, Gerchunoff says, "[Guedali, an old colonist] far from suggesting a colonist or farmer, his whole manner and bearing recalled the noble Jewish doctors, scientists and poets of medieval Spain" (Gerchunoff, 1955, p. 145). *The Jewish Gauchos* describes how the Spanish heritage of immigrant Jews was acknowledged and praised. Jews' immigration to Argentina was described as a continuation of the Spanish tradition that was interrupted in 1492 with the expulsion of Jews from Spain. In *The Jewish Gauchos*, Gerchunoff even tells a story of a wedding feast in which the main character is called Camacho, like the character Camacho in *Don Quixote*, the archetypal Spanish book. Argentinean Jews claimed that "[b]y settling in Argentina, Jews were simply recovering what was already theirs; they even learned Spanish easily, he averred, because they already possessed a Spanish spirit" (Elkin, 2011, p. 58).

By reenacting their Spanish roots, Argentinean Jewry merged with the emerging Spanish nationalistic trend. Not surprisingly, the Argentinean poet Francisco Luis Bernardez praised Gerchunoff, saying, "Being Jewish he had much of the Spaniard in him"(quoted by Elkin, 2011, p. 58). In sum, in the Argentinization of immigrant Jews, during the first decade of the 20th century, Catholic narratives were reenacted as a bridge to Argentinean life but within a seemingly secular discourse or republicanism, and the Hispanic heritage of the European Jews was deployed to validate their "right" to become "true" Argentineans.

Conclusion

The Jewish narratives represent a new complexity in the grids of narratives that shaped the Argentinean republican citizen. From an institutional perspective, Jewish religious narratives were perceived as an obstacle to national identity by Argentinean educational authorities. On the other hand, Gerchunoff's account of everyday life in the Jewish colonies shows how Jewish narratives intersected and assembled with already secularized Catholic narratives in the construction of the "secular" citizen. The Jewish religious narratives assembled with those about the Argentinean citizen, adding a new nuance to the construction of the secular Argentinean citizen.

First, Argentina was described as the new Zion. Although Catholic narratives about the Promised Land were already present in the secular understanding of the republic, the Jewish heritage gave a nuance to such sacralization of the republic. The understanding of Argentina as Zion brought all the salvific narratives not to a utopic future but to the actual Argentina that was receiving thousands of immigrants. The Jewish heritage brought to the table a bolder sacralization of the republic.

Second is the scope of political freedom. At the beginning of the 20th century, freedom was not an issue for Argentineans. Although the Argentinean national anthem refers to freedom several times, the target of such freedom was Spanish domination. Certainly, with a country full of Spanish immigrants, the initial target of such freedom was somehow an empty space. The persecution Russian Jews suffered incorporated a new layer to the understanding of freedom. In a rather explicit way, Gerchunoff explains that Jews were eager to live in Argentina only while their religious freedom was assured.

Third, the image of the "good" farmer enacted by the Jewish religious archetypical image of the shepherd assembled extremely well with the qualities of the "good" citizen constructed by the Argentinean liberal governments and later with the Hispanic nationalistic movement at the beginning of the 20th century. The notions of austerity and hard work that were present at the beginning of the republic during the Rivadavia years (*El Argos de Buenos Aires y avisador universal*, 1823, no. 43) acquired new tones. The hard work and frugality praised in the Jewish tradition reenacted those nascent civic virtues but now in the context of a political project that desperately required manpower.

The fine blend of Jewish narratives with the secular Argentinean citizen was possible for several reasons. First, the secular Argentinean citizen was not as secular as he seemed. On the contrary, the seeming secularization of the Argentinean citizen implied an internalization of Catholic principles in modern notions of the citizen and the republic. To the same extent, the assemblage of Jewish narratives was possible only because previously the republic had incorporated and naturalized religious ingredients—Catholic salvific narratives in the modern understanding of the republic. Second, the Hispanic heritage of Jews also helped to validate the Jewish ingredients in the discourses about the Argentinean citizen. However, this idea of Jews as Spanish acted more like a health certificate for Jews in the context of a pro-Hispanic nationalistic trend. The claim to Hispanic roots from Jews was not an idle topic, but it seems that somehow it was used by Argentineans—non-Jews—to rationalize or explain the fine assemblage between Jewish narratives and the Argentinean republic that I explained throughout the chapter.

Finally, educational authorities' critiques of Jewish students' lack of knowledge of the Argentinean national anthem resonate with Gerchunoff's description of the elder Jews saying "amen" at the verses of the Argentinean national anthem. I do not want to reduce the complexity of the nation-building process. Both narratives, the one of the educational authorities and Gerchunoff's depiction of everyday life at the colony, deserve attention. Gerchunoff's stories show the extent to which religious narratives could be perceived at the same time as fanaticism and stubbornness following educational authorities' accounts or as a complex grid of different narratives—Jewish, Catholic, and so forth—that intersect in the shaping of the Argentinean citizen. The different perspective relates to the understanding of religion. While considering religion from a functionalist perspective, religion was perceived as a threat to Argentinean national homogeneity. On the other hand, while considering religion as a cultural practice that shapes the grids of intelligibility, Jewish religious discourses of the colonists can be understood as overlapping narratives that shape the Argentinean citizen.

Notes

1. The book is included in the list of the 100 Greatest Works of Modern Hebrew Literature established by the National Yiddish Book Center (2001).
2. In the 80 square leagues of land that ICA had in Gualeguaychu, Uruguay, Colon, Villaguay y Concordia, there were, according to census, 3,400 boys that should go to school, but only 1,630 were attending school. The majority of students attended Jewish schools (*El Monitor*, 1909, s III, p. 14).
3. The United States is another example of how salvific connotations (Bercovitch, 1978) moved to national narratives. In the United States, with even a bigger wave of Jewish immigrants, the American exceptionalism—the new Zion rhetoric—although combined with a Calvinistic frame is even stronger and more resilient than in Argentina.
4. The extraordinary success of *Los gauchos judios* can be explained because the author was able to reconcile the pastoral ideal with a type of peaceful and laborious immigrant against the technical urban fears of dissolution of those years and the politically engaged immigrant of the city. The pastoral ideal of a golden past will shape the emerging Argentinean nationalistic narratives.

References

Avni, H. (1991). *Argentina & the Jews: A history of Jewish immigration*. Tuscaloosa: University of Alabama Press.

Bavio, A. (1908). *Las escuelas extranjeras en Entre Ríos*. In El Monitor de la Educación Común. Buenos Aires: Consejo Nacional de Educación. 1908. pp. 597–604.

Bercovitch, S. (1978). *The American Jeremiad*. Madison: University of Wisconsin Press.

Carranza, A. (1907). *El clero Argentino de 1810 a 1830*. Buenos Aires. Imprenta de M. A. Rosas.

El Argos de Buenos Aires y avisador universal. (1824). Buenos Aires: Impr. de los Expósitos.

El Monitor de la Educación Común. (1909–1910). Buenos Aires. Retrieved from http://catalog.hathitrust.org/Record/010314272

Elkin, J. L. (1980). *Jews of the Latin American republics*. Chapel Hill: University of North Carolina Press.

Elkin, J. L. (2011). *The Jews of Latin America* (Rev. ed.). Ann Arbor, MI: Mpublishing, University of Michigan Library. Retrieved from http://hdl.handle.net/2027/mdp.39015087418524

Faulk, K. A. (2008). *The walls of the labyrinth: Impunity, corruption, and the limits of politics in contemporary Argentina* (Ph.D. thesis). University of Michigan, United States. Retrieved from http://search.proquest.com.ezproxy.library.wisc.edu/pqdtft/docview/304572170/abst ract/13C6364AC2A2EFFC415/1?accountid=465

Gerchunoff, A. (1910). Los gauchos judíos. La Plata: Talleres Gráficos Joaquín Sese.

Gerchunoff, A. (1955). *The Jewish gauchos of the pampas.* New York: Abelard-Schuman.

Gomez Caride, E. (2014). Governmentality and religion in the construction of the Argentinean citizen. *Journal of European Education, 45*(3) 85–97.

Rojas, R. (1909). *La restauración nacionalista, informe sobre educacion.* Buenos Aires. Retrieved from http://hdl.handle.net/2027/loc.ark:/13960/t6c25qb6h

Rojas, R., & Rojas, R. (1922). *La restauración nacionalista; Crítica de la educación Argentina y bases para una reforma en el estudio de las humanidades modernas* (2. ed. [1. Millar]). Buenos Aires: J. Roldán y c.a.

Sarlo, B. (1988). *Una modernidad periférica: Buenos Aires 1920 y 1930.* Buenos Aires: Ediciones Nueva Visión.

Sarmiento, D. F. (1845). *Civilización y Barbarie.* Santiago de Chile. Imprenta del Progreso.

Smith, A. D. (2003). *Chosen peoples: Sacred sources of national identity.* Oxford, New York: Oxford University Press.

9

CHASING THE CHIMERA'S TAILS

An Analysis of Interest in Science

Lars Bang and Paola Valero

abyssus abyssum invocate
"deep calleth unto deep"
Psalms 42:7

Science Education and Being

Education produces specific desired expressions of Being. Nowadays we are surrounded by discourses stating that it is necessary and good for students to be interested in science and that *interest in science*[1] leads to effective learning and to scientific literacy. Thus, through science education, the student is transformed into a citizen or even a scientist—if he or she has the skills and aptitudes in that area. In a world where "the economy is increasingly driven by complex knowledge and advanced cognitive skills" (OECD, 2006, p. 3), the more natural scientists—and technologists, engineers, and mathematicians as well—society produces, the better economic competitiveness, progress, welfare, and enlightenment there will be for all. Science education, Being, and Becoming are linked in inexorable ways.

Problematizing the apparent force and unquestionable causality of these types of statements with tools from Foucault and Deleuze, the question explored is how scientific rationalities affect subjectivity and Being. Being-Scientist[2] is often portrayed as a monolithic, unified conceptual unit emerging from the particular universal enlightenment of reason. It is the purpose here to show that the constitution of the Being-Scientist has been effected in subsequent transformations taking place early in modernity as the sciences became differentiated and specialized (Daston & Galison, 2007). Thus Being-Scientist consists of ruptures and particular fragments rather than a uniform conceptual unit. It is composed of many different amalgamated rationalities, which often appear assembled in specific formations or hybrids, like a plethora of monsters; monstrous due to the often contradictory—still connected—construction of these particular formations.

One of these forms of Being-Scientist, namely the being who is driven by the *interest in science*, is identified and constructed as a new image of thought (Deleuze, 1994) for capturing one of these historical transformations in modernity. *Interest in science* is a concept that, since the PISA survey in 2000 (OECD, 2004) and the "interest" survey in 2006 (OECD, 2007), has been given a lot of attention internationally. The research in *interest in science* (e.g., Krapp & Prenzel, 2011) has spawned numerous projects (e.g., Sjøberg & Schreiner, 2010) and initiatives (e.g., OECD, 2006) to improve and facilitate youth's engagement with learning science and choosing a STEM course of study in higher education.

The mythical Greek *chimera* is used as the amalgam, hybrid, and new image of thought to explore and explain the folding and unfolding of how the construct Interest in Science frames a particular fragment of Being-Scientist. The mythical chimera is composed of a lion's head, a goat's body, and a serpent's tail. Its different animal traits changed place in various subsequent historical depictions. Sometimes the serpent would be the head, the lion the body, and the goat the tail. Like the chimera, the construct of Interest in Science transverses several discursive formations and adopts different forms in time and space. The process that leads to these transformations and reconfigurations of the chimera will be labeled *Chimestry*, as a nomenclature of the practices and events leading up to a transformation or a diagrammatic shift (Deleuze, 1986), though not enacting a direct causality.

The historical and contemporary discursive shifts of Being-Scientist are explored through the hunt of the Chimera, by positing the Archive, the Map and the Diagram of the various epochs in a new image of thought of the Chimera

PHOTO 9.1 The Chimera v. Anders Bang

(Photo courtesy of A. Bang)

(see Photo 9.1). The hunt pursues two particular claims, which are critical in understanding the power effects of contemporary science education. The first claim is that educational research in *interest in science* is framed by particular forma-tions of discourse—rationalities—that shape and ultimately limit the way research itself and educational practice address the concept and inherent problem of *interest in science*. Contemporary educational research in science education draws on three problematic premises:

1. Proposing a causal relationship between students' attitudes toward and *interest in science* and attainment in science subjects as measured in tests (Feist, 2012).
2. *Interest in science* is seen as a specific cognitive construct that can be measured for determining its degree and strength and thus has become a cornerstone in determining science learning (Gardner, 1975; Krapp & Prenzel, 2011).
3. The concept is linked unreflexively to notions of teaching, pedagogy, and curriculum, as well as to notions of the overall goodness of science (OECD, 2007).

Constructing a wormhole to the "history of the present" of the construct Interest in Science is a way to address, in a critical way, the problematic assump-tions listed: in other words, the issues of why it is important that youth are inter-ested in science and how society and our education system make that happen would become open to new thoughts and inventions.

The second claim of this chapter is that through tracing the hybrid construct of Interest in Science in its genealogy and archaeology, one can begin to shed light on the dispositive (Dreyfus & Rabinow, 1983) of the natural sciences (from now on, Science) and its effects of power on the contemporary expressions Being and Becoming. The central argument is that the construct of Interest in Science is intersected by at least three lines of thought: one about knowing, thinking, the mind, and cognition, increasingly colonized by psychology; a second about the possibility of mathematizing and measuring thinking and learning, increasingly colonized by a numerical rationality strongly represented by psychometrics; and a third about the sense of moral directionality of pedagogy, increasingly colonized by the field of education and didactics[3] research. Through chasing the chimerical construct of Interest in Science, it is shown how it is linked to and framed within specific rationalities in its contemporary manifestation.

Finding the Chimera: On the Surface of Interest in Science

The gaze employed here brings together some of Foucault's tools and Deleuze's appropriation of them: the Archive, the Map, and the Diagram and the methodol-ogy of archaeology and genealogy (Deleuze, 1986; Dreyfus, 1983; Foucault, 1972).

The Archive is the stratum in which the examination and gaze are turned to the discursive and historic formations within the specific thinkers and their time-space. The Archive is thus here the specific writings by Herbart, Dewey, and OECD. This could also be depicted as a kind of "depth." The Map is the stratum in which the discursive formations and the horizon of particular instances of the discursive formations are exemplified. This could also be depicted as a spread or frequency within the historical strata. The Map is the various historical curriculums, school reforms, and other educational practices linking the Archive to the horizon of instances. The Diagram is the set of relations and connections among the Archive, the Map, and the practices. A diagram is always a diagram of power relations. The Diagram is thus on the "outside" of the surface of the Archive and the Map. The Diagram is here the Prussian specific patriotic spirit of the state (Herbart), American progressionism (Dewey), and, finally, late capitalism (OECD). Deleuze (1986) elaborates these elements and their relationship, drawing on Foucault's conceptualizations:

> It is the Archaeology of Knowledge which will draw out the methodological conclusions and present the generalized theory of the two elements of stratification: the articulable and the visible, the discursive and the non-discursive formations, the forms of expression and the forms of content.
>
> *(p. 49)*

The nondiscursive and discursive formations are the elements in the three different "strata of thought" (Archive, Map, and Diagram). These two elements are entwined in the analysis of Interest in Science. The analysis is thus on the surface of thought and discourse and includes not only the concept *interest in science* but also a series of related statements and notions and other instances of linguistic forms. There is no singular unit of analysis but instead a *vivisection*[4] of the surface and of the discursive formations related to Interest in Science. To clarify, the nondiscursive element is not something beyond the discursive, a negative or a materiality, but the simply stratified content of an articulated discourse. Both the discursive and the nondiscursive are linked to practices, but there is no necessary causality between them.

The examination of the statements and concepts articulated in the writings of particular thinkers (the Archive) and the evidencing of how the conditions of

The Archive	The Map	The Diagram
J. F. Herbart	Prussian school reform towards mass schooling	The Prussian spirit of patriotism and the state
J. Dewey	American school reform	American progressionism
OECD	PISA (and various contemporary curricula in science education)	Late capitalism

FIGURE 9.1 The Archive, the Map, and the Diagram

possibility (the Map and the Diagram) shaped these statements and their subsequent concepts are the two analytical moves that constitute a gaze in a Foucauldian sense.

The analysis of the concepts, statements, and notions related to the construct Interest in Science makes it possible to point to their intersections with other discursive formations. This intersection of discursive formations is borrowed from Foucault's conceptualization of the statement and its linked concepts (Foucault, 1972). This means that concepts, statements, and notions related to Interest in Science will, here and in Foucault's terminology, be *treated* as statements in the analysis. Statements are the singular events that create the discursive formations. To do otherwise would be to miss the transversed discursive formations of the Chimera and the "thresholds" between the different parts of the construct:

> And then there are different kinds of statements, which are distinguished by certain "thresholds": a single family can pass through several different kinds, while one kind can incorporate several families. For example, science implies certain thresholds beyond, which statements attain an "epistemologization," a "scientificity" or even a "formalization." *But a science never absorbs the family or formation, which defines it.*
>
> *(Deleuze, 1986, p. 17, our emphasis)*

Deleuze's interpretation of Foucault's statements is one of the reasons Interest in Science can be seen as a chimera, a discursive formation, related to a desired expression of Being. Between the three discursive families under the gaze (the Mind, the Measurement, and the Morality), within the hybrid, the thresholds are the boundaries between the body, the tail, and the head. The specific families are not analyzed in their historical totality and genesis, which is again arbitrary, but in their form and shape within the specific historical manifestations of the Chimera. The method of using uppercase letters to signify discursive formations or families of discourses is inspired by Deleuze's nomenclature of Foucault's statements (Deleuze, 1986; Deleuze & Guattari, 1987).

The families will be termed as *rationalities*, as clusters of specific discourses, again containing statements and concepts related to the overall family or rationality (rationality of the Mind, the Measurement, and the Morality). Foucault used this term after *The Archeology of Knowledge* (1972) as a somewhat more plastic term than "discursive formations" (Dreyfus & Rabinow, 1983; Foucault, 2010). A rationality springs from the historical contingent episteme but is not a causal reenactment of it. Using the term "rationality" is also a way of stating that there is a specific causality linked to those respective families of discourses, a causality stemming again from the episteme of science.

This chapter will use research concepts, statements, and notions within theories. The rationalities of the Chimera are again very much on "the outside" and surface of the various thinkers (and PISA test) in the chapter and are shown in their discursive and nondiscursive elements. Thus a full "in-depth" textual analysis of the entirety of the thinker's theoretical work is unnecessary to identify the various rationalities at play and, in the methodology proposed here, would only depict the Archive and not the Map and the Diagram.

The thinkers here thus represent what Deleuze and Guattari (1994) called *conceptual personae*:

> The conceptual persona is not the philosopher's representative but, rather, the reverse: the philosopher is only the envelope of his principal conceptual persona and of all the other personae who are the intercessors [intercesseurs], the real subjects of his philosophy.
>
> *(p. 64)*

This line of thought, with the thinker as an envelope, is employed in the analysis here. This envelope contains not neat systematic packages of reason but chimerical conceptual monsters.

The Greek imagery of the Chimera is used as a new image of thought in an effort to show how this structure is connected to Nietzsche's problematization of Becoming and Being and Deleuze's reading of him (Deleuze, 2006; Nietzsche, 1894).

The Chimestry produces a full metamorphosis in the sense that the earlier discursive formation (and intersecting rationalities) undergoes a shift or reconfiguration. One may see the statement and its concept as Interest in Science; in practice and form, it has changed into a new mythological beast only connected in the linguistic form. The Chimestry of the Chimera and its transformations (see Figures 9.2, 9.3, and 9.4) is an attempt to grasp Foucault's notion of power and the Diagram in a new image of thought, which depicts rather than describes the transformations taking place (Deleuze, 1986; Foucault, 1970, 1972). Power is the exercise of the Chimera with regard to its specific rationalities and disciplines within the construct. It is the very practical strategy of the institutions, the realm of the visible, and how they enact the statements and their intersected family. Power is also the transformations, the involutions of the institutions, and how logic within the articulable is transferred to the visible. The mechanisms between the transformations, the Chimestry, are the ways in which power is exercised. Chimestry is the diagrammatic transformations of the Chimera qua the power relations. A shift in the Diagram shifts the Chimera and its intersecting discursive formations. Thus without stating specifically that power is at stake in the various transformations addressed in the chapter, power is very much the dynamo and engine behind the changes of the Chimera, and without that notion in mind, one will miss its crucial role behind the "necessary" shifts in the rationalities of the Chimera.

The PISA 2006 Interest Survey: A Reenactment of the Chimera

The PISA 2006 Survey was the first study to include a comprehensive international assessment of *interest in science* (OECD, 2007). The survey was a culmination of research showing "that an early interest in science is a predictor for late science learning and/or career in a science or technology field" (p. 122). In the beginning of the 21st century, there was an explicit political and economical aim and desire to secure more interest, learning, and engagement with science, thus producing more pupils Being-Scientific. The new regime of PISA has effected significant changes in the national and international configuration of science education (Dolin & Krogh, 2010; Grek, 2009; Osborne & Dillon, 2008). The reenactment of the Chimera is one of the catalysts of that change.

The PISA 2006 findings were not remarkable. Not much had changed since the PISA 2003 Survey, and the findings regarding *interest in science* seemed quite sociologically and statistically "typical": *Interest in science* has some correlation with gender and with social and economic background (Egelund, 2007, 2008). To examine the reasons for this surprising lack of new findings, one must look at the questions and the frame of the surveys. In other words, an analysis of the Chimera and its discursive formation is needed.

> Students' support for scientific enquiry and students' interest in learning science topics were directly assessed in the test, using embedded questions that targeted personal, social and global contexts. In the case of students' interest in learning science topics, students were able to report one of the following responses: "high interest," "medium interest," "low interest" or "no interest." Students reporting high interest or medium interest were considered to report an interest in learning science topics. For attitudinal questions measuring students' support for scientific enquiry, students were asked to express their level of agreement using one of the following responses: "strongly agree," "agree," "disagree" or "strongly disagree." Students reporting that they strongly agreed or agreed were considered to support scientific enquiry.
> *(OECD, 2007, p. 123)*

The quote evidences the clearly assumed causal linkage among attitudes, scales, and *interest in science*. It is a manifestation of the discursive formation of Interest in Science and the rationalities traversing it. It is a contemporary "fact" that youth's attitudes regarding science are measurable attributes within the students (Gardner, 1975). The attributes can be retrieved by questions and become an object of study to put on a scale. The transformation of qualitative traits into quantitatively reified facts is part of the modern rationality, where "numbers have come to epitomize the modern fact, because they have come to seem preinterpretive or even somehow noninterpretive at the same time that they have become the bedrock of systematic knowledge" (Poovey, 1998, p. xii). The mathematical measurement of the Chimera is labeled the Measurement, as a name for the family of discourses that all have the specific aim to measure, quantify, and enact statistical models and provide a numerical language of intelligibility to talk and think about education (Popkewitz, 2012).

Another important element in the framing of the PISA 2006 Survey is the assessment's goal in bonding the Measurement with the self, through the use of concepts such as the student's self-concept and self-efficacy regarding thinking and using Science (OECD, 2007, pp. 135–138). This bonding enacts a causality that produces questions in the survey to retrieve students' "sense of personal responsibility for maintaining a sustainable environment," "awareness of the environmental consequences of individual actions," and "willingness to take action to maintain natural resources" (OECD, 2007, p. 123). This trait of the Chimera, labeled the Morality, entails a family of discourses closely related to the normative, regulatory effects of pedagogy as a technology of disciplination and governmentality. In this enactment of the Chimera, there is an implied relationship between measurable psychological self-conceptualizations and moral self-regulation. This moral is expressed in, for example, Science's role in generating good conditions in society, larger issues regarding Science and the environment, and basic moral issues regarding ecological behavior.

The last trait is the visible head of the Chimera, the controlling discourse. Interest in Science is connected to enjoyment, motivation, and learning and various other concepts, which are given an intrinsic psychological meaning (OECD, 2007, pp. 139–150). The psychological trait of the Chimera is labeled the Mind. This family of discourses or rationality is of a cognitive and inner nature, an ontology, which states that *interest in science* is a domain-specific cognitive construct, a trait of personality, or even a psychological attribute from which learning emerges (Krapp, 1999). In this enactment of the Chimera, it is possible to measure the combined psychological construct "interest," through indicators of attitude in the survey.

The construct of Interest in Science in the PISA06 Survey, the contemporary chimera, is thus intersected by three different rationalities. The head of the

The Parts of the Chimera	The Rationalities	The Manifestations and Links Between the Rationalities
The Head	The Mind	*Linked to Measurement and Morality.* A specific cognitive domain.
The Body	The Measurement	*Linked to Mind and Morality.* Psychometrics and statistical modeling.
The Tail	The Morality	*Linked to Mind and Measurement.* Questions within the survey connecting science to society and a holistic awareness of science's role in society.

FIGURE 9.2 The Chimera of PISA

contemporary chimera is the Mind, the proud regal lion's head of neuropsychological causality; it is dominating and controlling the body, which is the Measurement—the workings of psychometrics supporting the *logos* of the head. Finally the tail, the proverbial hidden trait, is the Morality, the steering intrinsic morality of the goodness of science for the betterment of a sustainable world, where citizens use science to do good, even to the environment. *All components are perfectly linked and entwined;* the thresholds between the rationalities have become invisible.

Herbart's Mathematical Psychology: The Measurement in the Soul

Krapp and Prenzel (2011) take Johann Friedrich Herbart's theory of education and mathematical psychology as the starting point—a milestone—for the concept of *interest in science*, since it was he who

> for the first time developed a general theory of education in which interest played a central role. He emphasized that interest must not only be regarded as a desirable motivational condition of learning but also as an important goal or outcome of education.
>
> *(p. 29)*

Johann Friedrich Herbart (1776–1841) provided a model of the mind that uses mathematical modeling akin to Sir Isaac Newton's model of the solar system. Herbart had discovered a way to expand the notion of Science and its laws and regularities into the science of psychology, which at that time was not regarded as one of the serious sciences and was still under the sway of religion and notions of the soul (Foucault, 1970).

Many thinkers were attempting, in the late 18th and the 19th centuries, to expand mathematics into the science of man (Leary, 1980). At the time of Herbart, psychology was still a dominion of the soul (Herbart, 1890). As an apprentice of Kant, he intended to expand Kant's notion of predicting physical events both in the body and in the brain to actual mental events, which went beyond Kant's explicit denial of a mathematical psychology (Kant, 2004; Leary, 1980).

Herbart's key notion of *Vorstellung*—which may roughly be translated to a sense, presentation, or idea—could be measured and predicted with mathematical accuracy (Herbart, 1890). A Vorstellung is for the mind as the atom is for the physical world: The consciousness is composed of combinations of these *Vorstellungen* behaving according to Newtonian mechanical laws (Herbart, 1891). The mental unit of Vorstellung entails thoughts, emotions, visual images, and "inner speech/voice." It is defined by a measurable strength in the consciousness reflecting the clarity of the Vorstellung (Boudewijnse et al., 1999; Herbart, 1890). Herbart's concept of Vorstellung is inspired by his education in music and the concept of *tonelehre*. From music he got the notion of strength and how Vorstellungen could cancel each other out. It is also the concept of *tonelehre* that allows him to go beyond Newtonian concepts regarding opposing Vorstellungen in the mind (Boudewijnse et al., 1999; Herbart, 1890). In his mechanical and abstract explanation of the behavior of Vorstellungen, he provides an explanation of how one Vorstellung helps another into existence or is fused by it. With this characterization, he argues that sequential learning is attained through *repetition* (Boudewijnse et al., 1999; Herbart, 1890). Herbart's concept of interest arises from the cited conceptualization of Vorstellung:

> Interest, which in common with desire, will and the aesthetic judgment, stands opposed to indifference, is distinguished from those three, in that it neither controls nor disposes of its object, but depends upon it. It is true that we are inwardly active because we are interested, but externally we are passive till interest passes into desire or volition.
>
> *(Herbart, 1896b, p. 129)*

The intrinsic inner nature of interest is thus revealed, and Herbart stresses the transformation from the inner Vorstellung of interest to external forms in desire and volition:

> Interest only rises above mere perception in that what it perceives possesses the mind by preference, makes itself felt among the remaining perceptions by virtue of certain causality. From the preceding is immediately deduced what follows.
>
> *(Herbart, 1896b, pp. 129–130)*

Interest brings a chain of causality represented in other activities or actions: (1) observation; (2) expectation; (3) demand; and (4) action.

Herbart's mathematical study of the mind in his following writings goes beyond a desire to predict and measure the mind and enters the practice of education and pedagogy. He follows other related thinkers from the 18th century by fusing the respective sciences with Kant's Dictum—"I assert, however, that in any special doctrine of nature there can be only as much *proper* science as there is *mathematics* therein" (Kant, 2004, p. 6)—and the mathematics of Newton/Leibniz (Leary, 1980). He introduces the concept of *pedagogical tact* (Pädagogischer Takt), which is a solution to unite the problematic duality[5] of educational theory and educational practice (Herbart, 1890). The duality is due to the problem of good and bad practice, and good practice is dependent on a scientific approach to pedagogy and educational theory.

In this there is a quite clear demarcation line posited by Herbart: An educational science may never follow the asserted causality of the natural sciences; hence the need for a clear distinction between educational theory and practice. To elaborate, educational theory gives the choice of action, but pedagogical tact makes the pupil select "the right choice." His moral and ethical thinking becomes evident through the concept of *aesthetic necessity*, which is the judgment of a specific situation—still a judgment of taste in Kantian terms and subjected to the rules of such, but one that the educator can support and improve upon (Kenklies, 2012). The improvement of the educators' and pupils' perception of the world is the cornerstone of Herbart's mathematical concept of Vorstellung and how it evolves (Boudewijnse et al., 1999; Herbart, 1890; Kenklies, 2012; Leary, 1980). The notion of repetition and attentiveness is therefore the link between the mathematic-psychology of Herbart and his educational and pedagogical theory.

Embedded in Herbart's project of uniting mathematics, psychology, and educational/pedagogical theory, there is also the grand failure of the enterprise: He did not manage to show how the micro level of his mathematical psychology was visible at the macro level of schooling and education (Boudewijnse et al., 1999; Herbart, 1896b). The Dark Side of Pedagogy (Herbart, 1896a) was attributed to general problems regarding education, especially from his followers in both Europe and America (Dunkel, 1970). Herbart saw his mathematical psychology and theory of attention in the mind as being in direct conflict with the temporal and unsystematic nature of pedagogy and education. In other words, demands from elsewhere disturbed and "darkened" education and pedagogy and the pure instruction according to Herbart's principles.

Herbart's solution was to emphasize repetition as the method to achieve learning, repeating and reinforcing the pupil's previous knowledge, interest, and experience (Erfahrung), and abstaining from artificial rewards to the pupil. The Dark Side of Pedagogy transformed into a specific form of disciplination through repetition far from the pure mathematical psychology originally intended by Herbart's writings.

The Chimera of Herbart's Interest in Science is composed of mathematics, psychology, and educational/pedagogical theory. This trinity of the Measurement, the Mind—or the Soul in early psychology—and the Morality of pedagogy are the head, body, and tail of his Chimera.

In this historical episteme, the proverbial head of the construct of Interest in Science, openly and proudly displayed, is thus the regal mathematical lion of causality and encompasses the totality of the soul. The goat's body and main functioning of the concept of Interest in Science is a notion of psychology founded not in biology and physiology but in Vorstellung and abstract notions of repetition, fusion, and attention—still in the nomenclature of the Mind/Soul.[6] The tail of the Chimera, the hidden and steering manifestation of the construct, is morality emphasized by educational and pedagogical theory. The concept of *interest in science* is, in the 19th century, not explained as a "thing in itself" but as a measurable, internal structure and unit that should be developed according to a judgment of taste. This Chimera remains, though, a creature of mythos in the various discursive formations of the century. Herbart's Dark Side of Pedagogy evidences the failure of linkage between the various parts of the beast, a creature of mythos, only partly actualized, in the various discursive formations of the century. The relation among measurement, soul, and morality is never fully realized in Herbart's discourse.

The Parts of the Chimera	The Rationalities	The Manifestations and Link Between the Rationalities
The Head	The Measurement	*Linked to the Mind/Soul.* The mathematical model of Herbart.
The Body	The Mind/Soul	*Linked to the Measurement.* The notion and concept of Vorstellung. The unit in the Mind.
The Tail	The Morality	*Unlinked.* The pedagogy of Herbart. The disciplination of the child. Dark Side of Pedagogy.

FIGURE 9.3 The Chimera of Herbart

Dewey's Interest versus Effort: The Fragmentation of the Concept

Krapp and Prenzel state that Dewey adopted Herbart's ideas regarding *interest in science* (Krapp & Prenzel, 2011). Specifically, the text *Interest and Effort in Education* (Dewey, 1913) is central in the analysis of how the construct Interest in Science was composed in 1913 in the United States and shows the early form of Dewey's Chimera. Henry Suzzalo, president of the University of Washington at Seattle, in his editorial comment on this text spells out the reason for Dewey's importance—the failure of the spirit of the Prussian School Regime through repetition and physical disciplination:

> To this end we have established a compulsory school attendance age, forbidden child labor, and provided administrative machinery for executing these legal guarantees of the rights of children. Yet, a guarantee of school attendance will never of itself fulfill the purposes of state education. The parent and the attendance officer, reinforced by the police power of the state, can guarantee only one thing—the physical presence of the child at school. It is left to the teacher to insure his mental attendance by a sound appeal to his active interests.
>
> *(Dewey, 1913, p. viii)*

There is a dichotomy between physical attendance and mental attendance of school, and the editor appoints Dewey's thinking as the solution to the problem. Dewey's discourse in *Interest Effort in Education* (1913) proposes a reform of how to think and do education in line with his new philosophy. He constructs a theoretical binary between interest and effort and proposes a stance and practice between these two poles. Both the contemporary theories of effort and interest are wrong, and both are "intellectually and morally harmful" (Dewey, 1913, p. 97). Dewey proposes that interest be placed at the center of a theory of education. A twofold or binary position is then enunciated:

The positive contributions of the idea of interest to pedagogic theory are two-fold. In the first place, it protects us from a merely *internal* conception of mind; and in the second place from a merely *external* conception of subject matter.

(Dewey, 1913, pp. 91–92; Dewey's emphasis)

Dewey tries to escape the binary of interest and effort by internalizing subject matter and externalizing the mind. In the terminology of the Chimera, he creates a clear connection between the Mind and the Morality, which in this historical configuration becomes subject matter leading to democracy. He proposes that interest cannot be understood without this binary.

The Mind in Dewey's terms is very much a psychological phenomenon, with a basis in stimulus and motor response. He uses the physiological discourse on the brain and perception:

The teachings of Pestalozzi and of the sense-training and object-lesson schools in pedagogy were the first important influence in challenging the supremacy of a purely formal, because inner and abstract, conception of self-activity. But, unfortunately, the psychology of the times was still associated with a false physiology and a false philosophy of the relations of the mind and the body.

(Dewey, 1913, p. 70)

In this quote he emphasizes how his conception of Mind has moved beyond the accounts of the 19th century, indirectly implicating Herbart, and into a new line of thought. What is of interest here with regard to the modern contemporary form of the Chimera is the direct link between the mind and the body in Dewey's terminology. Dewey has also previously stated the clear connection between moral (or ethical) behavior and psychology:

But when once the values come to consciousness, when once Socrates insists upon the organic relation of a reflective life and morality, then the means, the machinery by which ethical ideals are projected and manifested, comes to consciousness also. *Psychology must be born as soon as morality becomes reflective.* Moreover, psychology, as an account of the mechanism of workings of personality, is the only alternative to an arbitrary and class view of society, to an aristocratic view in the sense of restricting the realization of the full worth of life to a section of society.

(Dewey, 1900, p. 122; author's emphasis)

In Dewey's discourse, there is a clear link between the Mind and the Morality, between psychology and pedagogy, ultimately leading to democracy. Dewey—unlike Herbart—sees them as mutual requirements for achieving a just society. But what of the Measurement, so evident in Herbart's Chimera, vanished from the ratio-nalities of Dewey? In the discourse of Dewey in *Interest and Effort* (Dewey, 1913), measurement of the activity born by true educative interest is in fact immeasurable:

> The kinds of activity remaining as true educative interests vary indefinitely with age, with individual native endowments, with prior experience, with social opportunities. It is out of the question to try to catalogue them.
>
> *(Dewey, 1913, p. 67)*

In Dewey's later writings, however, he rescinds that limitation, especially in his text on building an education based on the concept of experience and of a specific organization of subject matter:

> I am aware that the emphasis that I have placed upon scientific method may be misleading, for it may result only in calling up the special technique of laboratory research as that is conducted by specialists. But the meaning of the emphasis placed upon scientific method has little to do with specialized techniques. It means that scientific method is the only authentic means at our command for getting at the significance of our everyday experiences of the world in which we live. *It means scientific method provides a working pattern of the way in which and the conditions under which experiences are used to lead ever onward and outward.*
>
> *(Dewey, 1938, pp. 87–88)*

In the terminology of this chapter, Dewey's specific form of the Measure-ment is thus specifically the scientific method, especially concerning the causal-ity regarding a proper organization of subject matter. This feature is, though, the least explored concept of Dewey's, because of the immeasurableness of his conceptualizations of the Mind and the Morality. The Measurement in Dewey's Chimera is only indirectly linked to the other two. What is interesting for the conceptualization and construction of Interest in Science is the introduction of the *scientific method* into the discourse on interest. No longer satisfied with edu-cation being merely linked to pedagogy, what took a warped and ultimately failed form in Herbart's writings is completed in Dewey's. Education is now regarded among the sciences as a specific application of psychology and ethical thought, and the link is ultimately in Dewey's terminology between education and democracy (Dewey, 1916).

To summarize, Dewey's Chimera consists of the Morality, which in his enact-ment is the proud head of democracy and pedagogy, the true aim of education, and the Mind, which is the body and functions perfectly linked to the Moral-ity through the conceptualization of experience, founded in a psychological and physiological understanding of the Mind; finally, the tail is a somewhat unad-dressed and hidden feature of Dewey's conceptualization, the Measurement.

The Parts of the Chimera	The Rationalities	The Manifestations and Links Between the Rationalities
The Head	The Morality	*Linked to the Mind through concept of experience.* The pedagogical writings of Dewey. Education and Democracy.
The Body	The Mind	*Linked to the Morality through the intrinsic concept of experience.* Thought and thinking. His biological and physiological notion of the Mind.
The Tail	The Measurement	*Unlinked in the early writings later connected to both the Morality and the Mind through a concept of scientific method.* Experience and Education. Notions on an educational science.

FIGURE 9.4 The Chimera of Dewey

Dewey's "tail" was first truly hidden in the "body of the Chimera"—only the inheritance from physiology contained "measures"; but later the tail becomes more and more visible, especially in his later writing, and he is forced to address the Measurement of education and experience. One never sees a perfect linked trinity in Dewey's Chimera, though one can glimpse the ascendancy of the Measurement in Dewey's later writings.

The Contemporary Chimera Revisited

The Chimera of today, as enacted in the PISA survey, is a perfect hybrid. The links, thresholds, and rationalities are faultlessly connected. We have a conceptualization of *interest in science* as something that is within the individual pupil and citizen (the Mind as the head). It is scalable and can be used to measure the effects of science education (the Measurement as the body) and, finally, Interest in Science is a good thing, connected to democracy, sustainable development, and a holistic awareness of natural role in society (the Morality as the connected tail). In short, we have tamed the Becoming-Chimera and resolved the intrinsic conflicts within the earlier transformations.

The tool of taming of the Chimera is closely related to an intricate dance between what Thomas Popkewitz (2004) calls Alchemy and the Chimestry proposed in this chapter. Alchemy is, in other words, the link and process of transformation between the rationality of the Mind and curriculum (here placed in the strata of the Map). The engine that drives this particular alchemy is the Chimestry—the outside of thought. The inscription on the pupil, in respect to Interest in Science, thus becomes something more than just the specific rationality of the Mind—the complete amalgam of the tamed contemporary Chimera.

Psychology, here called the rationality of the Mind, is enacted in the progress of scientifical of mind (specifically interest) in the curriculum, and this taming/scientifical of the Mind is critically related to the taming of the Chimera. To achieve a taming of the Mind, instances of Chimestry invoked the Measurement, and to reinforce that particular bondage, the Morality became the lever that pivoted the disparate parts into a perfect fit.

Something interesting appears when one compares the two earlier manifestations of the Chimera with the contemporary one. Herbart's Chimera (see Figure 9.3) had the Measurement as the proud head of causality. This was coupled with a notion of the Mind or the Soul, founded not in physiology but in metaphysics, as the body. Last, he had the Dark Side of Pedagogy, the educational science, which can never be a true science and is thus a hidden necessity and doomed to a pragmatic stance, the tail of the Morality.

Dewey's Chimera (see Figure 9.4) had undergone a Chimestry from Herbart's 19th-century construct. The Chimera of Dewey had the Morality (or pedagogy) as the head of the construct of interest, ultimately leading to democracy. The body consisted of the Mind, a psychology founded in physiology, and "modern" psychological theory, though with Dewey's notion of experience, bridging the Morality and the Mind. The tail was the Measurement, first in his writings deemed impossible, but later surfaced as the specific scientific method. Education as a specific science is the discursive result of Dewey's conceptualizations.

The common feature of the two earlier chimeras was their *brokenness*, or their various failed links, and the incoherent nature of the two Chimeras. Even though Dewey encapsulated a watered-down form of the Measurement, it was never in the form of the causality of attitude measurement or statistics; he did not dare to put the Mind into the form of numbers as Herbart tried to do.

The critical question thus arises: Is a tamed contemporary perfect Chimera, a stunted Chimestry, productive for the conceptualization of *interest in science* and ultimately Being-Scientist and in whose interests is it that the Chimera is so perfectly linked?

In other words, what process of Chimestry led to the taming of the Chimera and which "will" willed it?

Researchers in the social sciences have pointed out problems in the increasing trend of measurement and comparativeness in educational research (Grek, 2009; Grek, Lawn, Lingard, & Varjo, 2009; Lawn & Grek, 2012), and the claim of this chapter is that the Chimera "resolved" acts as a dogmatic image of thought to obscure the effects of the scientification of education and ultimately hinder Becoming-Chimera. The contemporary Chimera has thus become truly monstrous—not in the form of a chaotic eternal return, pure chance, but as a cybernetic Chimera of late capitalism caged in fixed structures of science education.

Acknowledgments

We would like to thank Gelsa Knijnik from University do Vale do Rio dos Sinos, Brazil, for her contribution to discussions while shaping this chapter. The research in this chapter is part of the "Youth-to-Youth" project, supported by the educational development initiative of the Northern Denmark Region and the Nordic Center of Excellence in Education "Justice through Education."

Notes

1. The concept/notion will here be called *interest in science*. The discursive formation (the construct of the Chimera) will be termed Interest in Science.
2. Being-Scientist is here assembled as a construct of thought and discourse, a discursive formation, not actual Being in the Deleuzian terminology. Being-Scientist, and the related becoming-Chimera, is though related to Being in the Deleuzian sense as a mode of thought and an *expression* of the univocity of Being (Deleuze, 1988, 1990).
3. The term "didactics" refers to the European tradition of systematic thinking about teaching and learning (Hopmann, 2007).
4. A *vivisection* of the surface refers to a movement, which cuts up and exposes the plane of immanence. It is thus directly opposed to transcendental deconstruction or similar movements.
5. In this historical epoch, a duality is instated in both the statements and the concepts of Herbart. He uses the German word for soul as the anchor of a psychology but avoids religion in that regard; it is only brought to the field when issues of disciplination and instruction are at hand (Herbart, 1890).
6. An extensive analysis of the duality of the Mind/the Soul in this epoch has previously been undertaken by Foucault (1970).

References

Boudewijnse, G.-J. A., Murray, D. J., & Bandomir, C. A. (1999). Herbart's mathematical psychology, *History of Psychology, 2*(3), 163–193. doi 10.1037/1093-4510.2.3.163

Daston, L., & Galison, P. (2007). *Objectivity.* New York: Zone Books.

Deleuze, G. (1986). *Foucault* (S. Hand, trans., 2006 ed.). London: Athlone Press.

Deleuze, G. (1988). *Spinoza: Practical philosophy.* San Francisco: City Lights Books.

Deleuze, G. (1990). *Expressionism in philosophy: Spinoza.* New York: Zone Books.

Deleuze, G. (1994). *Difference and repetition.* London: Continuum Group.

Deleuze, G. (2006). *Nietzsche and philosophy.* London and New York: Continuum International Publishing Group.

Deleuze, G., & Guattari, F. (1987). *A thousand plateaus: Capitalism and schizophrenia.* Minneapolis: University of Minnesota Press.

Deleuze, G., & Guattari, F. (1994). *What is philosophy?* New York: Columbia University Press.

Dewey, J. (1900). Psychology and social practice. *Psychological Review, 7*(2), 105.

Dewey, J. (1913). *Interest and effort in education.* London: Forgotten Books.

Dewey, J. (1916). *Democracy and education.* New York: Dover Publications.

Dewey, J. (1938). *Experience and education.* New York: Touchstone.

Dolin, J., & Krogh, L. (2010). The relevance and consequences of PISA science in a Danish context. *International Journal of Science and Mathematics Education, 8*(3), 565–592. doi: 10.1007/s10763-;010-;9207-;6

Dreyfus, H. L., & Rabinow, P. (1983). *Michel Foucault: Beyond structuralism and hermeneutics.* Chicago: University of Chicago Press.

Dunkel, H. B. (1969a). Herbartianism comes to America: Part I. *History of Education Quarterly, 9*(2), 202–233.

Dunkel, H. B. (1969b). Herbartianism comes to America: Part II. *History of Education Quarterly, 9*(3), 376–390.

Dunkel, H. B. (1970). *Herbart and Herbartianism: An educational ghost story.* Chicago: University of Chicago Press.

Egelund, N. (Ed.). (2007). *PISA 2006—Danske unge i en international sammenligning.* København: Danmark Pædagogiske Universitetsforlag.

Egelund, N. (2008). *PISA og ungdomsuddannelserne 2006—kompetencer hos 16½-årige elever i fire typer af danske ungdomsuddannelser foråret 2006.* København: Danmark Pædagogiske Universitetsforlag.

Feist, G. J. (2012). Predicting interest in and attitudes toward science from personality and need for cognition. *Personality and Individual Differences, 52,* 771–775.

Foucault, M. (1970). *The order of things: An archaeology of the human sciences* (2nd ed.). New York: Routledge.

Foucault, M. (1972). *Archaeology of knowledge* (A. M. S. Smith, trans., 1st English ed.). London: Routledge.

Foucault, M. (2010). *The birth of biopolitics: Lectures at the College de France, 1978–1979* (G. Burcell, Trans.). New York: Palgrave Macmillan.

Gardner, P. L. (1975). Attitude measurement: A critique of some recent research. *Education Research, 7,* 101–109.

Grek, S. (2009). Governing by numbers: The PISA "effect" in Europe. *Journal of Education Policy, 24*(1), 23–37.

Grek, S., Lawn, M., Lingard, B., & Varjo, J. (2009). North by northwest: Quality assurance and evaluation processes in European education. *Journal of Education Policy, 24*(2), 121–133.

Herbart, J. F. (1890). Psyuchologie als Wissenschaft [Psychology as science]. In K. F. Kehrbach (ed.), *Jon. Fr. Herbart's sämtliche Werke in chronologischer Reihenfolge* (Vol. 5, pp. 177–434). Lagensalza, Prussia: Hermann Beyer und Söhne.

Herbart, J. F. (1891). *A textbook in psychology: An attempt to found the science of psychology, on experience, metaphysics, and mathematics* (M. K. Smith, Trans.). London: Forgotten Books.

Herbart, J. F. (1896a). *Herbart's ABC of sense-perception, and minor pedagogical works* (Vol. 36). New York: D. Appleton.

Herbart, J. F. (1896b). *The science of education, its general principles deduced, from its aim and the aesthetic revelation of the world.* London: Forgotten Books.

Hopmann, S. (2007). Restrained teaching: The common core of Didaktik. *European Educational Research Journal, 6*(2), 109–124.

Kant, I. (2004). *Kant: Metaphysical foundations of natural science.* Cambridge: Cambridge University Press.

Kenklies, K. (2012). Educational theory as topological rhetoric: The concepts of pedagogy of Johann Friedrich Herbert and Friedrich Schleiermacher. *Studies in Philosophy & Education, 31*(3), 8. doi: 10.1007/s11217-;012-;9287-;6

Krapp, A. (1999). Interest, motivation, and learning: An educational-psychological perspective. *International Journal of Science Education, 14*(1), 23–40. doi: 10.1007/BF03173109

Krapp, A., & Prenzel, M. (2011). Research on interest in science: Theories, methods, and findings. *International Journal of Science Education, 33*(1), 23.

Lawn, M., & Grek, S. (2012). *Europeanizing education: Governing a new policy space.* Oxford: Symposium Books.

Leary, D. E. (1980). The historical foundation of Herbart's mathematization of psychology. *Journal of the History of the Behavioral Sciences, 16,* 150–163.

Nietzsche, F. W. (1894). *Die Geburt der Tragödie aus dem Geiste der Musik.* Leipzig, Germany: C. G. Naumann.

OECD. (2004). *Messages from PISA 2000.* Paris: OECD.

OECD. (2006). *Evolution of student interest in science and technology studies. Policy report.* Paris: OECD.

OECD. (2007). *PISA 2006 science competencies for tomorrow's world (Vol. 1—Analysis).* Paris: OECD.

Osborne, J., & Dillon, J. (2008). *Science education in Europe: Critical reflections* (A report to the Nuffield Foundation). London: Nuffield Foundation.

Poovey, M. (1998). *A history of the modern fact: Problems of knowledge in the sciences of wealth and society.* Chicago: University of Chicago Press.

Popkewitz, T. S. (2004). The alchemy of the mathematics curriculum: Inscriptions and the fabrication of the child. *American Educational Research Journal, 41*(1), 3–34.

Popkewitz, T. S. (2012). Numbers in grids of intelligibility: Making sense of how educational truth is told. In H. Lauder, M. Young, H. Daniels, M. Balarin, & J. Lowe (Eds.), *Education for the knowledge economy? Critical perspectives* (pp. 169–191). Florence, KY: Routledge.

Sjøberg, S., & Schreiner, C. (2010). *The ROSE project. An overview and key findings.* Oslo, Norway: Oslo University.

10

NUMBERS IN TELLING EDUCATIONAL TRUTH

Fabrications of Kinds of People and Social Exclusion

Thomas S. Popkewitz

In an important book about numbers and social affairs, Theodore Porter (1995) begins by asking, "How are we to account for the prestige and power of quantitative methods in the modern world? . . . How is it that what was used for studying stars, molecules and cells would have attraction for human societies?" To consider these questions, Porter continues that only a small proportion of numbers or quantitative expressions have any pretense of describing laws of nature or "even of providing complete and accurate descriptions of the eternal world" (pp. viii–ix). Numbers, he argues, are parts of systems of communication whose technologies create distances from phenomena by appearing to summarize complex events and transactions. As the mechanical objectivity of numbers appears to follow *a priori* rules that project fairness and impartiality, numbers are seen as excluding judgment and mitigating subjectivity. Porter continues that numbers are a technology of distance and used as a claim of objectivity instantiated by moral and political discourses.

The importance of numbers to contemporary societies is easy to demonstrate, ironically, by citing numbers. It is almost impossible to think about schooling without numbers: children's ages and school grades, the measures of children's growth and development, achievement testing, or league tables of school success/ failures and statistical correlations among social, economic, and family characteristics and school completion.

This discussion extends and refocuses Porter's notion of the technologies of numbers to consider how numbers are inscribed within a grid of historical practices that generate cultural thesis about who the child (and teacher) is and should be. Further, the making of equivalencies embodies comparability that creates differences from some sameness that differentiates and divides in the impulse to include. The argument is pursued in the following way.

First, I briefly consider the historical "making" of numbers as "social facts." This production of "social facts," I argue, fabricates "kinds of people" who are to be acted on and are to act as if they are such "people" (Hacking, 1999). The sections following focus on the New Public Management strategies in the making of kinds of people: research on "the effective teacher" to identify "value-added" factors to improve student achievement, the Organisation for Economic Co-operation and Development's (OECD) Program for International Student Assessment (PISA) international comparisons of children's curriculum knowledge, and the school curriculum standards reform movement. I explore these numbers as inscriptions of cultural theses about who the child/teacher is and should be—in effect producing particular human kinds. The third section historicizes the contemporary tropes of neoliberalism and markets as homogeneous to PISA and "the effective teacher" in that it assumes numbers whose effects fabricate human kinds. The fourth section extends and integrates the previous discussions to explore how principles are generated that exclude and abject in the impulse for inclusion.

The analysis is about the politics of schooling. This notion of politics focuses on the historically generated principles that govern what is thought, acted on, and hoped for; and divisions produced that embody differences registered as the dangers and dangerous populations. The approach works against the grain of the common sense of how change is considered. It poses the problem of change as making possible resistance to the frameworks of the contemporary rules and standards of "reason" (see, e.g., Foucault, 1984; Rancière, 2004).

Numbers as Fabricating Kinds of People

I begin the inquiry into numbers through, first, considering numbers as an "actor" that produces things through processes that seem to be merely representing and describing. Numbers order thought and action by visualizing "social facts" that in the 19th century were thought necessary for republican government and democracy. The seemingly objectivizing and standardizing through numbers were to equalize processes and practices of the new republican governments. That equalizing enabled the systems of planning to tame the uncertainty associated with democratic life and provide for the social administration for making the citizen that is historically inscribed in modern schooling (see, e.g., Popkewitz, 2008).

Numbers and Governing

The belief in the truth-telling capacity of numbers to establish values about social and personal life has not always been the case. Prior to the 18th century, truth was told through the manners and rhetorical qualities of the speaker that established one's social position (Poovey, 1998). The emergence of statistics as "facts" about social life was part of broader changes that traversed economy, statecraft, and culture during the 18th and 19th centuries. For example, considerable numerical information collected by the British government in the first three quarters of the 18th century was not collected in the context of coherent theory about statecraft (Poovey, 1998, p. 214). Numbers as representative of observed particulars were devalued through the priority given to Newtonian universals and the invisible laws of nature. In Sweden, numbers were an official part of governing through registering the reading ability of the population. That register of numbers was individual and without the probability reasoning for ordering populations that appeared in the 19th century.

The use of statistics as a numerical expression of human activity emerged from 18th-century German "cameral statistics" as a science of the description of the varied aspects of the state. Later and through successive (re)visioning of the word, "statistics" separated the political management of people from the scientific management of things and the autonomy of statistics as a field of knowledge. To consider these changes, it is possible to trace "statistics" in the 18th century as a literary term—the numerical part of the description of the state in the 19th century, and by the 20th century tied to mathematical techniques for numerical analysis of data whatever type (Desrosières, 1991, p. 200). The apparently quantitative precision and specific delineations of social and personal life lent authority to the new regimes of government. Numbers standardized the subject of measurement and the act of exchange so that they were no longer seen as dependent on the personalities or the statuses of those involved.

Numbers are a social technology that seems to instantiate a consensus and harmony in a world that appears, otherwise, uncertain, ambiguous, and contentious. The uniformity given by numbers brings unlike orders in social life into a system of magnitudes that regularize relations among social and psychological components (Rose, 1999, p. 206). If I use contemporary policy and research about poverty in the UK and the United States, numbers establish categories of equivalence and correlate them to identify factors about the family "unit" such as physical, social, and psychological characteristics of the home and parental relations. By correlating the statistical magnitudes of these characteristics of populations to achievement levels of children, it is thought that a more equal and democratic society can be achieved. Numbers perform as technologies to map boundaries and the internal characteristics of the spaces to be managed as a strategy to make judgments seem as not subjective. Yet while the categories of people given in the numbers of statistics "act" as if they are real, the distinctions embody implicit choices about "what to measure, how to measure it, how often to measure it and how to present and interpret the results" (Rose, 1999, p. 199).

The use of numbers and social science, it should be noted, were not central to the late-19th-century U.S. social sciences (including economics), as the sciences were more speculative than empirical. The insertion of statistics into social theory had the effect of reducing what seemed uncertain. Statistics, to borrow from Hacking (1990), tamed chance. It gave stability to things in flux and inscribed an apparent consensus that made phenomena of the world seem amenable to control.

Notions of decision making, human interest, and problem solving, for example, are ways to order and regularize the processes in a world in which the conditionality of the future seems under control.

The inscription of numbers in the systems of reason governing social life was not the logical outcome of disciplinary knowledge; nor was it the result of an evolutionary process from a single origin, such as capitalism or liberal political regimes. The movement of statistics from the concern with individual phenomena to its 19th-century notions of statistical knowledge as expressed through probability theories about large groups occurred through work in different and unrelated areas that overlapped 19th-century statistics with discoveries in physics and the needs of statecraft to monitor large groups for taxes and disease (Desrosières, 1993/1998).

Numbers as administration were continually fraught with multiple outcomes. One can consider historically that the French system of household taxes counted the doors and windows in a dwelling into the 20th century. To counter this system, peasants redesigned their houses with as few openings as possible to reduce taxes, which has long-term effects on their health. Monocropped scientific forestry developed from about 1765 to 1800 brought an administrative grid of straight rows of trees for more efficient growth; such growth was stunted, however, by the second planting because the nutrients produced with mixed growth were eliminated. And the rational planning of the city in the 19th century into gridlike streets created a particular spatial order that also produced anonymity, alienation, and feelings of loss of community (Scott, 1998, p. 58). The dark images of Expressionist art in the 1920s and Fritz Lang's silent film *Metropolis* testify to this other side of life in the city as well.

Fabricating Kinds of People

Numbers are *inscription devices*. The collection and aggregation of numbers participate in a "clearing" or space where thought and action can occur (Rose, 1999, p. 212). That cultural space in schooling entails the fabrication of human kinds. Fabrication is to think about the double and simultaneous qualities of the distinctions and classifications about people. If I use the category of adolescent, it is a fiction in the sense that the notion of adolescence was brought into and made a part of the early-20th-century American child studies of G. Stanley Hall to respond to changes in the populations of children coming to mass schooling. Older pedagogical distinctions of children no longer seemed appropriate (Popkewitz, 2008).[1] Adolescence was a classification for thinking about children, what pedagogical practices of school could be organized to govern children, and the role of the new psychological theories about development and growth in this governing.

That fiction to respond to things happening is no longer merely that. It "acts" in the world to simultaneously "make" or manufactured certain kinds of people. The classifications and distinctions of the child studies entered into structuring experience and as ways for people to think of themselves, their choices, and what is practical and useful within this apparatus of thought (for more general discussion of this phenomena, see Hacking, 1986; Rose, 1999, p. 203). Today, adolescence is not only a way of thinking about the child. Its principles are taken as what children are to organize parenting, schooling, and medicine. Adolescence is also how a child is to think about his life as a process of development.

My uses of fabrication and the making of kinds of humans are to provide analytic "tools" to pursue numbers in the governing of schooling without falling into the unfruitful philosophical dualism between discourse (nominalism) and realism. The argument, however, is not about the categories and classifications. It is about the rules and standard of reason embodied in contemporary assessment practices as *simultaneously doing something to us!*

Fabrications: "The Effective Teacher" and PISA Lifelong Learner

Measurement devices give magnitudes and correlations to particular abstractions (fictions) that work their way into the conduct of the world and as the potential to be materialized as what is taken as real in education. This can be explored in two seemingly different reform practices. One is research to identify the *effective teacher* and the other is the PISA, an international comparative assessment of children's application of curriculum knowledge. Each embodies a style of reasoning that is associated with the New Public Management in social, political, and educational reforms. The New Public Management links expectations about performance to strategies for achieving those outcomes, such as setting curriculum standards, benchmarking, and identifying "best practices"(see, e.g., Lindblad, 2014).[2] The style of reasoning circulates in the accountability movements of testing children and teachers in U.S. efforts to create equitable schools from the 1970s to the present, such as in No Child Left Behind mandates for school testing and the "Race to the Top" tests of teacher effectiveness.

The Effective Teacher: An Abstraction in Search of Being Real

An article in a leading educational research journal focused on the methodological design for identifying "the effective teacher" who enables successful achievement of "all children" (Day, Sammons, & Gu, 2008). Drawing on the language of the New Public Management about setting goals/expectations about performance (e.g., benchmarks, good practices), the research talks about identifying "value-added" dimensions in teachers' practices to make "a more robust" relation between the capabilities of the teacher and the children's achievement results.

The research described in the article begins with the assumption that the capacities of the teacher are part of a system of psychological and organizational qualities whose identification will enable children's success in school achievement.

Achievement is placed as existing within a system described as an integrated "wholist, nuanced understanding of teachers' work and lives" (Day, Sammons, & Gu, 2008, p. 330) given credence through the seemingly economic language of "value added." The economic language, however, is not about economy in the sense of the skills and knowledge necessary for the world of work. The value added is directed to cultural and social practices. The wholism is described, for example, as student motivation, school culture and leadership, and the biography and career of the teacher that combine to enable student attainment and achievement.

The research is described as innovative because of its use of a mixed-methods approach. The mixed-methods approach is called "the third way," to play off a term used in political arenas to describe the better of two different ideological worlds. The third way is the combining of quantitative and qualitative techniques for improving the quality of instruction. Rather than ask about the internal adequacy of the techniques applied, I want to ask about the particular space cleared for reflection and action inscribed in the numbers and the principles generated by the human kind of "the effective teacher."

The effective teacher is an abstraction designed to respond to the events of the school. It is not something "there" to be touched and felt. Nor is it something "there" for research to recoup and empirically "discover." The "effective teacher," like the adolescent, and discussed later in Adam Smith's "markets," is an invention whose conceptualization is in search of data that can be correlated and identified as the qualities and capabilities through which the concept is filled in. The fiction of "the effective teacher" relies on theories about schooling, teaching, and children that give that notion of "effective" intelligibility in the ordering and classifying procedures.

The theories are elided in the measurements that make the effective teacher into an ahistorical "fact" about the calculated potential of the teacher. The materialization is given through magnitudes and equivalences that define the effective teacher as the "contextual value added using multilevel models . . . that identifies differential qualities that relate to sustaining commitment ($n = 189, 61\%$) or sustaining commitment despite challenging circumstances ($n = 39, 13\%$)" (Day, Sammons, & Gu, 2008, pp. 334–335). The subject, the effective teacher, is given magnitudes and correlations charted as the teacher profession life trajectories and correlated with children's achievement. The particular kind of human—the effective teacher—statistically joins the different factors that "add value" to efforts to improve achievement scores (p. 335).

The relations are called "robust" to suggest that the principles are "real" and no longer abstractions about a particular human kind to be administered through school reform. The numbers shape and fashion a cultural thesis about a mode of life that a teacher should live to be "effective." Particular magnitudes are given as providing the value of the "value-added measure" to define that mode of life as the abstraction is filled in with data that is to serve as a kind of person to be sought. That person entails psychological stages of the teacher as expressions of commitment, agency, life–work management, and well-being. Without going into the how the categories embody assumptions that are not empirical (such as what constitutes management and well-being), the value-added measures are policing practices that inscribe a harmony and consensus to what is done, hoped for, and to be accomplished as sensible teaching.

International Assessments and Comparable Human Kinds

A different kind of human is generated in international comparisons of students' school performances in OECD's Program for International Student Assessment (PISA); the Progress in International Reading Literacy Study (PIRLS) conducted by the International Association for the Evaluation of Educational Achievement (IEA); Trends in International Mathematics and Science Study (TIMMS); and the Adult Literacy and Lifeskills Survey (ALL) conducted by Statistics Canada. As part of the New Public Management, the measurement devices focus on school inputs and output/performances as "benchmarks" to assess the progress of national school systems.

The shift is in governance from institutional indicators and audit and performance monitoring to governance that mixes technical components of measuring and procedures that produce principles to order the capacities and qualities of individuality (Lascoumes & Le Galès, 2007). The individuality in OECD's PISA is expressed through a missionary theme about progress and creating a better life. PISA, it is argued, is not directed to achievement measures, as was the research on effective teaching. The PISA testing in reading, mathematical, and scientific literacy is to measure "practical" ability to apply skills in everyday-life situations believed related to labor market core skills and future participation in society.

While international comparisons would seem different than the research on effective teaching, they overlap in generating principles about who "we" are and should be. PISA's identification of curricular competences is not merely about what a child knows and clearly cannot be about the practical knowledge of the future. PISA measures of "practical knowledge," when examined, are to assess and bring into being the abstractions (theories) about a particular kind of person that are described as psychological states. These states of the child are "motivation to learn," "self-esteem," and adapting appropriate "learning strategies" in organizing one's life.

The psychological categories about "motivation to learn and learning," for example, are not merely about the child's solving problems that will "open life opportunities" for them, as suggested. Motivation, as Danziger (1997) historically explicates, is an invention to design the interior of the child's desire. Early psychology did not provide explanations of everyday conduct. It was not until the emergence of mass schooling that an interest emerged about removing children's "fatigue" in learning through calculating and influencing the children's will, motives, interests, needs, and desires. This treatment of inner thought, daily life, and experience were objects of administration. Motivation became a key player in this administration: It is neither disinterested nor impartial, nor does it exist as objectively outside of the historical grid through which it is given intelligibility. Today, motivation is articulated and given nuance through notions of self-esteem and efficacy in social and educational planning and as part of the system that defines "the effective teacher."

Further the principles of "practical knowledge" in PISA assume that what is translated and transported into schooling is a reliable, objective representation of disciplinary fields. Yet the pedagogical principles that classify and order disciplinary knowledge, how that knowledge is made knowable and to be acted on in pedagogy, has little to do with disciplines (Popkewitz, 2004).

The procedures of classification and ordering in school subjects can be viewed as an alchemy. Analogous to the alchemists of the Middle Ages, academic practices (performed in labs, university science buildings, historical societies, etc.) are translated and transformed into the spaces that embody school curriculum (theories of learning, age and grade organizations of children, and didactic practices, among others). The tools of translation provide rules and standards for recognition and enactment (participatory structures) that give school subjects their identities as objects as well as the conditions of their operation in schooling. The practices of translation in the curriculum, however, are never just a copy of the original.

The practical knowledge assumed in PISA embodies pedagogical principles generated about particular cultural theses about modes of living related to governing conduct. It is not the practical knowledge of science or mathematics. The "eyes" for ordering and classifying the curriculum are psychologies about child development, communication competences, and "learning." The concepts of motivation, problem solving, and "lifelong learning" have little relation to the patterns of interaction and communication of the academic fields (Popkewitz, 2004, 2008). Further, the alchemy of school subjects assumed in PISA has a double quality. If I use science "literacy" as examined internationally (McEneaney, 2003a), there is a dramatic shift to emphasize greater participation and increased personal relevance and emotional accessibility in the science curriculum. That participation, however, links the child's "expertise" in solving problems to the iconic stature of professional knowledge and learning the majesty of the procedures, styles of argument, and symbolic system that assert the truthfulness of the expertise of science. The given conclusions of academic expertise (the generalization and conceptualizations) are located outside the bounds of children's questioning and problem solving. Further, when scientific literacy is examined comparatively, the individual capacities and dispositions are tied to national identity and citizenship rather than to science (McEneaney, 2003b).

The determinate category of this kind of person who is given as successful is named the lifelong learner. The cultural thesis generated in PISA about the lifelong learner embodies a cultural thesis about a mode of life. That mode of life is a never-ending process of making choices, innovating, and collaborating (see, e.g., Fejes & Nicoll, 2007; Lawn, 2003; Popkewitz, 2008). The life of choice is guided by pedagogical theories expressed as maximizing happiness through continual processes of rationally planning and organizing daily events to bring a better future. Personal responsibility and self-management of one's risks are tied to continually maximizing the correct application for making choices to create a new existence. The only thing that is not a choice is making choices! Virtue is managing effectively the limits and opportunities of the environment through steering one's performances in a continual feedback loop of self-assessment (Simons & Masschelein, 2008).

The lifelong learner recalibrates political aspirations and collective belonging through principles generated about community, participation, and collaboration. Its "agency" is shaped and fashioned through problem solving and collaborating in multiple communities—communities of learning, discourse communities. Choice in individual life sanctioned by acts of working collaboratively in community that tells of the collective obligation. That individual obligation gives expression to a particular liberal political theory whose universality provides the norms of diversity, self-emancipation, and social progress.

The technologies of comparing through numbers are navigational tools that bring into view a universe of capabilities to place the child ordered through standardized properties that enable comparisons (Lindblad, 2008). Simons and Masschelein (2008) argue that this new individuality entails the shift from earlier notions of emancipation to empowerment in which individual life becomes a continual process of learning as the capacity for appropriations that engage the uncertainties of the present. Virtue is managing effectively the limits and opportunities of the environment through steering one's performances in a continual feedback loop of self-assessment. The assessments embody environmental feedback loops that functions as a permanent "global positioning" that provides the criteria to judge someone and oneself in the choices that are made for seeking to be permanently "empowered" (Simons & Masschelein, 2008).

The measurements of PISA and "the effective teacher" do not act directly on people but act on the principles generated where individuality is enacted. If I return to the comparative measurements of PISA and the "effective teacher" research, the distinctions about its human kinds are posited as universal, global, and outside of history. Yet the universality has its particularity. In the context of the European Union, the research and assessment devices instantiate a European space through establishing equivalences in categories from which difference is measured (Grek, 2009; also see Stråth, 2002). Grek and colleagues (2009), for example, trace how the data produced of PISA acts as they circulate through different institutions such as OECD to perform as an actor that crosses borders by positioning the measures and magnitudes as "International Comparisons Programmes Manager" (p. 15).

Markets as Desired World Filled in With Numbers

I have been arguing that numbers are never merely numbers when entering into the cultural and social spaces of schooling. They entail cultural theses about modes of living that govern what is possible and not possible. The lifelong learner is one such cultural thesis. But is it also important to ask about the epistemological principles embedded in the distinctions and differentiations that order and make possible the characteristics and capabilities given to people. One of the principles is "systems." "System" is to see different parts (grammar and syntax, for example) as interrelated into a whole to give it comprehensibility, stability, and functionality. System is a theory of relations, inputs, and outputs that "acts" to govern what is said, thought, and done. The expression of "wholeness" in the effective teacher research and PISA's measurements identifying the social and psychological qualities of the child perceived as functional for performances in economy and as a citizen embody notions of system to give intelligibility as "robust" data. Terms like "systemic school reform" and "backward design" in curriculum models embody notions of "systems" that make possible the self-referential qualities of research. Identifying performance outcomes is part of a system of elements through which to design the curriculum and organizational patterns that will produce that outcome.

Here I want to use the notion of "system" to talk about the grid through which numbers are given intelligibility in schooling.[3] The notion of *social* systems in theory and policy studies related to this inquiry is one that crosses into the notion of market that appears in the late 18th century and again in today's debates about neoliberalism.

If I again draw on Poovey (1998), the notion of system was embodied in the work of David Hume, the Scottish Enlightenment philosopher who was concerned with the explanation of phenomena through natural causes and laws.[4] He and other British theorists of wealth, society, and political economy deployed systems to realize a desired world about what the philosopher hoped for, but not necessarily through numbers. Hume's naturalist philosophy, Poovey argues, was not interested in empirically exploring the effects of that system (Poovey, 1998, p. 264). Hume and other political economists saw notions of equity and equivalence between objects as less questions of knowledge than as questions of justice in the law governing market exchange. Numbers did not play a part in deciding justice and equity.

Adam Smith's *Wealth of Nations* (1776), in contrast to Hume, was not interested in calculations about particulars that were considered doubtful and speculative. Smith posited the notion of markets as agents through which national wealth would be increased through "the invisible hand" of human motives and competition. The heart of Smith's moral economy, the "market system," created a new role for numerical representation as descriptors of the products (actually and theoretically) created by institutions. Numbers did not exist in the abstraction of markets, so Smith set up ways of measuring and calculating as if they did exist to say something about wealth and governing (Poovey, 1998, pp. 240–1). The numbers applied "embodied [Smith's] *a priori* assumptions about what the market system *should be*" (Poovey, 1998, p. 216, italics in original). The sciences would "solve" the problem of studying the particulars observed so as to standardize in a manner that could be projected into a semblance of the future.

The task of philosophy was as an actor of change. The significance of Smith's sciences of society and wealth was in its possibility for tracing the movement from systemic philosophical claims about universals (human nature) to descriptions of abstractions (the market system) and then to the quantification of the effects or products of these abstractions (labor, national prosperity) as "social facts" that enable comparisons (Poovey, 1998, p. 237). The numbers, to be useful information about how the system worked, had to assume a consensus about what the truth of numbers rested on (Poovey, 1998, p. 243).

The philosophical operations of abstracting and generalizing markets re-inscribed conjectural history into the philosopher's hope that its knowledge would lead to action and "if the action was diligently pursued, it could actualize the future of which the philosopher was the first to dream. Markets became a historical agent of 'human nature,' a philosophical universe that could be named and quantify the effects of the abstraction" (Poovey, 1998, p. 247). By privileging the abstraction of "markets," Smith constructed the aggregates to "register the significance of these phenomena which could only be known in retrospect and discounting what diverged from type so as to describe 'nature'" (Poovey, 1998, p. 226).

Smith's use of numbers as "abstract spaces" about markets embodied the notion of system as a presupposition. A theory of systems provided Smith with a new basis for connecting the individual pursuit of profit with the growth of collective wealth; and to show the incompatibility between optimal development of economic process and the maximization of governmental procedures (Foucault, 2004/2008, p. 321). The historical schema was not only about economy. It gave importance to domesticity, manners, women, and commercial society as "the most sophisticated incarnation of human sociality through which the human mind would be collectively revealed. . . . The second order abstractions such as labor and happiness that was no longer a universal claim but a non-rhetorical (nonsuasive) place for a kind of representation that described what *could be* as if this potential was simply waiting to materialize" (Poovey, 1998, p. 248, italics in original).

Smith's science of wealth appealed to government officials interested in consolidating and theorizing government's relations with its subjects at home and abroad. Numbers appealed to the British government as a mode of representation less imbued with providential overtones or theoretical prejudices (Poovey, 1998, p. 265). Political economic facts were to be understood as impartial, transparent, and methodologically rigorous. Further, abstractions like the market system set limits on the kinds of legislative interference yet enabled mandates for the implementation and enforcement of other kinds of laws and policies (Poovey, 1998, p. 217).

The abstraction of markets is given a materiality as legislative principles in organizing institutions and people. In contemporary discussions of neoliberalism (re)visions and assembles a "method of thought, a grid of economic and socio-logical analysis, an imagination, and a method of governing that moves into non-economic phenomena" of behavior rather than on process (Foucault, 2004/2008, p. 218). The individual is *homo oeconomics*, but not in its classical meaning as the partner of exchange and theory of utility (Foucault, 2004/2008, p. 225). The individual is an entrepreneur who has his own capital and the producer of his own satisfaction where innovation and self-improvement instantiates an ethical-economic system and psychological qualities (Foucault, 2004/2008, pp. 229–311). This kind of person is an entrepreneur, if I return to the earlier discussion, homologous to the cultural thesis of the lifelong learner. The rationality of the "self" is inscribed and transmogrified in the distinctions and classifications of the effective teacher and value-added "teachers."

Numbers, the Democratic Citizen, and the Clearing of Spaces in School Standards

> Would it not be a great satisfaction to the king to know at a designated moment every year the number of his subjects, in total and by region, with all the resources, wealth & poverty of each place; [the number] of his nobility and ecclesiastics of all kinds, of men of the robe, of Catholics and of those of the other religion, all separated according to the place of their residence? . . . Would it not be a useful and necessary pleasure for him to be able, in his own office, to review in an hour's time the present and the past condition of a great realm of which he is the head, and be able himself to know with certitude in what consists his grandeur, his wealth, and his strengths?
>
> *(Marquis de Vauban, proposing an annual census to Louis XIV in 1686, cited in Scott, 1998, p. 11)*

After the discussions of numbers and fabricating kinds of people, it might seem unrelated to start with this quote by the Marquis de Vauban in 1686. But it is not. My use of the quote is to direct attention to how numbers circulate with a grid of practices to change conditions of people that change people. The standards that the marquis talks about fabricate kinds of people—in the name of the state and later in the name of modernizing and equity among people. My focus is directed to the "reason" of curriculum standards that brings into focus the New Public Management of establishing the benchmarks of outcomes and performances given plausibility in PISA and the value-added measures. Here I explore how the standards of schooling are not just about the content to learn. They embody principles generated about human kinds that paradoxically exclude and abject in the impulse to include.

The "benchmarks" of school reform standards are to establish a system of alignments between assessment and educational aims and curriculum. The popular strategy mentioned earlier of "backward instructional design" places the problem of teaching first to decide on the appropriate measurable instructional outcomes and then to design teaching to best achieve the outcomes. The standards and the backward design form a system that seems commonsensical for schooling: What is assessed should make visible what schools are to teach (curriculum standards), then identify the parts that are believed to influence it, and then try to make each of its parts efficient to achieve the learning outcome.

The search for "standards" can be related to creating the capacity for direct knowledge about what was previously opaque about the territories and populations the Marquis de Vauban spoke about. Prior to this, measurement was almost random, because each local area had its own system of measurement (a hand, a foot, cartload, basketful, handful, within earshot) that prevented any central administration (Scott, 1998). The standardization was to enable the state to know who fell under its domain and to provide a less variable and systematic tax system. The reliable means of enumerating and regulating the populations of the realm, numbers were to gauge the wealth, and maps of land resources and settlements produced.

The production of standards was important to Enlightenment notions of equality and justice and inscribed in the formation of the modern republican and liberal forms of government. The academicians of prerevolutionary France, for example, saw the standardized measurements of the metric system as important for creating equal citizens. The Encyclopedists prior to the Revolution saw the inconsistency among measurements, institutions, inheritance laws, taxation, and market regulations as the greatest obstacle to making a single people (Scott, 1998, p. 32). They believed that there could be no equality with unequal measures and sought to standardize through the metric system. If the citizen did not have equal rights in relation to measurements, then the citizen might also have unequal rights under the law.

Standards were placed "in service of the democratic ideal" in the formation of modern schooling. The sciences of American Progressive education at the turn of the 20th century, for example, were to make the child legible, easily administrable, and equal in the name of the freedom of the future citizen (Popkewitz, 2008). Notions of child development, cognition, and learning, for example, installed standards that were directed to the interior of the child. These standards about behavior, problem solving, and attitudes overlap moral qualities about the future citizen with physiological and biological ones.

But equality implied in the imposition of standards embodied double gestures. The qualities and characteristics instantiated as the standards of the mind embodied a double gesture. It engendered the hope of the child as the future cosmopolitan citizen that coexisted with fears of the dangers and dangerous populations to that future. American pedagogical science of Edward L. Thorndike's Connectionist psychologies and psychometrics, for example, embodied the Progressive hope of establishing standards about the self-motivated and self-responsible individual whose participation was necessary for the functioning of the republic. But that hope of the future simultaneously embodied threats to the envisioned future. Thorndike wrote of the double gestures of the hope and fear in saying that "only cure" for the nation's ills was through education to "prevent each new generation from stagnating in brutish ignorance, folly and pain" (Thorndike, 1912/1962, pp. 142–143). The narratives of recognition of difference, however, inscribe differences and processes of abjection, as the child (female, racially defined, for example) could never be "of the average."[5]

The double gestures are embodied in the contemporary "standards"-based reforms whose principles intersect with PISA and the "effective teacher" research. The comparativeness is expressed through the *topoi* of "Education for All." The "all" signifies calls for equity that ensure that "every child matters," "all children learn."

The "all" is the gesture of hope to make all children equal that overlaps with fears of children whose characteristics are different and thus a threat to the moral unity of the whole. If I return to PISA, the "practical" skills of the assessment are based on the inscriptions of comparative equivalences. The comparative equivalences are about the child who is not the lifelong learner, classified through data about student, family, and the child whose capacities are outside of the borders of normalcy given in the presumption of consensus. That space of fears is ordered by categories about social-cultural disintegration and moral disorganization, such as in the psychological classifications of the child's disabilities, low self-esteem, and poor self-concept. The psychological qualities overlap with social characteristics of the dysfunctional families, juvenile delinquency, poverty, being "at risk," and the needy or urban child.[6] The system of psychological and social factors that recognize the child as different makes difference, abjecting the particular characteristics and capabilities of the child into unlivable spaces.

Some Concluding Comments: Critical Inquiry and the Problem of Change

My focus on numbers is to explore the principles of assessment in a grid of practices that generates cultural theses about modes of life. This was explored through different sites of educational policy and research: the notion of markets in the sciences of wealth in the 19th century, the effective teacher and value-added measures, the "practical knowledge" of PISA, and curriculum standards. The categories of equivalence constitute domains rendered as stable, representable forms that can be calculated, deliberated about, and acted on. The stability and consensus, I argue, fabricated kinds of people for school to act on and for individuals to act as if they were those "people."

The interest in numbers as an embodied "reason" is to engage the political aspect of schooling. My use of the political aspect is different from the notion of politics that circulates in critical studies of schooling. The politics of schooling can be thought about in the curriculum question of whose knowledge is privileged in schooling, locating which actors and agents are favored and handicapped through the processes of schooling. It is also located in modern political science notion of politics as the allocation of values. While the general question of whose knowledge is sanctified in social institutions is important, that question by itself is not sufficient. The principles of reflection and action are not just there as part of the nature of phenomena but are formed through the historically inscribed rules and standards that differentiate, distinguish, and divide what is constituted as sensible/ not sensible as thought and action. The focus on numbers in making of human kinds is to consider this quality of the politics of schooling.

If we think about the historical construction of the subject as the political aspect, it is possible to challenge and (re)vision elements of the common sense of contemporary reforms and research. One is about producing *useful* knowledge. That notion of useful assumes a consensus and harmony by naturalizing the "lived experiences" of the teacher and child or identifying the phenomenological/structural concern of "whose knowledge" is missing in school, with the politics of change to give "voice" to subaltern groups. As Joan Scott (1991) argued about the notion of experience, such views of "use" are not there merely to be recouped as some natural element of life by researchers. It is a theoretical concept and an effect of power. Perhaps what is of more "use" in articulating social commitments, if I can play with the word, is examining and making problematic the very frameworks that order and constitute experiences and their limits.

This notion of "use" is to make the naturalness of the present strange and contingent. It is a political strategy of change; to make detectable the internments and enclosures of the common sense of schooling is to make them contestable and thus possible as an object of change itself. Critical thought is directed to "what is accepted as authority through a critique of the conditions of what is known, what must be done, what may be hoped" (Foucault, 1984b, p. 38). Agency is in the testing of the limits of making visible the particular dogma of the present through a resistance to what seems inevitable and necessary by "modifying the rules of the game, up to a certain point" (Foucault, 1984b, p. 48). Curriculum study, as a tactic of change, is tracing epistemological shifts in the cultural theses of schooling to challenge the habitual ways of working and thinking in school reform, teacher education, and the sciences of education.

Finally and ironically, the policy, research, and approaches to assessment start with the assumption of inequality as the goal is equality. But as Rancière (2004) has argued, the very commitment that begins with inequality to potentially compensate by devising well-placed strategies actually (re)visions equality as inequality. The comparative inscription of difference to address the fundamental wrong produces the precondition of difference and re-inscribes divisions that are to be erased at every step by the philosopher and social scientist as the shepherd. Rancière (2007) argues that this epistemological position embodies a fear of democracy itself.

Notes

1. "Adolescence" was a word that existed prior to Hall but was brought into a realm of the new sciences of psychology to rationalize, classify, and administer children.
2. The notion of benchmarks circulates in the business efficiency models, EU and U.S. government reforms, the military, and the way to express how current U.S. wars in Afghanistan and Iraq have achieved their goals, for example. But it would be historically incorrect to assume that such language emerges unidirectionally from business to social and political logics of change and assessment (see, e.g., Vann & Bowker, 2001).
3. I realize the irony of "systems" as a concept deployed to think about the cultural inscriptions in numbers and my use of systems of reason to engage in that analysis. My excuse of "system" is analytical, first, to historically give attention to different trajectories that overlap to produce the objects seen and acted on. The notion of "system," then, has no theology or single origin. Second, the coherence given is about the epistemology as it relates to ontology; that is, the relation of how one is to know and the objects produced through that knowing. Third, my use of the notion of grid to talk about "systems of reason" is to suggest incompleteness and its processes of deferral.
4. The Scottish Enlightenment philosophers, as David Hamilton (1989) explores, were influential in the development of modern schooling and its notions of "knowledge" in curriculum theory.
5. I use Thorndike in this section, as he is considered important to the emergence of American psychometrics. But the comparative style of thought embodied in this psychology is embodied in the social sciences that emerged at that time and needs to be considered as a historical phenomenon rather than as unique to Thorndike.
6. An ethnographic study of urban education teacher education reforms (Popkewitz, 1998) illustrates the constituting of standards through the making of difference.

References

Danziger, K. (1997). *Naming the mind: How psychology found its language.* London: Sage.

Day, C., Sammons, P., & Gu, Q. (2008). Combining qualitative and quantitative methodologies in research on teachers' lives, work, and effectiveness: From integration to synergy. *Educational Researcher, 37*(6), 330–342.

Desrosières, A. (1991). How to make things which hold together: Social science, statistics, and the state. In P. Wagner, B. Wittock, & R. Whitley (Eds.), *Discourses on society: The shaping of the social science disciplines* (pp. 195–218). Dordrecht: Kluwer Academic Publishers.

Desrosières, A. (1993/1998). Camille Naish, Trans. *The politics of large numbers: A history of statistical reasoning.* Cambridge, MA: Harvard University Press, 1998.

Fejes, A., & Nicoll, K. (2007). *Foucault and lifelong learning: Governing the subject.* London: Routledge.

Foucault, M. (1984). What is the Enlightenment? Was ist Auflärlung? In P. Rabinow (Ed.), *The Foucault reader* (pp. 32–51). New York: Pantheon Books.

Foucault, M. (2004/2008). *The birth of biopolitics. Lectures at the Collège de France 1978–1979* (Michel Senellart, Ed., G. Burchell, Trans.). New York: Palgrave Macmillan.

Grek, S. (2009). Governing by numbers: The PISA effect in Europe. *Journal of Education Policy, 24*(1), 23–37.

Grek, S., Lawn, M., Lingard, B., Ozga, J., Rinne, R., Segerholm, C., & Simola, H. (2009). National policy brokering and the construction of the European education space in England, Sweden, Finland, and Scotland. *Comparative Education, 45*, 5–21.

Hacking, I. (1986). Making up people. In T. C. Heller, M. Sosna, & D. E. Wellbery (Eds.), *Reconstructing individualism: Autonomy, individuality, and the self in Western thought* (pp. 222–236, 347–348). Stanford, CA: Stanford University Press.

Hacking, I. (1990). *The taming of chance.* Cambridge: Cambridge University Press.

Hacking, I. (1999). *The social construction of what?* Cambridge, MA: Harvard University Press.

Hamilton, D. (1989). *Towards a theory of schooling.* London: Falmer Press.

Lascoumes, L., & Le Galès, P. (2007). Understanding public policy through its instruments: From the nature of instruments to the sociology of public policy instrumentation. *Governance, 20,* 1–21.

Lawn, M. (2003). The "usefulness" of learning: The struggle over governance, meaning, and the European education space. *Discourse, 24*(3), 325–336.

Lindblad, S. (2008). Navigating in the field of university positioning: On international ranking lists, quality indicators, and higher education governing. *European Educational Research Journal, 7*(4), 438–450.

Lindblad, S. (2014, in press). Observations on European education and educational research: The European Educational Research Journal at work 2002–2014. *European Educational Research Journal.*

McEneaney, E. (2003a). Elements of a contemporary primary school science. In G. S. Drori, J. W. Meyer, F. O. Ramirez, & E. Schofer (Eds.), *Science in the modern world polity: Institutionalization and globalization* (pp. 136–154). Stanford, CA: Stanford University Press.

McEneaney, E. (2003b). The worldwide cachet of scientific literacy. *Comparative Education Review, 47*(2), 217–237.

Poovey, M. (1998). *A history of the modern fact. Problems of knowledge in the sciences of wealth and society.* Chicago: University of Chicago Press.

Popkewitz, T. (1998). *Struggling for the soul: The politics of education and the construction of the teacher.* New York: Teachers College Press.

Popkewitz, T. (2004). The alchemy of the mathematics curriculum: Inscriptions and the fabrication of the child. *American Educational Research Journal, 41*(4), 3–34.

Popkewitz, T. (2008). *Cosmopolitanism and the age of school reform: Science, education, and making society by making the child.* New York: Routledge.

Porter, T. (1995). *Trust in numbers: The pursuit of objectivity in science and public life.* Princeton, NJ: Princeton University Press.

Rancière, J. (2004). *The flesh of words: The politics of writing* (C. Mandell, Trans.). Stanford, CA: Stanford University Press.

Rancière, J. (2007). *The hatred of democracy* (S. Corcoran, Trans.). New York: Verso.

Rose, N. (1999). *Powers of freedom: Reframing political thought.* Cambridge: Cambridge University Press.

Scott, J. (1991). The evidence of experience. *Critical Inquiry, 17,* 773–797.

Scott, J. (1998). *Seeing like a state: How certain schemes to improve the human condition have failed.* New Haven, CT: Yale University Press.

Simons, M., & Masschelein, J. (2008). "It makes us believe that it is about our freedom": Notes on the irony of the learning apparatus. In P. Smeyers & M. Depaepe (Eds.), *Educational research: The educationalization of social problems* (pp. 191–205). Dordrecht: Springer-Science+Business Media B.V.

Stråth, B. (2002). Introduction: The national meanings of Europe. In M. A. Malmborg & B. Stråth (Eds.), *The meaning of Europe: Variety and contention within and among nations* (pp. 1–26). Oxford: Berg.

Thorndike, E. L. (1912/1962). Education. A first book. In G. M. Joncich (Ed.), *Psychology and the science of education. Selected writings of Edward L. Thorndike* (pp. 69–83, 141–147). New York: Bureau of Publications, Teachers College, Columbia University.

Vann, K., & Bowker, G. (2001). Instrumentalizing the truth of practice. *Social Epistemology, 15*(3), 247–262.

PART III

The Alchemy of School Subjects, Exclusion/ Abjections

11

TRANSGRESSION AS DEMOCRATIC *CONVIVENZA*

Italian School Policy and the Discourse of Integration

Jamie A. Kowalczyk

Italian Prime Minister Letta named Italy's first minister of African origin, Dr. Cecile Kyenge, to head the Ministry for Integration.[1] One of Kyenge's primary aims was to change Italian citizenship requirements from a *jus sanguinis* policy to *jus soli*. She declared on the Ministry website and was quoted in newspapers: "Whoever is born and raised in Italy is Italian" (Indini, 2013). In an effort to bring attention to this issue, she has promoted the documentary "18 jus soli," which has evolved into a movement of sorts. The documentary's webpage contains the following information: "932,675 foreign minors live in Italy; 572,720 were born in Italy; . . . every 7 minutes a child is born to foreign parents [in Italy], 9 every hour, 214 every day" (www.18-ius-soli.com). According to the Ministry of Instruction, University and Research (MIUR), during the academic year 2012–2013, 786,630 non-Italian students were enrolled in Italian schools, and 47.2% of those students were second generation (Integrazione Migranti, 2013).

The discussion surrounding citizenship policy in Italy precedes Kyenge. In 2011, the former center-right Italian Speaker of the House, Gianfranco Fini, who in the past had coauthored legislation with the xenophobic Northern League's Umberto Bossi intended to restrict immigration, raised the question as to what it meant to be an Italian citizen. He argued that ". . . 60% of young foreigners that reside in Italy were born here among us and . . . in fact, they are already, for all practical purposes, real and proper Italian citizens, even if they do not yet have juridical recognition or status as such"[2] (Seconde generazioni, 2011). While he did not define "practical purposes," he suggested that, in addition to living in Italy and speaking Italian, it is also necessary to consider how these young people feel, stating that "[t]he extremely restrictive criteria set out for the obtaining of Italian citizenship . . . become yet another burden for these young people who by now identify as Italians"[3] (Seconde generazioni, 2011). While this ought to be strictly a question of legislation, Fini concluded with an address to Italian schools which, as he puts it, are "called upon to be a driving force in the new processes of integration"[4] (Seconde generazioni, 2011). Thus, one can see proponents on both the political left and right challenging the current ethnocentric citizenship policy, arguing that not to do so is to make the project of social integration ever more difficult.

Transgression and Integration

Foucault offers a reading of transgression that discards its usual negative connotations; transgression is that which "designate[s] the existence of difference" (Foucault, 1977, p. 36). The designating of difference is never a final or stable act but rather an ongoing process, because the relationship between the limit and transgression "takes the form of a spiral which no simple infraction can exhaust" (p. 35).

Transgression could refer to the very act of immigration itself—"to walk across" a border or limit is to transgress. Drawing upon the connotations of the sacred that are embedded in the idea of transgression, the immigrant renders profane a sacred "homeland" and, by her very existence, embodies a threat to the home's limits that must be protected and its purity that must be maintained. What is more, transgression is not a natural given: It does not just locate a limit for protection and a transgressor to be redeemed. It is productive. Transgression work—its recognition and policing—draws attention to the making of limits, putting them into discussion for resetting or reaffirming.

> [T]ransgression incessantly crosses and recrosses a line which closes up behind it in a wave of extremely short duration, and thus it is made to return once more right to the horizon of the uncrossable. But this relationship is considerably more complex: these elements are situated in an uncertain context, in certainties which are immediately upset so that thought is ineffectual as soon as it attempts to seize them.
>
> *(Foucault, 1977, p. 34)*

On the one hand, the protection of limits is seen as a salvation project; but on the other hand, that kind of protection or management of the limit authorizes the very practices of exclusion and marginalization that contemporary cosmopolitan discourses like integration are said to combat. As Pickett summarizes, "The various rules, limits, and norms history has placed upon us, which are often seen as natural, are the source of exclusion, marginalization, and the resulting solidification of identity for those who 'confine their neighbors'"(Pickett, 1996, p. 450).

I examine in this chapter how transgression and difference figure into the construction of Italian integration, or *convivenza*, through two common requirements identified in the *convivenza* discourse: "democracy" and "civic participation." That is, to achieve *convivenza*, there must be the successful management of difference through the honoring of established common values and norms (or, to use Foucault's lexicon, limits). I suggest that this idealized Italian *convivenza* and its requisite limits for democracy and civic participation do not function to create anything new but rather seek to govern, and thus conserve/preserve, already established norms. However, another way of doing democracy and civic participation shadows ideal *convivenza*, where limits are in flux and transgression is the "staging of a nonexistent right" (Rancière, 1999, pp. 24–25; see also Honig, 2001). While the policy discourse calls for an integrated immigrant student who respects the limits of Italian-European common values as "universal" and who engages in democratic civic practice, I argue that such practice seeks to tame the transgressions that are necessary for democratic change, as limits are contested and the "commonly held" is transformed.

Within the Italian discourse on the education of immigrant students, while integration claims to be open to difference, it nonetheless requires transformation on the part of the immigrant in order protect the national community from transgression. Intercultural education policy, on the one hand, endorses mutual transformation, with immigrants and "natives" engaging one another in dialogue and thus growing and changing because of that engagement. While mutual transformation is the stated aim, it is regularly checked by the limits of "common values," "civic participation," and "democracy." Policy does not dwell on mutual transformation but instead rests on the "problem" of immigration and immigrants and their lack. Badiou (2011) reflects on how democracy can focus on lack and colonize the commonly held:

> In sum, if the world of the democrats is not the world of everyone, if tout le monde isn't really the whole world after all, then democracy, the emblem and custodian of the walls behind which the democrats seek their petty pleasures, is just a world for a conservative oligarchy whose main (and often bellicose) business is to guard its own territory, as animals do, under the usurped name world.
>
> *(pp. 7–8)*

Highlighting the imperial blurring that occurs when "integration" is conceived of as adopting "universal values," Badiou points out that the world's values are defined by particular kinds of people, such as European or Italian.

Similarly, Honig (2001) critiques the practice of cosmopolitanism, showing how it acts as another sacred space to be protected from transgressors. She echoes Badiou, stating that "[t]here is surely no way out of this paradox, in which cosmopolitanism must be striven for through the particular, albeit heterogeneous, (national) cultures that shape us" (Honig, 2001). In other words, the practice of cosmopolitanism as democracy or universal values necessarily undergoes a process of translation that is tied to the cultures and places in which it is performed. Honig argues—calling into question the taken for granted in the "processes of integration"—that by not recognizing the particularity of "universal" practices located in spaces with different histories and cultures, integration is evacuated of "the political work that always also involves critical self-interrogation and courts the risk of transformation" (Honig, 2001), producing instead a

> cosmopolitanism [that] already knows what it is—and what it isn't, and so it risks becoming another form of domination, particularly when it confronts the other that resists assimilation to it, another that is unwilling to reperform for 'us' the wonder of our conversion to world or [national] citizenship.
>
> *(p. 66)*

In the field of education, Popkewitz (2008) also takes up cosmopolitanism as referring to particular historical cultural theses that order "the reason of reason" and thus the vision and language of school reforms. Schooling, and school reforms in particular, are technologies that serve to manage the borders of the home and thus seek to protect the nation from transgression. While it may seem odd to speak of a national cosmopolitanism, Popkewitz argues that "[t]he universal values of the Enlightenment's cosmopolitan individual were inscribed in the new republics and its citizens as its transcendental values and purposes" (Popkewitz, 2008, p. 3). Therefore, there is no one cosmopolitanism or world, but rather an assemblage of Enlightenment principles and values that intersects with particular times and places to constitute different ways of practicing the universal and being in the world. Given this, the immigrant poses a special case, as one who has not yet adopted the national cultural thesis for living. "The immigrant lives in the in-between spaces between requiring special intervention programs to enable access and equity and at the same time established as different and the Other, outside the virtue of their qualities of life" (Popkewitz, 2008, p. 6). The immigrant student and the transgressions she threatens to commit by her very existence reaffirm the limits of national belonging and *convivenza*.

Italian Integration

Within the Italian immigration discourse, when the claim is not for "universal" values, it is for European values that are authorized through the universal. Consider, for instance, the following observation made by the Italian National Contact Point of the European Migration Network in its 2009 report: "when the European Union was joined by 10 new countries in 2006 and then by Romania and Bulgaria in 2007, immigration experts realized that EU citizens, even if protected by a broader regulation, are often still in need of protection, and sometimes share the same life style of non-EU citizens" (p. 40). (Callia et al., 2009, p. 57). While not specifying the qualities that make up the European "life style," or those that make up the non–EU "life style," there is the sense that to embody the latter is to put both the immigrant and the EU "at risk." The text suggests that the making of the European citizen is not just accomplished through the formal process of accession into the EU but is also something that is to be learned and achieved and thus something that produces uncertainty. To be integrated into Europeanness is to accept a particular "cultural thesis" for living, here referred to as a "life style." To not accept this European life style is to transgress the conceptual borders for living. In other words, one may physically reside within Europe but may still continue to live as non-European. Those who do not embody this life style are the objects of integration reforms and, in terms of school reforms, become objects of rescue through intercultural and civic education. They are to submit to the rules and norms that order European living.

The European Fund for Integration in Italy designates among its primary areas of need "language formation and civic orientation" and "school orientation and insertion" (Callia et al., 2009, p. 11). The text thus focuses on transgressions in the form of lack—those coming into European Italy are " backwards" or "deficient." Aside from lacking an ability to speak Italian or having necessary "job skills" to find employment, it is also assumed that the immigrant is in need of "civic instruction," in order to submit to the rules and standards for participation within a democratic society, both politically and socially. These needs are part of a double gesture that fears a loss of a unified citizenry and an increase in the burdens upon the state in terms of illiteracy, unemployment, and conflict.

Integration, then, is invoked as a strategy that will save the "original" community from conflict and dissolution. It places the immigrant in the impossible, abjected space of being at once included and separate from "us." According to the Italian Ministry of Public Instruction, intercultural education is the ideal pedagogical method for the integration of "non-Italian" students because it "refuses the logic of assimilation, as well as the construction and reinforcement of closed ethnic communities" (MIUR, 2006).[5] Integration, as it is referred to here and throughout Italian intercultural and civic education reforms, seeks to respectfully leave untouched the immigrant's personal culture and language while at the same time integrating her into the European and Italian public culture and dominant language. The aim is to engage with immigrants, but that engagement is only recognized as legitimate when performed in particular ways and in particular forms.

At the Italian Ministry of Education's website, one finds specific reference to the risks "different students" pose to quality public schooling, stating that due to the presence of "students of different social, cultural, ethnic backgrounds and with different learning capacities and experiences," Italian schools face a "complex phenomenon with problematic aspects that are without easy solutions" (MIUR, 2010).[6] It goes on to specify further risks related to foreign students, stating that

> [p]articular attention is given to the inclusion and integration of foreign students, in order to create equitable conditions that can prevent the difficult situations and problems that are part of living and studying in a new context and that contribute to creating the necessary sharing of norms for *convivenza* and social participation.[7]
>
> *(MIUR, 2010)*

In other words, the school is to concentrate on bringing foreign students within, integrating them in order to avoid two different kinds of risks—on the one hand, the potential problems foreign students will face as foreigners in Italian schools and, on the other hand, the potential problems that Italian students will have when attending school with foreign, "unintegrated" classmates who do not know nor adhere to Italian norms and ways of interacting.

Moreover, the text reaffirms this second set of fears, stating that the issues the schools must deal with "do not merely regard foreign students, but inevitably have an impact on the learning process of the entire class in which foreigners are present" (MIUR, 2010). Again, the risks that must be dealt with are not just those of foreign students but also those of Italian students and the Italian school. It is for this reason former Minister Gelmini created "limits as to the number of foreign students with a poor knowledge of the Italian language that can be present in individual classes" (MIUR, 2010). Integration has as much to do with protecting what are assumed to be normal ways of living that are not just "universal" but also particular to the nation or region where they are practiced.

Citizenship Regimes and Integration: National Models, *la via italiana*, and Normalization

While a degree of so-called juridical and political harmonization (or homogenization) occurs due to the circulation of EU policy discourse, EU member states' national narratives of integration also intersect with national histories and social practices. For example, Koopmans and colleagues (2005) argue that individual countries such as Germany, France, the Netherlands, and Britain "do" integration in very different ways, despite EU influence, and are perhaps now distinctive parts of their national narratives.[8] And what of Italy?

The Italian "citizenship regime" (Koopmans et al., 2005) is like that of Germany in that it is based on a *jus sanguins* model, meaning the children of nonnational immigrants, while born in Italy, are considered immigrants. Some proposals would make "the completion of Italian compulsory schooling" a requirement for minors who would like to acquire citizenship (Zincone, 2010, p. 5). Furthermore, the process for obtaining citizenship established in 1992 "was intrinsically ethnocentric" (Zincone, 2010, p. 2), changing the uniform period of residency of 5 years before application to varying periods of residency according to one's status: Those who are of Italian descent need only reside for 3 years,[9] while those who are EU nationals 4 years, refugees and stateless persons 5 years, and non–EU immigrants must reside legally for 10 years before being allowed to apply for citizenship (Zincone, 2010). The "*Pacchetto Sicurezza*," or Security Act, passed in July 2009, quadrupled the required residency period for the spouses of Italian citizens who wish to obtain Italian citizenship (Zincone, 2010, p. 4).[10] Thus, Italy's conception of citizenship is decidedly ethnic rather than civic-territorial.

Within this citizenship regime, two paths are regularly taken up and intertwined within the policy landscape: The first is a focus on intercultural education and dialogue, and the second is a focus on civic education, emphasizing the citizen's rights and responsibilities. The former calls, as said previously, for a mutual transformation, but discursive analysis of ministerial texts suggests that this mutual transformation gives way to a one-sided attention to the "at-risk" immigrant students. The latter sees a way forward, much as Italian scholars Guolo (2003) and Rusconi (1999) have suggested, in different keys: Italy must belong to a collective "We" established within the Constitution. Renzo Guolo has argued that, in terms of establishing a distinct Italian model of integration, neither of the two models present in Europe—assimilationist (as in France) and multicultural (as in Great Britain)—will work.

The assimilationist model fails in Italy because the country lacks the equivalent of "French 'republicanism'" (Guolo, 2003, p. 151), especially as Italy has had a history of weak national identity, making assimilation harder to enact. Furthermore, how can Italy assimilate immigrants of different faiths into an Italian culture that is so strongly tied to the Roman Catholic Church (Guolo, 2003, pp. 151–152)? On the other hand, the multicultural approach would risk the further weakening of Italy's already fragile unity (Guolo, 2003, p. 152). And so Guolo's thesis is for a political assimilationist approach that envisions a Habermasian "constitutional patriotism," founded on "universal" principles (Guolo, 2003, p. 153). He suggests an Italian model that conceives of integration as the adoption of cosmopolitan way of life that is democratic, civically responsible, and respectful of the Constitution and the rule of law, and that sustains a belief in the universal value of human rights (Guolo, 2003, pp. 153–154). In summary, this approach is meant to preserve national unity through its "universals."

In the 2004 to 2005 "Students with non-Italian citizenship" report, then Minister of Education Letizia Moratti suggested that Italy better fulfills its commitments to EC directives in comparison to other European countries, arguing that

> [f]or a long time now our school has chosen the full integration of all students and intercultural education as our cultural horizon. Our model of integration, different from the British and French, tends to refute the logic of assimilation and the construction or reinforcement of closed ethnic communities. It favors, instead, dialogue, reciprocal respect and engagement in order to make the most of the richness of experiences. . . . It favors, in summary, integration with complete respect of identities.[11]
>
> *(MIUR, 2005)*

Moratti argued that integration via intercultural education would guarantee a third way forward that is based on particular practices—dialogue, showing respect, and engaging with the other. Later policy meant to more fully elaborate these practices also claims those practices as national.

The 2007 report "The Italian way for an intercultural school and the integration of foreign students" (MIUR, 2007a), put out by the National Observatory for the Integration of Foreign Students and Intercultural Education, specifically speaks to the need for dialogue and mutual engagement. Interestingly, it also discursively renders "invisible," thus normalizing, the Italian who is to participate in this mutual project of engagement and transformation. The cover of the report is decorated with cartoon images of young students, presumably those who are to attend the intercultural school—and those who must integrate. Each cartoon figure is different, dressed in various "traditional" or "foreign" clothing and physically marked in terms of skin color, eye color, and facial features. There appears to be no "Italian" among the group, as the Italian exceeds representation as the "natural" or "normal." Each image, a transgression of the limits of the imagined Italian, captures the process of abjection that differentiates who is in need of being included through the remaking of an "Italian" border. While intending to call for a new kind of national belonging that is inclusive, the text reinvokes the processes of normalization that occurred during the early years of the Italian nation-state, with the task of uniting the various regions into a single, national identity.

The "Italian Way" report cover recalls the description of "the Calabrian" in De Amicis's (1886) *Cuore*, a popular children's book that was to be the diary of a young boy living in Turin. Within an opening passage, a new student from Calabria has arrived, and he is at once included while also being differentiated as at risk of marginalization. The teacher warns the students,

> Take care to remember what I am telling you. Because for the very possibility that this could happen, that a Calabrese boy could be at home in Turin, and that a boy from Turin could be at home in Reggio di Calabria, our country fought for fifty years and thirty thousand Italians died. You should respect one another, love one another; but if one among you offends this companion because he was not born in our province, he would not be worthy to ever lift his eyes from the ground when the tricolor banner passes.
>
> *(De Amicis, 1886/2000, p. 15)*

The "Calabrese boy," Coraci, is to be included as a fellow Italian student, and yet within the discourse he is also divided from the rest as "the Calabrese." Throughout the text he is rarely referred to by name, while the other classmates, such as Garrone, Derossi, Stardi, and Nobis are called by their proper names, as their Northernness is normalized as Italian and consequently not in need of differentiation. The othering of the Southerner carries with it a racialization, just as the 2007 "Italian Way" report cover does the same, focusing on his body while making the Northern students' bodies invisible. This racialization is expressed at the very same moment it seeks to "include" the "foreigner":

> The Principal entered with a new student, a boy with a very dark face, with black hair, with big, black eyes, with bushy eyebrows that met in the middle; he was dressed entirely in black, with a belt of Moroccan leather around his waist. The Principal, after having spoken in the teacher's ear, left, leaving next to the teacher the boy who was watching us with his big dark eyes, as if frightened.
>
> *(De Amicis, 1886/2000, pp. 13–14)*

In this entire section, which calls upon a unification of spirit among students from the North and the South, transgressions of the imagined Italian student are marked out in the description of the boy's face and dress, in his fear and in his lack of a name.

On the 2007 "Italian Way" report cover, the students' "foreignness" or difference is likewise represented in terms of skin color, eye color, facial features, and dress. In each instance, difference precedes inclusion into national "normalized" belonging. As the contours of the categories of intercultural and civic education are fabricated within policy, so too is the Italian cosmopolitan child and the internal borders of national belonging. The immigrant student is tasked with the impossible: to become an Italian cosmopolitan child and to represent the internal borders of national belonging that her presence transgresses. Is it, then, any wonder she is so easily figured in the unreality of the cartoon?

While intercultural education was the favored pathway for integration through 2007, in recent years interculturality has been coupled with an attention to the Italian Constitution and citizenship education. Indeed, returning to MIUR's website on foreign students within Italian schools, specific mention is made of the importance of the civic approach to integration.

> It is indisputable that knowledge of the Italian language represents one of the means by which harmonious social cohesion is achieved; meanwhile the teaching of 'Citizenship and Constitution' offers all students an opportunity to become familiar with and share the fundamental rules of *convivenza* and the principles of legality and democracy.[12]
>
> *(MIUR, 2010)*

Integration, or Italian *convivenza*, is reduced to the study of a language and laws. As was previously the case with Italy's linguistic minorities, non-Italian students are differentiated from an Italian majority, but are they protected under the universal values of the Constitution they are called upon to practice? Article III of the Italian Constitution declares that "all citizens have equal social dignity and are equal before the law, without distinction of sex, race, language, religion, or political opinion, personal and social conditions" (The Italian Republic, 1947/2006, p. 8). But what about foreign students who are not (yet) citizens? The non-Italian students are called to share in the principles of legality and democracy while being denied status as citizen.

Convivenza, Democracy, and Transgression

As we have seen, within the Italian education discourse, integration is intended to produce *convivenza*. The National Observatory's workgroup for "Intercultural education and the formation of *convivenza*" delineates the following aims:

- to define actions for the "integration" of foreign and Italian students who are called upon today to face a new scenario of pluralism and globalization;

- to identify strategies for the formation of *"convivenza,"* in particular for adolescents in high school (MIUR, 2007b).

Convivenza can be translated as either coexistence or cohabitation, as the word is made up of two parts: *con-*, which translates as "with," and *-vivenza*, which means "living." As the term has moved into the intercultural discourse, it calls for the making of a harmonious society that not only "exists" or "inhabits" the same space but also is engaged with one another in the making of that harmony and that society. Intercultural education, as the workgroup title suggests, is discursively tied to the making of *convivenza*, and this is tied to the learning of democratic practices. However, the making of *convivenza* is part of a double gesture that normalizes and divides. The *convivenza* imagined in intercultural and civic education is a way of distinguishing between acceptable ways of being and performing difference and those that are not acceptable. The latter makes visible who is at risk, lacking the necessary competencies for daily *convivenza*.

In other words, *convivenza* sets up limits, which are defined by their possible transgressions. Embedded within the *convivenza* discourse are the limits of what it means to be Italian and maintain *convivenza*. But transgression, I argue, can also be read as engaging in democratic practice by contesting current limits, opening them up for debate and revision. A good example of this is the presence of the issue of religion in Italian public schools. Calls for the removal of crucifixes in public schools or the inclusion of other religions within school curricula may be read as transgressions on Italian tradition and culture, a failure on the part of others to respect Italian heritage. However, by raising these questions, students would also be engaging in a democratic practice that seeks to enforce rights that are guaranteed under the Constitution. But how can immigrant students enforce those rights when they are restricted from the very citizenship that grants such rights? In the claiming of rights and privileges that they do not yet have—by transgressing current limits—immigrant students may be simultaneously engaging in democratic practice and being marked as not integrated into *convivenza*. By not accepting current limits and norms, they would be disrupting social cohesion through their unauthorized civic participation.

This question regarding religions, public schools, and transgression is significant because it points to an example in which the universality of democracy and equality is translated within a specific site in terms of its culture and history. The overlapping of the national with the religious in Italy is well illustrated in the 1920s legislation concerning the décor of the Italian classroom: "the national flag, the crucifix, and the portrait of the king" were all three to adorn Italian classrooms (Ergas, 2004, p. 14). This combination of symbols demonstrates the way in which the Church figures in the national imaginary, and in schooling in particular. Additionally, particular norms and values from the Church were purposefully established as national tenets of teaching, such as the new Republic's aim, under Christian Democrat leadership, to teach fraternity and morality as a way of undoing the effects of fascism.

While the school is represented in policy as a neutral space for intercultural dialogue, it has also been the site of a hotly contested debate over whether the crucifix may be displayed, with the majority of the Italian population identifying the crucifix as not just a religious symbol but also as a national one. Indeed, an editorialist from Corriere della Sera, Claudio Magris, argued that the displaying of the crucifix was compatible with the notion of laicity.[13]

> Laicity rests, Magris wrote, on the distinction between that which pertains to faith and that which pertains to reason—that which pertains to the Church and that which pertains to the state. Whereas compulsory veneration of the crucifix would be unacceptable, "only an obtuse mind can be scandalized by the presence of the crucifix in a school in our country because Christianity . . . is part of our civilization." In fact, its mere presence on school walls "offends no one."
>
> *(Ergas, 2004, p. 13)*

The bringing of the crucifix into the notion of laicity is part of a historical narrative that brings religion into the state, even as the state was created in "conflict" with the Church. What becomes "invisible" or part of the center of Italianness is expressed as "offending no one," even as particular families who are not Catholic have initiated legal battles to have the crucifix removed. The presence of the crucifix is "reasonable" and compatible with the state because Italy is a "Christian civilization," while the Constitution declares that all persons, no matter their religious creed, are equal. It is this particular overlapping of laicity with religiosity that continues to shape Italian cosmopolitanism, giving particular form to the practice of various "universal" principles such as dialogue, respect, and democracy.

In this way, all students—including immigrant students—are to practice a cosmopolitan belonging brought via "Italian traditions, first Roman, then Catholic." The "common values" of Italian citizens and those yet to be citizens are taken as stable, homogenous, and universally accepted. Difference is allowed so long as it is tamed by an already established set of "common values" and norms—and that commonality within Italy is informed by the country's historical overlapping of laicity and religiosity.[14]

The relationship between practicing democracy as a way of "being integrated" is limited by this preconfigured *convivenza*. The discourse constructs integrated students as able to live according to unquestioned common values and norms for civic participation that are informed by national culture and history. My aim in this chapter, through the rethinking of transgression, is to suggest another possible relationship between practicing democracy and the immigrant student, perhaps even as the "unintegrated." The democratic practice of the unintegrated, imagined as the shadow figure of current policy, would, through the recognition of limits and the transgression of those limits in the name of rights as yet not taken/given, reconfigure *convivenza* as a site of contestation rather than a status to be maintained or an objective to be met. As Honig argues, "The practice of taking rights and privileges rather than waiting for them to be granted by a sovereign power is, I would argue, a quintessentially democratic practice" (Honig, 2001, p. 99).

Conclusion

I have taken up Foucault's reading of transgression—the act of naming difference—in order to rethink what it means to be "integrated." If the integration of immigrant students is geared toward developing the habit of democratic living, then norms and values that shape daily life and schooling will necessarily never be final or stable as the new members, along with other "others," *transgress* and thus enrich the possibilities of collective living. Rather than aiming to transform non-Italian students through an assimilatory process of integration, thereby preserving a sacred notion of Italianness, I argue that a shift in focus on Italian cosmopolitanism itself opens up new possibilities in integration policy within schools. This shift draws attention to differences in cultural theses for living, producing the much-touted democratic *convivenza* of Italian policy through students', teachers', and administrators' regular transgression-reformation-submission to collective values and norms, to be repeated again and again.

How, then, is integration to be understood? If non-Italian young people are "for all practical purposes" Italians according to Fini and are unquestionably Italian if they are born and/or raised in Italy according to Kyenge, one might ask, what kind of further integration needs to occur aside from being granted legal citizenship? Why is the school called upon to play a further role in the "processes of integration"? Minister Kyenge has rallied for the disruption of the current patterns of growing "disparity and exclusion" regarding student success (Kyenge, 2013) and to instead aim for schools that are "a place of inclusion and plurality, where one learns how to be informed citizens, actors in their own rights and agents of their own lives" (Kyenge, 2013). Kyenge goes on to assert that the unification of a nation is not completed in one moment. She seems to capture the spirit of the 19th-century French historian Ernst Renan's reflection that the nation is a daily plebiscite, as she argues instead that Italy is meant to be "continually renewed as a collective work that succeeds best when it involves the most" (Kyenge, 2013). "In this chapter I seek to extend our understanding of what that "collective work" is to include by recognizing the role of transgression as part of democratic practice." Integrated schools are not just places in which one demonstrates knowledge of and abides by established norms of behavior but places in which norms are questioned, transgressed, or reaffirmed, in the very collective work to which Kyenge aspires.

Schools are not called upon to establish the juridical status of their students, but through national policies they are called upon to inculcate and offer students opportunities to learn and practice those rights and duties that are seen as part of being a citizen of the nation-state. This call to integrate the immigrant student is part of a double gesture that expresses not only a hope for what the country can be if integration is successful but also the fears that attend that uncertain process—fears of degeneration and loss. With such fears embedded within the logic of policy discourse, its calls for "democratic practice" undergo a kind of alchemy (see Popkewitz, 1998) in which the democratic practice that is part of Italian *convivenza* demands acceptance and honoring of already established norms, common values, and laws and thus maintains or takes as fixed the limits of the national cultural thesis as they were imagined to be before the arrival of immigrants. In doing so, democratic practice that transgresses limits in the demanding of rights before they are granted is read as a sign of not yet being integrated. This kind of "being integrated" leaves little discursive room for other ways of doing democratic practice, such as contesting and even transforming what are taken as current norms and values.

Notes

1. In 2011, under the interim government of Mario Monti, a new ministry was created: the Ministry for International Cooperation and Integration. This ministry was then renamed under Prime Minister Enrico Letta. Under the current government, led by Prime Minister Matteo Renzi, the Ministry for Integration was dissolved.
2. ". . . il 60% dei minori stranieri che risiedono in Italia sono nati qui da noi ed è anche a loro che dobbiamo guardare, dal momento che, nei fatti, sono già, a tutti gli effetti, veri and propri cittadini italiani, anche se non hanno ancora avuto i riconoscimento giuridico e lo status" (ibid.).
3. "I criteri molto restrittivi per ottenere la cittadinanza italiana . . . divengono un ulteriore peso per molti giovani che ormai si sentono italiani" (ibid.).
4. "E questa non può che essere la sfida che si consegna alla scuola del futuro chiamata ad assumere un fondamentale ruolo di traino dei nuovi processi di integrazione" (ibid.).
5. "L'Italia ha scelto, fin dall'inizio (C.M. 205/1990, 'La scuola dell'obbligo e gli alunni stranieri. L'educazione interculturale') la piena integrazione di tutti nella scuola e l'educazione interculturale come dimensione trasversale, come sfondo che accomuna tutte le discipline e tutti gli insegnanti" (MIUR, 2006).
6. "Rilevato che la presenza nelle scuole di alunni di diversa provenienza sociale, culturale, etnica e con differenti capacità ed esperienze di apprendimento costituisce un dato strutturale in continuo aumento, un fenomeno complesso con aspetti problematici di non facile soluzione, che incidono negativamente sull'efficacia dei servizi scolastici e sugli esiti formativi" (MIUR, 2010).
7. "Particolare attenzione va rivolta all'inclusione e all'integrazione degli alunni stranieri, al fine di predisporre condizioni paritarie che possano prevenire situazioni di disagio e di difficoltà derivanti dai nuovi contesti di vita e di studio e contribuire a creare l'indispensabile condivisione delle norme della convivenza e della partecipazione sociale" (ibid.).
8. Germany and Belgium, for example, tend still to base their conceptions of citizenship in terms of ethnicity, while Britain, France, and the Netherlands are more civic-territorial in their approach. In this, it is easier for immigrants of the latter group to obtain citizenship, notwithstanding further differences regarding the expression of cultural rights. For example, in France there continues to be an emphasis on assimilation to a universal French culture, while in Britain and the Netherlands there has been an emphasis on a pluralist model of multiculturalism.
9. Thus, in Italy, there is the peculiar situation in which "for minors born or educated in Italy it is still difficult to become citizens, descendants of a single emigrant can keep Italian citizenship and add it to that of the place where they reside" (Zincone, 2010, p. 5).

10. ". . . the Italian Government implemented gender equality . . . within the Family Reform Act (no. 151, 19 May) . . . which stated that loss of nationality for married women [with a foreigner] contravened art. 3 of the Constitution. In 1983, following a new Constitutional ruling (no. 30, 9 February 1983), a new Act (no. 123, 21 April) established the right for married women to transfer their nationality both to their children and to their foreign husband" (Zincone, 2010, p. 22).

11. "Da tempo la nostra scuola ha scelto la piena integrazione di tutti e l'educazione interculturale come suo orizzonte culturale. Il nostro modello di integrazione, a differenza di quelli inglese e francese, tende a rifiutare sia la logica dell'assimilazione, sia la costruzione o il rafforzamento di comunità etniche chiuse. Favorisce, invece, il dialogo, il rispetto reciproco e il confronto per valorizzare la ricchezza di esperienze e riflessioni compiute in questi anni, anche con il coinvolgimento delle famiglie. Favorisce, insomma, l'integrazione nel pieno rispetto delle identità" (MIUR, 2005).

12. "È innegabile che la conoscenza della lingua italiana rappresenta uno degli strumenti per costruire una armoniosa coesione sociale; mentre l'insegnamento di 'Cittadinanza e Costituzione' offre a tutti gli studenti l'opportunità per conoscere e condividere le regole fondamentali della convivenza e i principi della legalità e della democrazia" (http://hubmiur.pubblica.istruzione.it/getOM?idfileentry=199101).

13. This is similar to the French *laïcité*, defined by Ergas as "meaning, roughly, nondenomi-nationalism and secularism" (2004, p. 13).

14. "Allo stesso tempo si rinviene nel valore universale della persona il fondamento di una comune cultura e si riconosce nella Dichiarazione universale dei diritti dell'uomo (ONU, 1948) l'espressione di valori di generale consenso. Ad un approccio relativista viene dunque a corrispondere una visione universalista. . . . L'educazione interculturale si impernia, appunto, sui motivi dell'unità, della diversità e della loro conciliazione dialettica e costruttiva nella società multiculturale" (Ministero della Pubblica Istruzione, 1994).

References

Badiou, A. (2011). The democratic emblem. In G. Agamben, A. Badiou, D. Bensaid, W. Brown, J.-L. Nancy, J. Ranciere, K. Ross, & S. Žižek (Eds.), *Democracy in what state? (New directions in critical theory)* (W. McCuaig, Trans.; pp. 6–15). New York: Columbia University Press.

Callia, R., Pittau, F., & Ricci, A. (2009). EMN—The Organization of Asylum and Migration Policies in Italy. Retrieved from EMN: Rete Europea Migrazioni website:http://ec.europa.eu/dgs/home-affairs/what-we-do/networks/european_migration_network/reports/docs/emn-studies/migration-policies/it_20120412_organisation asylummigrationpolicies_en_version_final_en.pdf.

De Amicis, E. (1886). *Cuore: Libro per i ragazzi*. Milano: Treves.

Ergas, Y. (2004). Rome dispatch: When in Rome. *The New Republic, 231*(9), 13–14.

Foucault, M. (1977). *Language, counter-memory, practice: Selected essays and interviews*. Ithaca, NY: Cornell University Press.

Guolo, R. (2003). *Xenofobi e xenofili: Gli italiani e l'islam*. Roma: Laterza.

Honig, B. (2001). *Democracy and the foreigner*. Princeton, NJ: Princeton University Press.

Indini, A. (2013, December 26). "Ius soli, la Kyenge torna alla carica: 'Chi nasce o cresce qui è italiano.'" *Il giornale.it,* from www.ilgiornale.it/news/interni/ius-soli-kyenge-torna-carica-chi-nasce-o-cresce-qui-italiano-978402.html

Integrazione Migranti. (2013, November 22). *Pubblicato il Focus statistico del MIUR. Sono 800 mila gli alunni stranieri nelle scuole italiane: il 47% sono seconde generazioni*. Retrieved

December 16, 2013, from www.integrazionemigranti.gov.it/archiviodocumenti/minori-e-g2/Pagine/Alunni-stranieri-2012_2013.aspx

Italian Republic. (1947/2006). *Costituzione della Repubblica Italiana.* Roma: Senato della Repubblica.

Koopmans, R., Statham, P., Giugni, M., & Passy, F. (2005). *Contested citizenship: Immigration and cultural diversity in Europe.* Minneapolis: University of Minnesota Press.

Kyenge, C. K. (2013, January 27). Cécile Kashetu Kyenge—Deputato al Parlamento per il Partito Democratico. Retrieved June 6, 2014, from www.cecilekyenge.it/old/stampa/CecileKyengeProgramma.pdf

MIUR. (1994). *Circolare Ministeriale 2 marzo 73.* Retrieved December 16, 2013, from www.edscuola.it/archivio/norme/circolari/cm073_94.html

MIUR. (2005). *Editoria | Istruzione.it |.* Retrieved December 16, 2013, from http://archivio.pubblica.istruzione.it/mpi/pubblicazioni/2005/nonita_05.shtml

MIUR. (2006). *Normativa MARZO.* Retrieved December 16, 2013, from http://archivio.pubblica.istruzione.it/normativa/2006/cm24_06.shtml

MIUR. (2007a). *La via italiana per la scuola interculturale e l'integrazione degli alunni stranieri: Osservatorio nazionale per l'integrazione degli alunni stranieri e per l'educazione interculturale.* Retrieved June 4, 2014, from http://istruzione.comune.modena.it/memo/allegati/la_via_italiana.pdf

MIUR. (2007b). *Osservatorio nazionale per l'integrazione degli alunni stranieri e l'educazione interculturale.* Retrieved June 4, 2014, from http://archivio.pubblica.istruzione.it/dgstudente/intercultura/allegati/osservatorio.pdf

MIUR. (2010). *OGGETTO: Indicazioni e raccomandazioni per l'integrazione di alunni con cittadinanza non italiana, prot. n. 101/R.U.U., C.M. n.2.* Retrieved from http://hubmiur.pubblica.istruzione.it/getOM?idfileentry=199101

Pickett, B. L. (1996). Foucault and the politics of resistance. *Polity, 28*(4), 445–466.

Popkewitz, T. S. (1998). *Struggling for the soul: The politics of schooling and the construction of the teacher.* New York: Teachers College Press.

Popkewitz, T. S. (2008). *Cosmopolitanism and the age of school reform: Science, education, and making society by making the child.* New York: Routledge.

Rancière, J. (1999). *Dis-agreement: Politics and philosophy* (J. Rose, Trans.). Minneapolis: University of Minnesota Press.

Rusconi, G. E. (1999). *Possiamo fare a meno di una religion civile?* Roma-Bari: Laterza.

Seconde generazioni. (2011). Fini: *"Serve lungimiranza su scuola e cittadinanza"—Stranieri in Italia.* Retrieved December 16, 2013, from www.stranieriinitalia.it/attualita-seconde_generazioni._fini_serve_lungimiranza_su_scuola_e_cittadinanza_13342.html

Zincone, G. (2010). *Citizenship policy making in Mediterranean EU states: Italy.* Retrieved June 4, 2014, from http://eudo-citizenship.eu/docs/EUDOcom-Italy.pdf

12

BACK TO THE BASICS

Inventing the Mathematical Self

Jennie Diaz

In a May 1969 issue *of The Arithmetic Teacher,* a new footer appeared: *"Excellence in Mathematics Education—For All."* This call for excellent math in all schools for all children remained on each page thereafter. As if reminding the reader of the ways in which mathematics education had once again become an issue of educational reform, *excellence for all* seemed to demand something new.

The appearance of this message coincided with rising concerns about the previous New Mathematics curriculum that began to emerge in around the 1970s. In some ways, this reorganization of mathematics was thought of as a transition away from New Math toward basic math skills (Kline, 1973). In other ways, this particular period is thought to blend into New Math, as part of what historically came before the now-so-familiar Standards-based reforms (Hiebert et al., 1997). So, generally speaking, the Back to Basics reform does not get much individual attention in the history of math education. Yet it served as an important event in the history of working to organize math for *all* children.

In this chapter, I attend to how the *logic of equality* that is embedded in the notion of *mathematics for all* organized certain ways to see and think about children during the reform of math education during the 1970s and 1980s in the United States.

I examine this logic as a way of reasoning about and establishing what is equal, equivalent, and different. In this way, Basic math pedagogy was about much more than mathematics. It provided, I argue, new ways of seeing and classifying children as individuals with identities and differences linked to basic skills, interests, and abilities for participating in both school and society.

As a way to understand the production of identity and difference in the Back to Basics movement, I draw upon the notion of fabrication to explore how the math curriculum "invents" the child as a certain kind of self (Hacking, 2002).

Fabrication provides a way to think about how, in the (re)forming of the curriculum, there is an inscription of identity and difference that represents who the child is and should be. This is important because the representation of the child with certain psychological traits is not natural or neutral. Rather, it is a cultural invention of the *mathematical self*—a child whose traits of individuality and sense of self (in relation to the all) are ascribed in and through the Basic math curriculum.

The analysis explores the inscriptions of identity and difference as cultural principles organizing the child as a particular kind of individual through the use of the equal sign (=). On one level, I analyze the equal sign as a fundamental element of the skills-based curriculum that emerged in this period. As a symbol of mathematical logic, the equal sign ordered how children were to think of fundamental arithmetic relationships of equivalence and nonequivalence. On another, I examine the use of the equal sign in the curriculum as embodying a cultural logic about equivalences and differences between children.

To relate the basic problem solving in the curriculum to the representation of the child as a certain kind of self, I give attention to how mathematical skills were translated through psychology in this reordering of math education. This process of translation, what Popkewitz (2004) has called "alchemy," illuminates how principles of psychology and mathematics intersect within a broader system of reasoning about equality to invent cultural representations of equivalence, identity, and difference. On both levels, then, the analysis investigates how seemingly distinct "mathematical" and "cultural" equality related to (re)organize *excellence in mathematics education—for all*.

Attending to the Basics in Math: The Individual, Intuition, and Interest

> We do need to get back to the basics, but it is essential that we first identify the basics we want to get back to.
>
> —*W. Ross Winterowd quoted in Brodinsky, 1977, p. 523*

While the Back to Basics movement may be considered a move away from what came before in the New Math curriculum, it also expressed important continuities in terms of a link between math education and the reorganization of social and cultural life. What distinguished the Basics movement, however, were new modes of living this life. No longer simply about making intelligent citizens of the nation, mathematics education was related to "the development of life (or survival) skills—that is, competencies needed for personal growth and for successful existence as a citizen, consumer, jobholder, taxpayer, and member of a family" (Brodinsky, 1977, p. 524). Implicit in this statement of math skills as integral to life skills is a double layer of *competencies* whereby knowledge learned in school was to be related to one's participation in society as an individual—given multiple forms of expression and responsibility. This shift in the reorganization of math's basic skills as skills of *personal* survival and growth required a determination of the *basics* to get back to.

In grappling with *Why Johnny Can't Add: The Failure of New Math,* Kline (1973) suggested that the emphasis on structure and abstraction was the reason, not only for Johnny's[1] failure but also for math's inadequate contribution to the development of science and society. The so-called failures of New Math—marked as math's abstractness, disinterest, and inward turn—brought with them ideals of what would constitute the basic education for life in a progressive and democratic society. More specifically, while the modes of abstract reasoning emphasized in the previous New Math curriculum seemed to "destroy the spirit and life" of mathematics, a more "natural motivation" could be found in the study of problems that would "revivify math by the air of reality" (Kline, 1973, p. 149). In terms of curriculum redesign, math in its most basic form was to be motivating and interesting—not abstract or removed from what constituted the problems of real and everyday life.

Within this (re)connection of math to "natural" interests and motivations, it seemed evident that "the basic approach to all new subject matter at all levels should be intuitive" (Kline, 1973, p. 157). The basic mathematics curriculum was articulated within what were taken as inherent modes of reasoning, instinct, and awareness. This appeal to a "natural" intuition would seem to provide the sort of "natural" motivation that was deemed necessary for learning and success in the Basic curriculum. Supported by research concluding that even "infants have ample opportunity to learn about number, repetition, regularity, differences in magnitude, equivalence, causality, and correlation," notions of mathematical intuition would serve to create equivalences between children, all capable of the same basic mathematical insights and skills (Ginsburg, 1977, p. 30).

However, the assumptions of a natural intuition and motivation that were to organize the math curriculum and provide equal opportunities for success were not biological distinctions. This distinction between nature and culture is expressed as unproblematic in the following discussion of the math curriculum:

> [I]t is hard to see how any child, rich or poor, Western or non-Western can grow up in an environment which does not offer him or her the natural opportunity to learn about basic aspects of quantity. In this sense, environments are all similar and quantity is universally available. We shall see later that there is a sense in which all children take advantage of this natural opportunity.
> *(Ginsburg, 1977, p. 31)*

Expressed as skills and opportunities that would naturally develop, this notion of natural is a cultural standard. In other words, the opportunities that children had to take advantage of had to be first considered as such. What those opportunities were would have implications in how the idea of a basic, intuitive mathematics was to be made available to *all children.*

So, at the same time that it was possible to think that all children could naturally excel in basic math, it would become clear how some children did not adequately "take advantage" of the "natural opportunities" to be a part of school mathematics. When Kenneth, a child interviewed to better understand his "challenges" with math, "interpreted the + and = in terms of actions to be performed," his interpretation was seen as one that "can lead to trouble":

I: How would you read this? [$\Box$ = 3 + 4]
K: . . . Blank equals 3 plus 4.
I: O.K. What can you say about that, anything?
K: It's backwards! [He changed it to 4 + 3 = $\Box$] You can't go, 7 equals 3 plus 4.
(Ginsburg, 1977, p. 84)

Kenneth's opportunity to "see" the relation of equality was missed by an apparently limited, or backwards, logic. Taken merely as a truth of mathematical equality, this expression and the questions asked about it serve to highlight the ways in which Kenneth does not seem to have a natural intuition about equality as a relationship of like terms. Beyond that, the inscription of equality provided a way of organizing what was given as Kenneth's individual understanding—a lens into how he sees, thinks about, and interprets the mathematics. However, this is not simply "his," "natural," or "intuitive." Rather, this is a cultural distinction that provides a way to identify abilities that are given as his "own," not some one else's.

As part of a broader effort in math education research to identify individual abilities in the process of learning math, this signification of individuality importantly relates the organizing logic of math in schools to the notion of equality underlying excellence in math for all. This occurs through the psychology that defines the child's unique traits and differences as a way to think about producing equal opportunities for every one to learn math. But this individuality could not be understood without reference to some norm that represents an imagined *all*.

So, while the principles of identity and difference that were to express individuality may not be the same for Johnny, who has failed and been failed by New Math, as they are for Kenneth, the fundamental notions of interest, motivation, and intuition would establish equivalence between them. Similar to how the terms of equality could be reordered and seen as identical ($\Box$ = 3 + 4 to 4 + 3 = $\Box$), Kenneth and Johnny could be seen as distinct individuals—yet equal in their differences.

As stated, the analysis of the equal sign that follows is no mere example. It is examined in how cultural principles of identity and difference in what appears as mathematics in the curriculum is more than mathematics—ordering the thoughts and actions of the child as a "naturally" but differently motivated and interested in Basic mathematics. This ordering is visible at the intersection of research in the psychology of individual math learning and basic math skills that serve as the foundation of the elementary math curriculum. In the next section, I explore this intersection as a way to understand how a particular style of reasoning about equality, equivalence, and difference represents children as individuals—distinct in their abilities, skills, and interests.

Motivated to Learn Mathematics: Equalizing Opportunity and Access

With a "natural motivation" to learn basic math skills linked to children's interests, intuitions, and individuality, it seemed necessary to determine how to produce, maintain, and differentiate this motivation. Particularly in the context of *excellence in mathematics education—for all*, the focus on motivation to learn math assembled with a concern for equality of opportunity. So, while equal opportunities for all children to learn math could not technically be guaranteed, this equality was thought to be measurable as the effect of an "equality of optimum motivation" (Nicholls, 1979). In fact, it seemed fairly straightforward that "we can say that someone is not developing his or her potential in, for example, mathematics, if that person is not optimally motivated to learn mathematics" (Nicholls, 1979, p. 1072). With motivation as a factor of success in school mathematics, it would make sense for the curriculum to be organized to enhance the motivation of each individual student.

As a historical classification, motivation was deemed useful in the language of psychology to distinguish children who were/were not achieving (Danziger, 1997). The invention of this distinction was to give finer "scientific" classifications to understand and talk about differences between children. At the same time, motivation has become a category by which to establish equivalence between *all* children as equally capable of being "motivated." During the Back to Basics movement, it was this cultural notion of identity that was given as a way to establish a standard of equivalence by which to identify the ways in which all children could excel in mathematics.

Though it would seem that *all* children are or can be motivated to learn mathematics, it would become clear that some children could not excel. This was emphasized in *The Psychology of Mathematical Abilities in Schoolchildren*, stating, "even with perfect teaching, *individual differences in mathematical abilities* will always occur—some will be more able, others less. Equality will never be achieved in this respect" (Kilpatrick & Wirszup, 1976, pp. 6–7). Yet this was not the end of hope for equal access and opportunity for all to excel in mathematics. Together with the investigation of individual differences in interest and abilities in math education, it was thought that equal opportunities could be produced as an effect of equalizing children's motivations.

Self-Discovery: Starting With the Child

A commonsense idea organizing the Basics curriculum was that meaningful and motivating mathematics started with *each child*. By starting with the individual rather than with the mathematics, pedagogy was to "encourage young children to respond to situations using their own ideas, language patterns" (Price Troutman, 1973, p. 427). This way of thinking about the child as an individual, defined by his/her "own" ideas and language, required a way of thinking about this individuality and what its expression entailed.

This can be seen in a discussion of "Child-created Mathematics" (Cochran, Barson, & Davis, 1970). In solving the open sentence $\square - 3 = \triangle$, a child named Leslie chose numbers so as to create equivalence between $\square - 3$ and $\triangle$ on either side of the equal sign. This required her to replace the $\square$ and $\triangle$ with chosen numbers so as to identify the unknowns with known quantities. Then, to represent this equivalence as a comparison between the two quantities, Leslie produced a graph by translating the numbers and shapes to points on a grid. Through her "creation" (selecting numbers and plotting points), the shapes were given identity—representable and fixed as both a quantity and a point in space.

The openness of the expression provided more than an opportunity for this child to create a mathematical understanding of equality as a relationship of like/ unlike terms. In producing this graph, the act of identifying the mathematical objects that gave meaning to the equal sign—open symbols, numbers, point on a graph—represented a way for Leslie to "create" an understanding of her self and the choices she was to make as an individual. Apparently not satisfied with the way her graph of $\square - 3 = \triangle$ looked, she expressed that she wanted her graph to be more "straight up." Rather than correct her language use (by introducing the term "vertical") the teacher should provide Leslie with the opportunity to follow her hunch that the $\square$ and $\triangle$ were related and were not the same. In this, the child appeared to make choices about the language and task direction while also discovering that changing the $\square$ would change the $\triangle$. This discovery was to leave her feeling more satisfied with and motivated by mathematics.

On one level, developing basic math skills was associated with the ability to identify the shapes as distinct numbers and create a relationship of mathematical equality. On another level, the mathematics intersected with cultural expressions of individual identity. Given in psychological terms, children's interests, abilities, and feelings were categories deemed useful in motivating each individual child given their differences. This logic of cultural distinction assembled with the math. Related by the equal sign (=), to distinguish $\square$ and $\triangle$ while at the same time making them equivalent, it is necessary to identify the terms that hold their differences constant. In the case of the math equation, the 3 served to differentiate as well as identify the $\square$ and $\triangle$. In a similar way, a term of comparison must identify Leslie (or any other child) as different from yet related to another.

Defining terms of equivalence between children, research emerged examining how individuals thought about and learned mathematics differently. The focus on differential abilities invited new ways to distinguish between "the gifted or less able child" (Inskeep, 1970, p. 195). Within this range, "mathematical precociousness" provided a psychological category to identify the child presumed as mathematically talented. The classification and the traits attributed to this child were articulated in the language of interests, values, and personality. Further, the "mathematically precocious" or "gifted" child was characterized as a person who "liked finding out things, discovering things, and learning things" (Stanley, Keating, & Fox, 1974). S/he also appeared to have a positive attitude toward and a general "likeness of math." Together, these traits served to explain student success in school math. More than that, they provided a way for children to "see themselves" in their math classes. This seeing, however, was more than a reflection of who the child "naturally" was. It was an invention of a particular kind of self—motivated by self-discovery and general feelings of personal satisfaction.

Creating her own mathematics was to be seen as an opportunity for Leslie to enact what were given as "her" mathematical interests and intuitions. Not only that, it was to provide her with a way to feel personally fulfilled and express an unbound sense of self as a motivated individual, capable of excelling in math. Not every child would achieve like Leslie, however. But since "children's self-concept is usually bound up with their intellectual achievements," it became increasingly part of the common sense to identify individual strengths and weaknesses in learning math as factors impacting learning (Ginsburg, 1977, p. 130). Both were to be understood so as to provide all children with a better self-concept and an equal opportunity to be motivated to learn.

Informally interviewing children with "severe difficulties in the learning of arithmetic" is seen as a way to "discover" strengths and weaknesses, as though they were already there. In solving $21 - 5 = 24$, a child named Bob seemed to use an incorrect written, or what was considered a formal, strategy. The research emphasized Bob's self-realization that, "Oh, I think I added" (Ginsburg, 1977, p. 134). In the analysis, the mathematical understandings seemed deemphasized. Instead, the focus was on how Bob seemed to come to his own awareness of his miscalculation. Embodying a logic of difference and equivalence, this problem organized a way of thinking about children, like Bob, as different yet still having a sort of intuitive sense that he had done something wrong with his formal expression of understanding. Presumably, if Bob could identify when he made a mistake in translating his "informal" mathematical logic to "formal" strategies, then he could eventually find a way to establish equality between $21 - 5$ and its equivalent term. Until then, his self-awareness would motivate future success.

Organizing particular ways of thinking about identity and equivalence, the use of the equal sign is not isolated as pure mathematical reasoning. Translated through the language of psychology and connected to notions of self-expression and -discovery, the equal sign embodied a cultural way of identifying the child as motivated to learn mathematics.

This relation of mathematical logic to cultural principles of equality also functioned to produce a notion of difference. That is, certain kinds of kids were presumed capable of creating, discovering, and expressing their "own" mathematical ideas while others were not. This distinction was to be understood in terms of the psychological promise of "learning by discovery" (Gardner Thompson, 1973, p. 344). In solving the following series of problems:

$1 + 1 =$
$1 + 1 + 1 =$
$1 + 1 + 1 + 1 =$

"Caesar didn't seem to grasp that we were going in sequence and just adding one more each time" (Gardner Thompson, 1973, p. 344). In fact, this inability to intuitively "grasp" the pattern seemed to reinforce the use of what was taken as an inefficient counting strategy. In addition, "Caesar didn't seem to realize that problems like $8 + 1 = \square$ and $1 + 8 = \square$ were the same" (Gardner Thompson, 1973, p. 346). Given as obvious realizations, which Caesar did not immediately discover, the problems served as a way to identify his lack of self-awareness and rationalize the need for "continued practice" of predetermined concepts. The practice of establishing equivalence between like problems provided a way to produce a distinction between Caesar and the children that did have the ability to "realize" and internalize the mathematical rules. Again, as more than mathematical rules, the principles of identity and difference embodied in the use of the equal sign framed cultural standards by which to compare Caesar to the child who learned by discovery and was motivated by one's own sense of self-realization.

Enthusiasm, Choice, and Control: Games of Winners and Losers

"Fostering enthusiasm through child-created games" provided another mode of motivating learning, for children of all abilities (Price Troutman, 1973, p. 428). Following the assumption that "children are highly motivated to explain games clearly to others" (Golden, 1970, p. 114), games were to provide children with the opportunity to express mathematical ideas while encouraging cooperation and collaboration. Organized according to the rule that games provided a pleasurable medium through which to develop basic mathematical skills, they also embodied rules that ordered how the child was to enact that pleasure and play.

As part of the Basic curriculum, games were not to be enjoyed at the expense of building math skills. Rather, they were supposed to play an integral part in developing understanding. This included approaches to "mastering the basic math facts with dice" (Gosman, 1973). In this game, the dice and the mathematical expressions they represent are "loaded with activities to help children master basic number facts and enjoy the experience" (Gosman, 1973, p. 330). In one turn of "multiplication-addition double trouble," children might multiply the number on the dice by 5, following the formula $5 \times \#$ on the dice = total score. The math seemed fairly straightforward and basic. Mastering basic facts required children to think about each turn as establishing a single value (score) from the dice and the given number.

Aiming to reach a combined score of 100 without going over, the child would be expected to add each value to the total that came before it, giving a numerical identity to the total scores that were to be compared so as to determine the winner of the game. On one level, solving equations like *5 × # on the dice = total score* ordered children's understanding of how to establish basic equivalencies between numbers given in multiple forms. On another level, the equal sign carried rules for how to reason about and construct basic equivalences between objects that would otherwise have no relation or basis for comparison.

Thinking about and seeing equivalence in a given number, a die, a series of single values, and a total score arranged the game and children's thinking about how to play. But this mode of thinking was not just about mathematics—it was also about the game of making choices within a cultural system of a "game" in which self-realization was to occur. Like mastering the math skills by following a formulaic method, enjoying the experience of playing the game was not to be left to chance. Instead, kids were to enjoy that the game itself was "completely under the control of the children. They must roll the dice, keep track of their scores, and decide to pass or play after each throw of the dice" (Gosman, 1973, p. 331). This required children to make choices at every turn. How they made their choices was thought to impact not only the outcome of the game but also the extent to which they enjoyed it as a mode of living.

While all kids could presumably learn math from and enjoy the game, only some of them would win. Nevertheless, playing the game was to "guarantee participants an experience that is like the experience they would have in the real world" (Cruickshank & Tefler, 1980, p. 77). The experiences of taking turns, calculating outcomes, keeping score, and deciding what to do next were to provide all children with opportunities to "make decisions and live with the consequences" (Cruickshank & Tefler, 1980, p. 77). In this way, solving *5 × # on the dice = total score* was not only about following rules of mathematical logic. It was linked to a cultural standard of identity by which children were to embody norms for personal decision making, even if in the end they (their total scores) were deemed unequal to their competitors. At least the game was organized to offer equal opportunities and there was a value ascribed to children by which to identify, compare, and differentiate them as winners or not.

Living with the consequences of the game presumed some natural outcome of winning or losing—as the effect of one's own calculated interest, enthusiasm, and effort. Articulated as the opportunity "for participants to solve difficult problems themselves rather than to observe the way someone else solves them" (Cruickshank & Tefler, 1980, p. 76), the game was to model some notion of what children would encounter in the "real" world. That is, no one was going to do the work for them. They would need to decide to do it for themselves and take advantage of the situation. Together, "these exercises may give pupils a greater sense of control over their future" (Cruickshank & Tefler, 1980, p. 79). This sense of control was determined by how one played the game and what choices were made to impact the future outcome. With the game ultimately determined by how children were identified and given equivalence with a numerical score, the total score became more than that. Continuously multiplying 5 by the # *on the dice* = a measure of personal interest, decision-making ability, and sense of control over one's life.

The equal sign (=) used in the formula for play embodied a method of establishing equivalence between unrelated terms and making them equal to a value. Given as a way to identify both the result of the game and the child capable of winning, calculating the score was more than a mathematical skill. In relating basic math facts to cultural principles for how children were to make their own choices and control their own future, it embodied a skill for living as self-regulating individuals. Inscribing this as the standard, the mode of reasoning about identity carried in the equal sign also organized principles of difference. In other words, more than a series of basic facts, the equivalence calculated by throws of the dice became a mode of comparing things that otherwise seemed incomparable—children's abilities to control situations and make decisions.

The comparison was most easily made by using scores to determine the winner and loser. Whereas losing the game could be attributed to an unequal score, it could also be seen as a child's lack of control over the game and inability to make wise decisions. Importantly, this could also represent a child's incompetence with even the most basic facts. As mentioned earlier, the game was also about math skills. If a child was not learning them, then motivating him/her to learn them was to psychologically order self-directing thoughts and actions. That is, if a child does not want to play the game, cannot control it, or continuously loses, that can be rearranged.

Seen as a "psychological block" to learning even the most basic skills, a child's self-concept as a loser or failure intersected with a notion of "self-fulfilling prophecy" (Dreyfuss, 1973, p. 489). A child's idea of him- or herself in the math classroom was thought to either advance or inhibit future success. This student "had already decided somewhere back in the grades that the mention of the words like *inches, feet,* or *yards* spelled FAILURE" (Dreyfuss, 1973, p. 488). Comparing things that otherwise seemed incomparable did not seem to make sense. In this case, a sort of "mental paralysis" engendered the belief that something was too difficult or could not be done. Yet this could be undone.

As a way to provide equal opportunities for children to be motivated to learn math, certain practices of math pedagogy were linked to a psychologically (re)-ordering of self-directing thoughts and actions. So that any child could have the skills to play the math game, the equal sign reinscribed expressions of difference as a mode of mathematical thought that was thought to *undo the mental paralysis.* By "start[ing] out with a simple equality: If 2 zobos = 5 dingbats, then how many dingbats do 4 zobos equal? . . . the students responded admirably" (Dreyfuss, 1973, p. 488). That is, now believing they could solve problems that they previously thought were impossible, the students were "surprised," "happy," and "relieved."

This equality between zobos and dingbats seemed to provide a way for the child to think about the difference between the unlike terms by resignifying their identity and making it at once strange and familiar. Now, no longer thinking of units of measure, children were supposed to compare the zobos to the dingbats—presumed as nonequivalent and unnecessary to identify. One did not need to know what a zobo was to compare it to a dingbat. S/he just needed to follow the rule of making equivalences based upon what were already given as different. A dingbat was always already not a zobo.

At the same time, and following a similar way of reasoning about difference, the expression of equality in 2 zobos = 5 dingbats inscribed a psychological fix for the child who was thought of as nonequivalent to the self-directed, enthusiastic, and in-control student. This difference distinguished the kind of child who seemed to need a more direct form of instruction, did not appear to motivate him- or herself, and continuously fulfilled his "own" predetermined sense of failure.

The use of the equal sign in mastering basic math skills was about developing mathematical modes of reasoning about equality and equivalence that embodied rules for thinking about identity and difference. Yet it also entangled with the principles of psychology to identify individuality and ascribe norms of self-direction, -concept, -awareness, and -control as traits of the child motivated to learn math. In its various inscriptions, then, the equal sign was much more than a symbol of mathematical equality. It carried cultural standards for living as a self-motivated individual, as the basic element of all children having an equal opportunity to excel in school math.

To this point, I have looked at how the equal sign in the Basics curriculum organized a logic of equivalence and difference that worked to inscribe notions of identity as psychological traits of the motivated and self-directed individual. In the next section, I discuss how making the child motivated to learn mathematics historically assembled within broader social and cultural shifts that would give intelligibility to the skills that would seem basic to living and surviving in the 1970s in the United States.

Basic Principles of Self-expression, Individuality, and Personal Choice

To understand the shifts in curriculum that connected success in mathematics education to motivating the mathematical self, I place the Basics curriculum within a grid of historical, cultural, and political trajectories. This is in order to see how the child's identity as a particular kind of self made sense within this context of reform. It is to explore how mathematical and cultural ways of thinking about equality and establishing equivalence intersect outside of what is taken as the mathematics curriculum.

In other educational projects of reform, the individual was given as a basic and fundamental component of social progress within a web of economic, political, and cultural challenges about rights, equality, and freedom. In *The 1970s: A New Global History From Civil Rights to Economic Inequality,* Borstelmann (2011) asserted that these challenges of reform were undergirded by a "spirit of egalitarianism and inclusiveness that rejected traditional hierarchies and lines of authority, asserting instead the equality of all people" (p. 3). This notion of equality and inclusion is expressed as a logic of mathematics embodied in the equal sign, in how identity, equivalence, and difference are taken as representable in order to make this "spirit" visible.

The sociological, psychological, and cultural histories provide a way to see the connection between the particular discursive distinctions and classifications embodied in the use of the equal sign in the curriculum. More than a textual relationship, norms of identity and difference connect the logic of equivalence expressed in the equal sign that bear a logical resemblance to cultural standards in the curriculum as elements of the child's freedom, choice, motivation, and self-expression by which to live one's life.

Defining individuality and marking difference could be conceived not merely as self-serving but as within a broader responsibility for others, acceptance of difference, and an appreciation for pluralism (Yankelovitch, 1998). At the same time, this way of thinking about equality and inclusion entailed a consensus as to what constituted this difference, who was identified as the other, and what forms of plurality were to be appreciated. Thinking about equality within a diverse society required a norm by which to determine a basis on which equality was granted.

In a society that valued the individual in relation to others, differences and inequalities in the social, political, and economic challenges that characterized one's daily life were simultaneously troubled and presumed to be mutable. In this, unequal results and differential opportunities were taken to be the result of and therefore altered by individual actions. In the context of social sciences, the value given to reason and rationality as the basis for deciding was accompanied by a cultural pattern of thought that gave significance to notions of individual choice as the basis of good decision making (Heyck, 2012). Importantly, this interest in the individual also encoded new norms for discovering, identifying, and planning the self (Bellah et al., 1985; Thomson, 1992).

Working on the "self" was to be in the name of gaining a greater sense of freedom, finding one's place in society, and inspiring one's own commitments to personal fulfillment. In an issue of *New York Magazine* devoted to the "Me Decade," journalist Tom Wolfe (1976) noted that "the new alchemical dream is: changing one's personality—remaking, remodeling, elevating, and polishing one's very *self* . . . and observing, studying, and doting on it." Describing what seemed to be a new American preoccupation with self-awareness, Wolfe pointed to an individual and inward turn. This was not his view alone. Social psychologist Louis Zurcher (1977) conceived what he considered to be the mutable self as a response to rapid social change and an increasing fear of uncertainty of the future. In a similar sociological vein, Ralph Turner (1976) examined the impulse of individuals to identify what seemed to be inner, more personal thoughts and actions. Granted as more "real" than actions that aligned with what one "should" do, personal decisions seemed to be an expression of an internalized "want."

This relates to an earlier discussion of Leslie, enacting a sense of personal freedom to formulate her own mathematics rather than following the predetermined rules given by the teacher. This form of creating understanding for oneself and directing one's own satisfaction served as a cultural standard ascribed to the child motivated to learn. Inscribed as a principle of identity in the curriculum, this notion of motivation aligned with more nuanced ways to identify the very traits associated with motivation. One such measurement tool, the California Psychological Inventory (Gough, 1969), assigned equivalencies to traits of sociability, self-acceptance, well-being, responsibility, and self-control as factors of children's mathematical success (Weiss, Haier, & Keating, 1974). As people identified with these psychological characteristics, all children could be seen to have equal opportunities to choose to be motivated and control their own excellence in math.

Excellence in Mathematics Education—for All?

If the math in schools started with the natural abilities, skills, and interests of children rather than with abstract mathematical ideas, then each and every child could be motivated to master basic math skills. In this reorganization of the curriculum, motivation and its psychological traits served as the norms by which to identify equal opportunities for success. While this psychology seems to have little to do with mathematics, the very notion of in/equality could not make sense without a way of thinking about how to establish equivalence by assigning identity to things so as to compare them.

In this chapter, I have explored how the logic of equality embedded in what seems to be a purely mathematical symbol is transmogrified into a cultural way of representing identity and difference. By examining the use of the equal sign as related to the production of basic math skills, I have aimed to highlight how a cultural reason of equality is inscribed in and through the use of the equal sign in the math curriculum to produce new ways of classifying difference.

As it intersected with psychological notions of self-control, -esteem, and -direction, the equal sign itself embodied cultural principles ordering who the child is and should be as a mode of making the child into a certain kind of self. I have referred to this as the *mathematical self* to highlight the ways in which children's sense of individuality was organized through the relation of the equal sign and cultural modes of reasoning about equality. In this way, the equal sign was much more than a symbol encompassing basic math skills. It inscribed standards by which to identify the child as a kind of person who could be motivated to learn and excel in math— while learning basic skills to survive in life!

Although situated in the context of the Back to Basics reforms, roughly spanning the decade of the 1970s in the United States, the implications historically extend beyond this moment. This can be seen in how the distinctions to which the equal sign relate to represent cultural differences have changed over time—from classifications of citizenship to individuality to personhood.

In the period of math reform mobilized after World War II, New Mathematics was organized so as to include all children at all levels in modern math. As the equal sign ordered mathematical ways of thinking about equality and equivalence, it also embodied rules for how to live a modern life—defined by cultural norms of citizenship. As the equal sign intersected with cognitive psychologies, children were identified as creative, innovative, and abstract thinkers. This representation of children provided a cultural mode of seeing them *all* as similar in their process of learning math. In this, children's "mathematical" thought was associated with rules for how to live as citizens of a modern nation.

As discussed in this chapter, during the Back to Basics reforms, the inscriptions of equivalence by which to represent children and their mathematics were disarticulated from norms of citizenship, instead expressing forms of individuality. The mode of establishing a cultural norm of *all* also changed with the Standards-Based movement that mobilized in the 1980s. *All children* were thought capable of learning mathematics because math was about problem solving—something all people could do. Yet the cultural rules of this problem-solving capability were embedded in the math problems, given as the Standard. Following similar ways of reasoning about identity, equivalence, and difference, the mathematical logic overlapped with cultural distinctions to classify children as people—valued by their abilities to think, speak, and act "mathematically."

The stated historical perspective provides a way of seeing how the shifting significations of equality that order notions of identity, equivalence, and difference are etched into the present. Motivation, in its varying expressions explored here, has become a commonsense way of reasoning about how to reach *all children*. As a rationale for success and failure, attributing motivation to a child's achievement in school math gives meaning to the statement "If only s/he were more motivated, s/he would do better in math." Not a natural distinction, this "problem" of motivation gets assigned to particular children and is expressed as traits of certain kinds of people. How the assignments are made is not a question about a child's interest, abilities, or skills as motivation to learn math. Instead, the question is how it has become possible to see each individual child as part of the *all*, or not.

Note

1. Johnny is the name used by Kline (1973). I take the use of his name to represent the emerging impulse to situate mathematics education within each child, as a distinct individual. Throughout, I use the names taken from the original source documents. Although seeming to represent a particular child, any of the names could be substituted in the narrative without changing the way in which "mathematical" individuality was determined in reference to cultural norms of identity and difference.

References

Bellah, R. N., Madsen, R., Sullivan, W. M., Swidler, A., & Tipton, S. M. (1985). *Habits of the heart: Individualism and commitment in American life.* Los Angeles: University of California Press.

Borstelmann, T. (2011). *The 1970s: A new global history from civil rights to economic inequality.* Princeton, NJ: Princeton University Press.

Brodinsky, B. (1977). Back to the basics: The movement and its meaning. *The Phi Delta Kappan, 58*(7), 522–527.

Cochran, B. S., Barson, A., & Davis, R. B. (1970). Child-created mathematics. *Arithmetic Teacher, 17*(3), 211–215.

Cruickshank, D. R., & Telfer, R. (1980). Classroom games and simulations. *Theory Into Practice, 19*(1), 75–80.

Danziger, K. (1997). *Naming the mind: How psychology found its language.* Thousand Oaks, CA: SAGE Publications.

Dreyfuss, J. (1973). Filops, hahas, zobos, gripes, zillies, and dingbats. *Arithmetic Teacher, 20*(6), 488–489.

Gardner Thompson, M. (1973). Hidden implications for change. *Arithmetic Teacher, 20*(5), 343–349.

Ginsburg, H. P. (1977). *Children's arithmetic: The learning process.* New York: Van Nostrand Reinhold, Inc.

Golden, S. R. (1970). Fostering enthusiasm through child-created games. *Arithmetic Teacher, 17*(2), 111–115.

Gosman, H. Y. (1973). Mastering the basic facts with dice. *Arithmetic Teacher, 20*(5), 330–331.

Gough, H. G. (1969). *Manual for the California psychological inventory.* Palo Alto, CA: Consulting Psychologists Press.

Hacking, I. (2002). Inaugural lecture: Chair of philosophy and history of scientific concepts at the College de France. *Economy and Society, 31*(1), 1–14.

Heyck, H. (2012). Producing reason. In M. Solovey & H. Cravens (Eds.), *Knowledge production, liberal democracy, and human nature (pp. 99–116).* New York: Palgrave Macmillan.

Hiebert, J., Carpenter, T. P., Fennema, E., Fuson, K., Wearne, D., Murray, H., Olivier, A., & Human, P. (1997). *Making sense: Teaching and learning mathematics with understanding.* Portsmouth, NH: Heinemann.

Inskeep, J. E. (1970). As we read: Editorial comment. *Arithmetic Teacher, 17*(3), 193–195.

Kilpatrick, J., & Wirszup, I. (Eds.). (1976). *The psychology of mathematical abilities in schoolchildren* by V. A. Krutetskii (J. Teller, Trans.). Chicago: University of Chicago Press.

Kline, M. (1973). *Why Johnny can't add: The failure of new math.* New York: St. Martin's Press.

Nicholls, J. G. (1979). Quality and equality in intellectual development: The role of motivation in education. *American Psychologist, 34*(11), 1071–1084.

Popkewitz, T. (2004). The alchemy of the mathematics curriculum: Inscriptions and the fabrication of the child. *American Educational Journal, 41*(4), 3–34.

Price Troutman, A. (1973). Strategies for teaching elementary school mathematics. *Arithmetic Teacher, 20*(6), 425–436.

Stanley, J. C., Keating, D. P., & Fox, L. H. (Eds.). (1974). *Mathematical talent: Discovery, description, and development.* Baltimore, MD: Johns Hopkins University Press.

Thomson, I. T. (1992). Individualism and conformity in the 1950s vs. the 1980s. *Sociological Forum, (7)*3, 497–516.

Turner, R. (1976). The real self: From institution to impulse. *American Journal of Sociology 81,* 989–1016.

Weiss, D., Haier, R. J., & Keating, D. P. (1974). Personality characteristics of mathematically precocious boys. In J. C. Stanley, D. P. Keating, & L. H. Fox (Eds.), *Mathematical talent: Discovery, description, and development* (pp. 126–139). Baltimore, MD: Johns Hopkins University Press.

Wolfe, T. (1976). The "me" decade and the third great awakening. *New York Magazine, 1*(4), 27–48.

Yankelovich, D. (1998). How American individualism is evolving. *The Public Perspective, 2,* 3–6.

Zurcher, L. A. (1977). *The mutable self: A self-concept for social change.* Beverly Hills, CA: Sage Publications.

13

THE SOCIAL QUESTION REVISITED

The Configuration of the Social Dimension in the European Education Space

Kenneth Petersson, Ulf Olsson, and John B. Krejsler

The focus of this study is the reinstallation of the social question as a historical practice—or, in other words, the discursive reproblematization of social groups as dangerous and potential threats to societal hopes for the future. The purpose is to investigate how the historic figure of the social question returns and is applied in contemporary political discourses, more precisely in the context of education, education policy, and our main focus, teacher education. To highlight this, we use a genealogical method inspired by Michel Foucault, exploring the system of reason that ordered political discourses and policies in the early 19th century and at the turn of the 21st century (Foucault,1991). We are problematizing and mirroring the fabrication of the social question in two different historical discourses that both deal with social integration: the discourse of philanthropy and the contemporary discourse of the European Higher Education Area (EHEA). The question we examine is in what way, and under what circumstances, the relationship between included and excluded subjects and society is reproduced and operates from one period to another.

In the 19th century, the social question was raised within the context of the industrialization of society. It dealt with the fear and suggestion of the disintegration of predominant social structures and problems resulting from social and political unrest, poverty, and lack of morality, perceived as threats to the social order ordained by God (Popkewitz, 2008). The social question, the fear of social groups constructed as in need of special care, is far from being lifeless compared with the past. Quite the reverse; it is still alive but today invested with new thoughts and material. In the frame of higher education, including teacher education, the social question appears in terms of social groups and individuals that don't live their lives as lifelong learners, entrepreneurs, or problem solvers and thus are considered threats to the contemporary vision of a lifelong learning knowledge society.

In this chapter, we explore the differences and similarities between contemporary European discourses about higher education and the early 19th century's discourse about philanthropy as the link among governance, knowledge, and political reason. In both discourses, the social question operates in contexts of fears and hopes for the future, and education becomes the key solution for integrating the dangerous groups in the political visions for the future (cf. Olsson, Petersson, & Krejsler, 2014). But of course, the future, the hopes, the fears, and the educational solutions are constructed very differently. We start with a discussion about the contemporary fabrication of the social question followed by another about the philanthropic one. We examine the historical narrative of philanthropy produced by some influential philanthropists from the 19th century. Finally we present a deeper concluding analysis comparing the two versions. The contemporary documents selected are white papers, scripts, and memos from the EU Commission concerning political arenas such as education policies, the Bologna process, and lifelong learning and their relation to the Nordic countries.

When reading this text, one thing is important to have in mind, namely that the teacher education in the Nordic countries is included in the higher education system and thus belongs to EHEA. On a policy level, this means that what counts for higher education also counts for teacher education.

The Problematic of Foucault and (Re)configurations of the Subject

In the past, the configuration of subjects took place within a national context. Today the context is global and supranational. In our analysis, we connect with Foucault's concept of governmentality, as this kind of analysis has the advantages that it does not require us to define political spaces like Europe and subjects like the individual in advance (Foucault, 1994; Larner & Walters, 2004). Instead, it becomes possible to scrutinize how these concepts and other floating signifiers acquire meaning within particular regimes of discourse and practice. Governmentality studies pay particular attention to the relationships among governance, knowledge, and political reason, in relation to questions such as how to govern those who are expected to govern themselves and how much to govern. The analytical potential of governmentality analysis shows itself in its potential to bring together and unify studies of governance of self with governance of other entities such as the state, the nation, the local, and the supranational. Notwithstanding this boundless openness to different types of governing processes, the majority of studies have focused mainly on political, social, and economic processes within the political spaces of nation states. In other words, these studies have concerned themselves principally with a kind of bio-political project that Foucault calls the governmentalization of the state (Foucault, 1994). In this study, however, attention is directed toward governance that goes beyond states: supranational and global contexts and processes. Since our attention is mainly concerned with so-called

European integration, we principally deal with what is called the governmentalization of Europe, that is, those processes of bio-political governance that target the population within the European Union as a political space (cf. Olsson, Petersson, & Krejsler, 2014).

Genealogically, our study deals with the question: What are the contemporary subjects in terms of history? The genealogical approach is to be understood as an attempt to problematize notions that are often taken for granted in the formulation and solution of contemporary problems.

The European Higher Education Area as a Technology of Inclusiveness

According to the European University Association (EUA), contemporary Europe's future as a dynamic competitive global region is threatened by global competitors investing heavily in universities (EUA, 2011). Thus, when stressing the necessity for increased investment in higher education, the Association is reproducing the hope and fear for the future that is operating in the European Commission's (COM) document *EUROPE 2020: A Strategy for Smart, Sustainable and Inclusive Growth*.

> Either we face up collectively to the immediate challenge of the recovery and to long-term challenges—globalisation, pressure on resources, ageing—so as to make up for the recent losses, regain competitiveness, boost productivity and put the EU on an upward path of prosperity ("sustainable recovery"). Or we continue at a slow and largely uncoordinated pace of reforms, and we risk ending up with a permanent loss in wealth, a sluggish growth rate ("sluggish recovery") possibly leading to high levels of unemployment and social distress, and a relative decline on the world scene ("lost decade").
>
> *(COM, 2010, pp. 6–7)*

According to the document, Europe is now facing clear threats and challenging choices. The threat is that of a sluggish recovery caused by member states only caring for themselves, and the hope is a sustainable recovery as a result of member states meeting the threats collectively. If the community and the spirit of European integration are strengthened, Europe can become a union with smart, sustainable, and inclusive growth and with high levels of employment and social cohesion. However, if the union does not act collectively as a community but acts uncoordinatedly, the union is at risk of being left behind as a result of permanent loss in wealth and potentials for future growth (COM, 2010).

In this narrative about contemporary Europe, the lifelong learner provides the technology to inscribe the hope of the future and the engendered fears of those populations dangerous to its making. The collective and overarching strategy of lifelong learning, including the EHEA, operates as a technology of hope for the future (LLP, 2011; Prague Communiqué, 2001). The contemporary way of reasoning in terms of lifelong learning is not something new but rather a reproduction of historical thoughts. But it is not a simple process of reproduction. In contemporary political texts and documents from the European Union, education is not restricted to the notion of school teaching or to the classroom in a physical sense. The citizen has to be engaged, in historically and discursively different ways, in an endless process of learning and skilling, lifewide as well as lifelong (Fejes & Nicoll, 2008). Furthermore, higher education, including teacher education, considered as a crucial part of the lifelong learning project, is constructed as a key player for Europe's future and successful transition to a smart, sustainable, and inclusive knowledge-based economy and society. According to the narrative, higher education delivers exactly what Europe needs, namely "Smart People for Smart Growth" (EUA, 2011). In the context of EHEA, "Improving the quality of teacher education" is considered "an important goal for Europe's education systems if quicker progress is to be made" (COM, 2007, p. 1). Teacher education becomes a central issue for policy making in securing the European Union's leading position among future knowledge-based societies in globalization.

In this sense, the EHEA operates as a technology of hope in the European dreams of a successful, sustainable, and inclusive knowledge-based economy. However, the EHEA also operates as a technology of fears, not only for what is considered external global threats but also for internal threats in the contemporary social question. Since the lifelong learner is embedded in the knowledge society as the hope for the future, the opposite is constructed as an internal fear, namely the non–lifelong learner, fabricated as a threat to the vision of future.

Fabricating Contemporary Social Questions in the Space of Europe of Knowledge

One may consider, historically, the social question as a way of constructing political fear and hope in the name of individuals, groups, and societies in need of special care. In this perspective, our concern is the understanding of how the social question is reconfigured in the contemporary space of EHEA and teacher education.

Usually we refer the notion of the social question to the 19th century and the political administration of poverty and pauperism and the hope and fear of the population as its target, something we will return to later on. Contemporary European production and formation of matters in terms of social question/social dimension is no longer confined to particular groups of "others" but encompasses the whole population as its target, but now guided by principles and strategies of lifelong learning (COM, 2011; LLP, 2011). The Prague Communiqué, for example, claims that "lifelong learning strategies are necessary" to face the community challenges of the future, and in one of the latest strategy documents, it is said that lifelong learning needs to be a priority in an ever-changing world. "However, in a rapidly changing world, lifelong learning needs to be a priority—it is the key to employment, economic success and allowing people to participate fully in society" (COM, 2011).

The subject, the European citizen, included in the vision of the European Union is coded as a lifelong learner employable and fully participating in the community. However, the hope of inclusiveness that operates in terms of the necessity to become a lifelong learner simultaneously produces principles about its opposite, namely the excluded subjects, non–lifelong learners who don't participate fully in the community and are at risk of unemployment. Embedded in the lifelong learner is the threat to the vision of a sustainable and inclusive future. What one sees operating here are processes of abjection that are excluding particular subjects from the space of inclusion in the very talk of subjects recognized as included (cf. Popkewitz, 2008).

The shift of the social question of the 19th century to contemporary knowledge society moves from the governing of certain social groups, the poor, to a double strategy of governing all in the name of lifelong learning as well as certain groups in terms of the social dimension. The shift also shows itself in that the administration of dangerousness is not governed by the prescriptions of an existing religious order but through the construction of a knowledge society. It is a transformation from the religious way of saving the soul during the 19th century to salvation projects during the 20th and 21st centuries that assemble the soul in a different way through the sociology of teaching and cognitive and learning psychologies (cf. Olsson, Petersson, & Krejsler, 2014; Popkewitz, 2008).

In the context of the social dimension, certain individuals, groups, and categories are fabricated as being in need of specific care to be able to be included in the knowledge society. They are, for instance, students from poor study traditions and with lower socio-economic backgrounds and ethnic groups and individuals not motivated for lifelong learning (London Communiqué, 2007). This fabrication of groups in need of special care is reproduced in the Nordic member states' teacher educations as they are developing strategies and action plans for management of the social dimension (SOU, 2008, p. 109; St. Meld. 11, 2008).

Considering teacher education, even the students of teacher training and teacher educators are fabricated as groups in need of special measurements. In a somewhat similar way to the philanthropic welfare assistant becoming an exemplary operator in putting poor people's lives in order during the 19th century, the contemporary teacher becomes a welfare assistant who is problematized as the most significant subject of lifelong learning, since teachers are supposed to have a "crucial role in supporting the learning experience of young people and adult learners" (COM, 2007, p. 3). The teacher becomes a prototype for children and young people when it comes to investing lifelong and lifewide learning. What's being put in focus is not so much learning in terms of subjects or of cultural heritage but rather how to prepare for sudden changes of society, preparation for a condition that forces us to believe that nothing is the same from one time to another, to be prepared to redress from one change to another in a rapid way and prepare for new lifestyles.

Inscribed in the political thought of improvement, Nordic teacher education during the last decades has been witnessing several evaluation systems and accreditation regimes as an expression of the governing agenda. In Norway, for example, there is a recurrent fear that the population has a lack of competence and knowledge-based experience (St. Meld. 11, 2008). The dropout of youngsters from school reminds the politicians that something has to be done. This in turn puts the system in a situation in which questions embedded into the social dimension are reproduced: Who is dropping out? What's the reason? What's the background? What is the condition of the pupils dropping out? What actions and solutions have to be found? A big part of this problematization can be seen as reminiscences of the past, as teacher education has been and still is one of the most politically debated and criticized phenomena in what we call the welfare society. In this context, there is also a unanimous fear of a weak point when it comes to the provision of the competence of the teacher. For example, the last Norwegian and Swedish reports on teacher education are permeated with anxiety about insufficient skills and qualifications among teachers and students applying for teacher education. In the Norwegian report, it is emphasized that a good teacher has to "develop professionally as well as personally throughout his/her whole working life" (St. Meld. 11, 2008, p. 31). It is emphasized that the whole school system has to be a learning society, which means that there will be the expectation of the teacher to be more entrepreneurial, more of a problem solver, more proactive, and more social and have more multicultural understanding and so forth. Once again, a "better teacher" and a teacher of tomorrow are operating as visions for the future.

The political rationalities and assumptions of ends and goals in the kind of policies that are illustrated here will produce expectations of, for example, a specific kind of society or community, of citizens, teachers, and pupils and so forth, with specific descriptions, behaviors, and attributes, all of which have to be achieved and included as a technology of the hope for the future. However, this hope is just one side of the governmental coin; the other is the fear of the future that operates side by side with the hope. This fear not only involves various social dimensions, groups, and individuals in need of special care, it also includes students of teacher training and teachers; for instance, teachers who are considered to be non-eager lifelong learners, that is, not work hard enough to become better teachers in terms of, for instance, active and problem-solving entrepreneurs. In the context of EHEA and the teacher education programs of the Nordic countries, teachers are constructed as threats to the utopian dreams of the future.

Today the social question is not governed by religion or by God, as was the case during the age of philanthropy, but through never-ending supranational measurements, comparisons, and classifications—that is, another kind of religion governed by numbers and ranking procedures. But above all, the supranational stocktaking regime is a producer of particular political technologies that enable measurement and comparison through the fabrications of indicators, benchmarking, account-ability, standards, guidelines, outcomes, reports, and so forth (Rauhvargers, Deane, & Pauwels, 2009). The reasoning of comparability as political technology in the case of education and lifelong learning leads to member states, without force, being measured and compared to each other in terms of how far each member state attains the object of common European goals.

This also means, as Thomas Popkewitz has stressed, that ". . . benchmarks and comparison do more than measure productivity" (Popkewitz, 2013, p. 451). The contemporary reason of education tells something about all of us and at the same time about the difference. Popkewitz exemplifies:

> The standards of the human kind who knows the future (or the future skills of science and mathematics) entail a double gesture of inscriptions of dif-ference. [. . .] The classifications and measurements are part of a grid that moves between psychological and social characteristics that place the disad-vantaged, urban and immigrant youth in in-between spaces to be included and, at the same time, abjected.
>
> *(Popkewitz, 2013, p. 451)*

In connection to this politics of making up educable people, there will be social categories included, but to be included, they first of all have been excluded and become target groups for normalizing measurements. In this way, measurement and comparability are arts of governance.

In this context, certain social groups, in terms of social dimension, are fabricated as threats in relation to the hope for the future, and education is constructed as a crucial technology for successful inclusion of these social groups. However, this is not something new. Despite different conditions in terms of historical periods and societies, educational politics have always been about varying constructions of poli-tics of future, hope/fear, and exclusion/inclusion. To come to a further understand-ing of what is in progress today, we are, as we have mentioned previously, going to be deepening the philanthropic discourse from the early 19th century.

The Genealogy of the Social Dimension

The characteristic of the early 19th century was the rise of the industrial and urban society combined with the social fear of breaking up hierarchical social structures.

> [A] horrible figure is marching through the most educated part of the world, Europe, which poisons with its dreadful presence, attacking all social classes [. . .] It is called pauperism, poverty, destitution, misery and so forth. It rather often paves the way to the path of crime and disgrace.
>
> *(Ellmin, 1847, p. 56)*

This kind of worry was a common thread in the organization of both the Swedish and the European caretaking of the poor. Ultimately, the fear was of a societal development that threatens the social order ordained by God. In these contexts, ideas of how to solve the so-called social question were raised. How should problems of pauperism, political unrest, lack of morality, and criminality be managed? Aside from these, the question of how to educate the poor away from indigence and bad manners was also raised.

As we have seen, a similar kind of worry is present when it comes to questions of education in the contemporary European education space. The difference, however, is that the administration of dangerousness, about fear and hopes and about the future, is not governed by the prescriptions of God and the existing religious order but through the construction of a social dimension that targets groups and individuals that don't live their lives as lifelong and lifewide learners, entrepreneurs, problem solvers, and so forth.

One of the most influential institutions that administered and managed the social crusade toward a hope of future during the early 19th century was the European Christian project of philanthropy. It worked as a technique or politics of hope to overcome what was imagined as a fear in the present and what was thought of as becoming a threat in the future. Within this framework, there was no necessity to draw up plans for the future, as this had already been done by Providence. Life was already put in order, and the responsibility for the creation of local contexts that would develop individuals' moral dispositions and willingness to adhere to the future plan did not rest with the common man but with society's financial, cultural, and moral elites. According to this narrative, the way to freedom for the poor was to accept this fabrication of the future and their position in the society ordained by God. Thus, in the narrative of the early 19th century, to be free was to obey.

According to the European philanthropists, it was a moral obligation of the enlightened and wealthy social classes to lead and supervise the manner of living and the morality of the less well-favored classes. If they didn't want to do that for the sake of the poor, they had to understand that it was important to do so out of pure self-preservation. The philanthropists conjured up horror scenarios of what would otherwise happen if the masses went on to revolutionary means. The Swedish philanthropist, officer, entrepreneur, and publicist Carl af Forsell was warning the favored classes, "the power is on the side of the many," and as there are "those who diligently work on the perception of the masses," there's a great risk that the masses "will move to action" (Forsell, 1831, p. 173). In this situation, the responsibility to prevent the existing order is not of the government alone, "but each enlightened and concerned man must, according to his or her ability, participate" (Forsell, 1831, p. 173). To manage these threats to the God-ordained order, not only charity but also education became crucial technologies of hope of the future.

> It is necessary to the good order of society that the poorer classes should learn to behold the more prosperous conditions without a feeling of bitterness, and to respect the distance which Providence has established between the different ranks in society.
>
> *(Gérando, 1832, pp. 96–97)*

Education could contribute to the Providence-ordained "natural" and pastoral world order, an order in which the wealthy belonged in the highest order of rank and the poor and less wealthy in the lowest. Not only children but also adults were obliged to learn. The schooling of adults could take place in Sunday schools or evening schools, where they were given the opportunity to study after work. The importance of building some kind of public libraries was also included as a tool in the philanthropic mission for adult learning.

In one sense, lifelong learning is not a new phenomenon; it has more or less existed as long as life itself. Compared to yesteryear, there are contemporary homologous trends in terms of the demands that are made upon the contemporary European people to be included in a knowledge-based, lifelong-learning society. The shift of the social question of pauperism to the social question of the organization of a knowledge society moves from the governing of the poor but god-fearing citizen to the lifelong and lifewide learner. The moral obligation of the enlightened and wealthier social classes, in the context of the philanthropy of the 19th century, to lead and supervise the manner of living and morality among the poor is today put into secularized and culturalized moral obligations in terms of the lifelong learner and his or her significant expertise.

The achievement that was so characteristic for the philanthropic project, established on all sides of Europe, was the endeavor to manage the social question through multiple actors. As Dave Jones has declared, "philanthropic evangelists, the established church, utopian socialists, and utilitarian radicals expressed from different perspectives a concern about the moral and intellectual condition of the urban poor" (Jones, 1990, pp. 57–58). From different perspectives, they agreed on that cheap education could be a solution to the social question and thus "introduced a pedagogical machinery to normalize the poor" (ibid.). A similar kind of discursive networking is put at stake in the contemporary European education complex. The EU is considered "the network of the networks" in terms of stakeholders as public authorities, higher education institutions, students, staffs, employers, quality assurance agencies, international organizations, and European institutions (EUA, 2010).

From the early 19th century, education became an active tool in a regime that would manage the social question, and education became an important technology, since there was a firm conviction that Europe was "the most educated part in the world" (Ellmin, 1847, p. 56). In terms of moral education, there was a wish that the poor would improve their circumstances, but not at the expense of groups in the higher social strata. A strengthening of morals in terms of diligence, order, and piety became the key concepts contributing to achieving this end. Increased knowledge would result in increased prosperity and increased human freedom, but also in diminishing conflicts in society. If it became clear to the lower classes that each and every one, according to the divine order, had their given place and task, that society was based on the idea that all work for their own good and thereby also for the common good, there would no longer be any reason for envy and pride. The innate, natural, and necessary sense of community/fellowship must therefore be reinstated within the framework of the societal changes of the time. Thus, the narrative of philanthropy is also operating within processes of sustainability and inclusion, not in terms of economy and changing of the existing order but in terms of religion and preservation of the existing order. The fear of the European society during the early 19th century was a fear of a population losing its religious orientation and becoming lost in a predestined social order. The fear of the contemporary European context is the fear of being left behind in the global race for the most eminent and sustainable knowledge society.

The Technology of Providence on Earth

One of philanthropy's methods, advocated by the French statesman, philosopher, and philanthropist Joseph-Marie, baron de Gérando, was "volunteer outreach" to the poor. His writing on welfare assistants came to influence the way in which the care of the European poor in the 19th and early 20th century was developed. The work was translated into a number of different languages. Thus, you can consider philanthropy a historical example of fabrication of a European project in terms of a social order ordained by God. Of those belonging to the wealthier groups, it was expected "that each and every one" make contact with the poor families with a view to "visit them in their homes, get to know about their living conditions" (Gérando, 1832, p. 1). The goal was to create possibilities to save human souls that have lost their orientation because of the changes brought about by the industrialized society. The method for solving these problems was to understand the lifestyles and moral ideas of the poor and thereby the preconditions for poverty and moral breakdown. "Penetrate the secret of that afflicted heart. By giving inward peace, you will do more than by appeasing hunger. By restoring moral energy, you will give the courage to perform useful labour, and better to support privation and suffering" (Gérando, 1832, p. 42).

In order to make this possible, Gérando developed an investigative method, a system of classification, and a pedagogic method with the purpose of dividing the poor into separate groups to enable the welfare assistant to decide who deserved financial aid. Who was in need of support and who was not? Whose poverty was self-caused and whose was caused by accident? Who could take responsibility and was capable of self-help? Individuals whose poverty was self-caused and who were deemed irresponsible or weren't capable of self-help were excluded from assistance.

Gérando was not in favor of the general handouts that were common practice. Handouts did not even touch the problems that the new investigation into poverty aimed at solving. On the surface, Gérando's project was concerned with financial support. At a deeper level, it was about finding a knowledge-based method for conflict resolution and the formation of a moral order of community/fellowship between the social strata and classes. For Gérando, help was synonymous with moral teaching and influence. Gérando's aspiration was to replace earlier emotionally motivated and unconsidered acts of charity with more considered, evidence-based, and forward-looking social arrangements. Armed with this insight, the welfare assistant was presumed able to help the recipients to gain insight about their moral qualities and become able to govern themselves. The poor must acknowledge their true nature, confess their sins, and face their blameworthy way of life. It is thus the "innermost recesses" that are the principal objects of influence and thereby the uppermost targets for policy on poverty. It is not material deprivation that is the primary focus but the deprivation of the soul. "Therefore, a cure of the sickness of the soul would also become 'a cure against need'" (Gérando, 1832, p. 49).

The linchpin of his pedagogic mission was to teach the poor about the unthinkable in imagining a different social order than the one prevailing. In a contemporary European context, the educational mission is, however, to create technologies that empower and promote the excluded to be included in one single thinkable world, that of the learning society.

The point of Gérando's teaching was to get the poor to learn the principle of the by-Providence-already-created plan. According to Gérando, the idea of "love to humanity" was to unify all classes in society into one harmonious community/fellowship. The societal group that lived in affluence and the group that lived in poverty were drawn to one another according to the plan of Providence and "the holy principle of humanity" (Gérando, 1832, pp. 2–3). The differences between the groups were thus no cause for complaint; they were, so to speak, part of the plan ordained by God. In other words, guided by a higher moral order, the work of outreach was to further the sense of fellowship and community among different groups in the local community and build self-regulating networks. However, to be able to support the poor in a proper way, the welfare assistants had to work with and educate themselves to become better assistants not only for the sake of the poor or themselves but, in a deeper sense, to become better assistants to Providence on earth: "To be able to do this one have, of necessity, to control the conduct of one's own, and by this means much has already been won" (Gérando, 1832, pp. 2–3).

In Gérando's project, there is a search for or construction of "the good welfare assistant" homological to the search or construction for "the good teacher" permeating society's educational projects from the first part of the 19th century and onward. The welfare assistants as well as the teachers are expected to constantly become better teachers and better welfare assistants (Gérando, 1832).

A short historical retrospective of teacher education indicates a genealogical conversion of what could be thought of as moral technologies. The genealogical character of the teacher has always been surrounded by suspicion and is for that reason in great demand for reconsideration and examination. The teacher is historically considered, according to Jones,

> a suspicious figure that requires continual examination within an examining technology—the school—which attempts to establish a disciplinary utopia based on a felicific calculus. Subsequently, the teacher through a process of self-examination is transformed into a moral exemplar to project an ethical verity into the unknown of the Victorian city.
>
> *(Jones, 1990, pp. 56–57)*

In a genealogical sense, the fabrication of technologies in the philanthropic world, with the aspiration to gather different social groups into one harmonious community, has today a homological trend on a supranational level. At present, the governing principle is not "humanity" but rather "learning outcomes" in a world that at the same time is concerned with winning a position in the global race and constructing a political spirit of European community. But what put the two social questions together are the fear and the hope of the future in different ways.

Concluding Words

In spite of the obvious differences between contemporary European discourse about higher education and the early 19th century's discourse about philanthropy, there are also obvious similarities in their way of putting the relationships among governance, knowledge, and political reason at stake. Scrutinizing these similarities and differences, we can also understand that there are differences within similarities: for instance, a concept of the future operates in both discourses, even though the futures that are constructed are very different. There are also similarities within differences: for instance, constructions of concepts of democracy operated as a threat in the early 19th century, while a construction of democracy in contemporary discourse operates as a technology of hope. However, in both narratives, both concepts operate as political technologies.

The focus has been on the conditions through which the relationship between included and excluded subjects and society is reproduced and fabricated in different periods. In contemporary European narrative, historical figures of thoughts—for instance, the problematization of groups of citizens as being in need of special measures, as they are considered threats against the vision for sustainable and inclusive futures—are revisited in a new context. The dangerous individuals and groups excluded for inclusion in the narrative of philanthropy were the poor, in particular those who didn't accept their position in the social order ordained by God and who didn't take responsibility for their own situation or weren't capable of self-help. In contemporary European educational discourse, the dangerous groups are constructed in terms of the social dimension and in terms of individuals that don't live their lives as lifelong learners, entrepreneurs, problem solvers, and so forth. Today there is less emphasis on poverty or pauperism but more on exclusion/inclusion, which is a wider concept than poverty and opens up for wider interpretations.

Both the included and the excluded subjects of the two discourses are inscribed into very different constructions of the concepts of future, sustainability, and inclusion. According to the narratives of the 19th century, the future was already predetermined by Providence and is finally stationed in heaven. The only hope of the future becoming truth was a preservation of existing social order, which is making the order ordained by Providence sustainable through inclusion of the groups fabricated as threats. Contemporary thinking on governance in the name of future is on the contrary, not stressing preservation of existing social order but rather challenges, uncertainty, and plurality. The social order is anything but nature given and must constantly be recreated in a continually changeable world. The future in today's narratives is not planned and is not plannable. Rather, the future is determined by situations and constructed by responsible subjects in a continually ongoing process. In contemporary European narrative, sustainability and inclusiveness are to be found not in preservation of an existing religious order but through cooperation toward common economic goals in a constantly changing world. This means that we today exchange philanthropy's "nature-given" sense of community and inclusiveness for a culturalized version—that is, we launch ourselves as culturalized beings, lifelong learners, active, cooperatively creative, and responsible. Integration is therefore thought of differently today than in the early 19th century. However, in contemporary narrative, the spirit of European integration is operating as a technology of inclusion homologous to the operation of the spirit of God in the narrative of the philanthropy. But what are being emphasized in contemporary narrative are not only similarities but also diversity, variability, and instability. It has to do with developing a plurality within the framework of community, about unifying the norms of community with ever-increasing individual variations. It also attempts to unify the prevailing with what is new in a new combination through the liberation and increase of plurality and simultaneously regulate this plurality and variation in a perspective of community and fellowship.

Another genealogical observation is that education, including lifelong learning, is reconfigured as a technology of hope for the future in both discourses. In both discourses, it relates to a mode of governance based on influencing the dispositions of the subjects and tying together the wills and interests of the citizen subjects with the interests of society. Notwithstanding historical preconditions, it concerns moral projects with the purpose of governing human dispositions, wills, and behaviors in both a certain predetermined direction as well as in a more or less non–predetermined one. In this context, systems of education, in our case, teacher education and lifelong learning, can be considered bearers of the hopes and fears for the future held by states and supranational organizations. If the fear during the early 19th century was of the consequences of a degenerated population losing its religious orientation, the fear today is of "losing the game" in the economic competition in a global arena. Teacher education, in this context, becomes an arena for the formation of teacher subjects and, in a wider sense, the citizen identities that are considered a precondition for the safeguarding of the European Union's identity as well as the future of its nations.

The political thoughts about change and future orientation are inscribed in teacher education and in the becoming teacher herself. The other side of the coin is the fear for teachers and students of teacher training that are considered not matching these expectations and thus are excluded. In this way, teacher education is embedded in the genealogy of the social question and the teacher and students of teacher training become objectives for political problematization and solutions. The fear today is how to create qualified teachers and other educable subjects that fulfill the demands of a knowledge society. The fear is linked to the question of how to recreate a teacher and other subjects as fully fledged lifelong learners and a teacher that is good enough to be an educational designer and how to educate the population for democratic responsibility. In a similar way, the welfare assistant as well as the teacher were linked during the 19th century to a fear of failing to live up to the demand of teaching the poor to accept the God-given social order. The welfare assistants and the teachers are both expected to constantly become better through different kinds of improvement measures that can be thought of as moral technologies operating in a space in which human bodies are organized in terms of the future.

References

COM. (2007). *Common European principles for teacher competences and qualifications.* Brussels: European Commission: Directorate-General for Education and Culture. http://docs. china-europa-forum.net/doc_48.pdf

COM. (2010). *Europe 2020. A strategy for smart, sustainable and inclusive growth.* Brussels: European Commission: Communication from the commission. www.elgpn.eu/ elgpndb/fileserver/files/39 (Accessed June 9, 2014).

Ellmin, J. (1847). *Om folkets bildning och bildningscirkeln i Stockholm första år* (About citizen education and study circle in Stockholm). Stockholm: Förlaget Frilansen.

EUA. (2010). *Budapest-Vienna declaration on the European higher education area.* Brussels: European University Association. www.ehea.info/Uploads/news/Budapest-Vienna_ Declaration.pdf

EUA. (2011). *Smart people for smart growth. Statement by the European University Association on the EU Flagship Initiative "Innovation Union" of the Europe 2020 European. Strategy for smart, sustainable, and inclusive growth.* Brussels: European University Association.

Fejes, A., & Nicoll, K. (2008). *Foucault and lifelong learning. Governing the subject.* London: Routledge.

Forsell, af C. (1831). *Underrättelser om de i America nyligen stiftade måttlighetsföreningar, jemte förslag till dylika I Sverige* (Advisement for people recently legislated in the American constitutions of the association of proposal, drawn upon a nomination list of the same of Swedish people). Stockholm.

Foucault, M. (1991). Governmentality. In G. Burchell, C. Gordon, & P. Miller (Eds.), *The Foucault effect: Studies in governmentality* (pp. 87–104). Chicago: University of Chicago Press.

Gérando, J. M. de (1832). *The visitor of the poor.* Boston: Hilliard, Gray, Little and Wilkins.

Jones, D. (1990). The genealogy of the urban schoolteacher. In S. Ball (Ed.), *Foucault and education. Disciplines and knowledge.* London, New York: Routledge.

Larner, W., & Walters, W. (2004). Introduction: Global governmentality. In W. Larner & W. Walters (Eds.), *Global governmentality. Governing international spaces* (pp. 1–20). London: Routledge.

LLP. (2011). *Lifelong learning programme, Guide 2012.* Brussels: European Commission: Directorate-General for Education and Culture.

London Communiqué. (2007). *Towards the European higher education area: Responding to challenges in a globalized world.* www.ond.vlaanderen.be/hogeronderwijs/bologna/docu ments/MDC/London_Communique18May2007.pdf (Accessed Jan 10, 2011).

Olsson, U., Petersson, K., & Krejsler, J. B. (2014). On community as a governmental technology. The example of teacher education. In M. Pereyra & B. Franklin (Eds.), *System of reason and the politics of schooling. School reform and science of education in the tradition of Thomas S. Popkewitz.* London: Routledge.

Popkewitz, T. S. (2008). *Cosmopolitanism and the age of school reform. Science, education, and making society by making the child.* New York, London: Routledge.

Popkewitz, T. S. (2013). The sociology of education as the history of the present: Fabrication, difference, and abjection. *Discourse. Studies in the Cultural Politics of Education, 34*(3), 439–456.

Prague Communiqué. (2001) *Towards the European higher education area. Communiqué of the meeting of European ministers in charge of higher education in Prague on May 19, 2001.* www.ehea.info/Uploads/Declarations/PRAGUE_COMMUNIQUE.pdf (Accessed June 9, 2014).

Rauhvargers, A., Deane, C. & Pauwels, W. (2009). *Stocktaking report.* www.ond.vlaan deren.be/hogeronderwijs/bologna/conference/documents/Stocktaking_report_2009_ FINAL.pdf

SOU. (2008). 109. *En hållbar lärarutbildning* (Governmental report: A Sustainable Teacher Education). Stockholm: Utbildningsdepartementet.

St. Meld. Nr 11 (2008). *Læreren. Rollen og utdanningen* (Governmental report: The Teacher. The role and the teacher education). Oslo: Det Konglige Kunskapsdepartement.

14

FICTIONS OF THE TRANSCENDENT AND THE MAKING OF VALUE IN MUSIC EDUCATION IN THE UNITED STATES

Ruth I. Gustafson

> Music has always sent out lines of flight . . . "transformational multiplicities" overturning the very codes that structure [it]. Musical form, right down to its ruptures and proliferations, is comparable to a weed, a rhizome. . . . A rhizome is made of plateaus designating something special: a continuous self-vibrating region of intensities. . . .We call a [rhizome structure] any multiplicity connected to other multiplicities by superficial underground stems.
>
> *(Deleuze & Guattari, 1987, pp. 11, 12, 22)*

This chapter is about public music instruction in the United States. It extends the thesis of this book by outlining how notions of reason and progress penetrated and misrepresented the curriculum history of music education. In prevailing narratives, music educators have, by and large, framed this school subject as evolution from its "origin" in Northern European pedagogy to universal ideals of liberty, aesthetics, and reason in the child. Here I argue that the fabrication of an evolutionary narrative obscures its operations as a social discipline that differentiates worthiness and abjection. The discussion highlights the way in which new configurations of merit emerge not only in concert with the inscriptions of music pedagogy but also in contradiction to formal, pedagogical ideals. In effect, school music, linked to the technologies of the self, has a double action in various historical periods. By bringing this dual capacity, seemingly an incompatible process, to the fore, I attempt to demonstrate the complex relation of musical practices to changes in social anxieties and the political economy of the United States. Throughout the discussion, racial anxieties are treated as an omnipresent register of school music. Notions of Blackness and Whiteness complement each other to fabricate differences in musical dispositions. A similar thematic redundancy occurs in the use of the term "Western" to contrast with the generic category of multicultural music.

Neither is historically exclusive of the other, yet they operate to separate the classical canon from the discourse of world music practices. The chapter is in four parts, corresponding to four large epistemological breaks in the constitution of music and reason.

Part I: Historical Shifts in the Definition of Music and the Production of Social Types in Music Pedagogy

Historically, the fabrications of race in the music curriculum are responsive to the pressure of new social concerns and technologies. Two metaphors capture the complex rapport between music and the ranking of human types. The first metaphor depicts curriculum construction as an alchemic process. Like the medieval practice of turning base metal into gold, the mixture of pedagogy and social anxieties in the school subject of music produces comparative standards of enlightenment, moral character, aesthetic taste, and reason (Popkewitz & Gustafson, 2002). For example, in the early 19th century, Horace Mann argued for including music instruction in public education. His main theme was a concern for public health in which lung exercise would combat tuberculosis. This amalgam of disease, wellness, and singing appears to make school singing emerge from the base metal of an ordinary pastime into a "golden" remedy. The lyrics of songs, however, also divided schoolchildren into those who would contaminate society and those who would build the new nation (Gustafson, 2009).

The second metaphor, the rhizome, depicts unexpected offshoots from the curricular alchemy. Following Deleuze and Guattari, the branches of the rhizome or "lines of flight" broaden the historical lens beyond the alchemic formation in that the very standards of personhood (abject versus worthy) also produce new combinations of meaning: "For good and bad . . . [the rhizome can] re-stratify everything . . . and reconstitute a subject . . . Good and bad are only the products of an active and temporary selection" (Deleuze & Guattari, 1987, pp. 9–10). Examining the corpus of school songs, we observe a consistent and obvious division of the abject from the worthy. But in transmission from school to home and community over decades, especially in the protocols of music appreciation, the curriculum challenges the totalizing categorization of human types, producing opportunity for advancement as well as remediation. In this sense, the music appreciation curriculum, coming half a century after Horace Mann, fostered a rhizomic process whose fruition depended upon shifts in religion, technology, the political economy, and music instruction. Music education divided auditory experience, forming new audiences commensurate with aspirations for social mobility.

In the Renaissance, Copernicus and Galileo offered a different paradigm in which the heavens lost centrality and theories of music revolved around national styles and composers. Church rules about music began to loosen their hold around 1550 when Northern European composers initiated a discourse of "true" and "false" tonality, exploiting a larger range of musical expression. The availability of printed music and the salience of regional styles to music composition gave rise to bourgeois patronage of music "masters." Consequently, individual composers outside the control of the Church shaped the Renaissance art music tradition of Europe with the support of a merchant class who prized secular "art" as marks of the prosperity and good taste of their households.

Analogous ideals and values appear in the early curriculum documents of music education in the United States. In the written record of school boards, references to enlightened "masters" is part of the alchemy that persuaded educators to support music instruction as an enduring school subject in America. Early 19th-century pedagogical texts often invoked the Swiss educational philosopher Pestalozzi to enhance what American educators called "object lessons." But ruptures as well as continuities occurred in the history of music education. In the mid-1840s when formal vocal instruction entered public schools, Northern European musical pedagogy represented the finer sensitivity and reason of the ideal citizen. This was the alchemy that would transform a rough-hewn people into a golden citizenry and distinguish citizens from abject sectors of the population. By 1890, a curriculum for listeners, borrowed from the European tradition of concert pamphlets, manuals of etiquette, and master pedagogical "systems," redefined music, creating new standards for public schools across the country. For example, the French music pedagogue Dalcroze became famous for his kinetic rhythmic exercises. His use of the body to teach musical beats was adapted in some American public schools to enhance public instruction methods. Each foreign master, whether French, Central European, or Asian, promised to lift public school music education and students' taste above popular music, turning the base metal of the miscreant listener into golden exemplars.

In the early 20th century, public school music teaching played a major role in advancing the consumption of radio and gramophone and thereby disseminating new categories of "art" music to the growing population. Due to the growth of the recording industry and the radio, public schoolchildren comprised a national audience for the auditory demonstration of spiritualism in particular kinds of folk music. However, the Negro spiritual (vocal music), previously labeled "slave music," took its place in the curriculum as an example of Negro inspirational music rather than American folksong. As the field of psychoacoustics developed in the land-grant universities in Iowa, Wisconsin, California, New York, and elsewhere, this new science stressed the study of human responses to music in terms of pitch, volume, and rhythm, linking neuromuscular phenomena to comparative scales of race and ethnicity. This new science, circulating nationally in professional journals and conferences, exerted influence on music methods, fabricating a "scientific" basis for comparing the internal, psychological characteristics of schoolchildren as qualities of reason and citizenship.

From the discursive connections between psychological theories, classical music, and the radio/recoding industry, music educators claimed that proper listening habits would identify superior personhood and increase mental capabilities. Thus

classical music and particular "ethnic" forms such as the African American spirituals were key ingredients in the alchemy, producing protocols to divide music heard
in school from popular forms of expression. Yet, ironically, this alchemic process
in the curriculum of the early 20th century with its capacity to disseminate new
technologies of the self also raised the aspirations of excluded populations, opening new opportunities in music for African Americans and Southern and Central
Europeans. This was especially the case given the expanding recording and radio
industries. As discussed in greater detail further on in this paper, the irony was
that while the comparisons between musical tastes and perception were brought
into the public school curriculum as procedures to identify "deficits" linked to
race and ethnicity, the consumption of music via radio and gramophone, both
inside and outside the school, produced new classifications of listeners who could
mobilize musical knowledge to change their social status in spite of and sometimes due to the curricular codes themselves. For example, as blues recordings of
African American singers were exemplars of a folk style in the curriculum, their
imitation and availability became new forms of cultural capital or "art" music for
professional musicians such as Gershwin, Ravel, and Milhaud. That is to say, the
fabrications of abjection in the alchemy of the music curriculum may determine
some aspects of citizenship, but they also generate lines of flight and new ruptures
from the "golden" system of instruction.

   We are now in the midst of another turning point in the alchemy of school
music in which digital technology and demographic change create conditions for
the facile electronic composition of global musical idioms. The process generates
new definitions for music teaching ("multicultural" or "global") as well as comparisons between musical tastes (worthy or abject). These comparisons emerge
from the teaching of world music and Western classical music and students' competence with electronic technology. The multicultural curriculum not only classifies listeners but also produces new orders of merit and abjection corresponding
to racial, ethnic, musical, and social categories. What follows is an analysis of
early 19th-century, mid-20th-century, and present curricular reforms. Each section discusses the relation between music as an object of study and shifts in the
recognition of what constitutes meritorious music makers and listeners in relation
to citizenship.

Part II: Saving the Republic Through Vocal Music

Music education in public schools in the United States emerged from the concerns of social degeneracy of the new republic in Boston, Massachusetts, around
1840. There, the Boston School Committee, with the urging of Horace Mann as
state secretary of education, pioneered singing instruction in the public schools as
a pedagogy that "moulds the character of this democracy . . . setting in motion a
mighty power which . . . will humanize, refine, and elevate a whole community"
(Boston School Committee, 1837, p. 141). Mann delivered these words to the

Committee: "[Music will] . . . subdue the hearts of the people . . . make them yielding and receptive . . ." (Mann, 1844, p. 151). As social reformer, Secretary Mann sought to replace the autocratic doctrines of religious institutions with secular principles. By borrowing the much-admired Prussian models of education, Mann inscribed American themes of progress on to the verses children sang in school. Threats of contagious disease in Boston, how to educate the children of freed slaves, and Irish Catholic immigrants were the main social anxieties of this era and the major alchemic ingredients educators combined with the discipline of music. According to one historian, 19th-century Boston was "crowded, noisy, decaying . . . covered with shanties and refuse" (Schultz, 1973, p. 32). Even so, school singing depicted the city as pastoral. The reality was that the slums housed many Irish Catholics and freed slaves who were to be made "reasonable" through the social direction of music education. Vocal instruction's alchemy was to mix music education with social prescriptions, inscribing each sector of the population with categories for their musical disposition, race, and religion.

In addition to this imaginary of a pastoral Boston, Emerson's concept of choral harmony of the nation fabricated a notion of mutuality between citizen and state. This ideal was strikingly different from the cultivated inwardness of German *Bildung*. The latter sought to distinguish individual spirituality from politics and state. American school songs celebrated hard work and outward success, not self-scrutiny or inward contemplation: "When I play, I will play, like a pleasant boy / And my play shall be cheerful and free. When I work, I will work, like a Yankee boy / With a right good will it shall be . . ." (Bradbury & Sanders, 1831, p. 111). "This idle boy no comfort had / His face was gloomy, dull and sad" (Fitz, 1846, p. 82). Such sentiments were stark contrasts to Northern European values of the same period in which work was the necessary fate of the low born. "What most astonished Tocqueville was that Americans thought work itself was an honourable public service" writes Gordon Wood (1991, p. 285).

Drawing upon the idea that social mobility rewards hard work, school singing became a performance of endless possibilities for industriousness. These songs amplified the mission of secular educationists, replacing clerical authority and making the Boston music curriculum a uniquely American method of fabricating enlightened citizens. In this sense, the alchemy—turning social principles into pedagogical "gold"—produced a double action and a paradox. One effect was to identify the unworthy. The other was to assert the radical idea of equality and freedom for all. The music curriculum had thus established its role in propagating multiple versions of reality, disrupting stark differences between what one might desire and what one might possibly achieve. Pastoral and patriotic school songs branched out in all directions like the rhizome, celebrating a spectrum of geographical and social imaginaries. But what is central to the trajectory of public school music is that these visions also asserted possibilities for the achievement of what was denied by historical circumstance. The "double" action of alchemy and rhizomic lines of flight is not a dialectic structure but a depiction of the entanglement of the real and the imagined that remakes social identities. As Henry James's novel *The American* depicts, the prevailing social dynamic of the 19th century in the United States was to make individual labor the key to the removal of social limitations (James, 1878).

The music curriculum also inscribed moral limits on the virtue of overindustriousness. School documents on the risks to health in repetitive factory and academic work described how these evils were overcome by lung and muscular-skeletal exercises. Boston educators prescribed vocal instruction as a tuberculosis preventive in which singing enriched the blood to protect the individual from disease and overwork (Mann, 1844). Progress in singing was a sign of the child/ citizen's reason as well as health. On the one hand, participation in school singing fortified barriers for those who, *a priori*, were thought to lack reason and a work ethic in the early 19th century, namely, Irish Catholic immigrants and African Americans. On the other hand, patriotic songs promised access to better social conditions *for all*. Reciprocity between imaginary ("for all") and real limits, however tenuous, formed a symbolic space in which all were released from restrictions of birth and property. And while the song repertoire inscribed a severe social hierarchy in endless comparisons of the idleness, industriousness, comportment, and moral virtue of human types, the ideals of liberty for all propagated in the new communities across America during a period of rapid social change. In Boston, New York, and Philadelphia, the moral mission of music educators met and mixed with the popular ballads of taverns, theaters, homes, and streets. What would be seen today as odd combinations of classical music and satiric songs were a familiar staple in popular theaters. Concert music and other forms of entertainment overlapped on the same program, and audiences increasingly contested notions of "low" and the "high" culture throughout the 19th century. Theaters offered blackface (White men dressed as stereotypes of African Americans), Shakespeare, opera arias, virtuoso violinists, and irreverent ballads, all on the same program. African American entertainers learned classical music and White Shakespearean actors took up blackface. This combination of popular stage events was censored in school songbooks, but the overlap of mixed modes of entertainment in both private and public venues compelled integration of musical content rather than separation.

It was no contradiction that patriotic songs, blackface minstrel performances, religious hymns, and school ballads appeared together. Racial imaginaries of Whiteness in the alchemy of school songbooks were deeply embedded in the idea that Blackness represented a lack of civilization. There was ridicule of Africans Americans singing "Yankee Doodle" in Southern dialect and humorous imitations of didactic health prescriptions. Often, White men dressed as slaves defied existing power relations and overturned the racial order onstage. The theatre was a "backstage" of American society where fissures in the social and racial hierarchy foreshadowed a central theme of the brutal Civil War. At this moment in history, vocal music manuals and songbooks underlined the "primitive" nature of Negro song, praise for national geography, and imaginaries of worthy citizens versus abject groups.

The school music curriculum played a role in social parody as well as edification. Inexpensive sheet music circulated across the continent, feeding the appetite of a populace eager, no doubt, to display its patriotism and gentility but also keen to gain competence with a satiric repertoire that took aim at the social control and puritanical ethos of schools, civic organizations, and churches. The result was not only the production of a uniquely American politics of aesthetics that manipulated institutional musical traditions but also the creation of popular forms of entertainment challenging elitism and social inequality. Above all, performances of so-called Negro dialects and comportment, while forbidden entertainments in public schools, drew widespread attention to the fragility of the concepts of Whiteness. In social debates leading up to the fateful court decisions in the 1850s over the fate of a runaway slave, John O'Sullivan, the source of the phrase "manifest destiny," wrote, "American patriotism is not of the soil . . . nor of ancestry . . . for we are of all nations; but it is essentially personal enfranchisement" (Wald, 1995, p. 111).

With the political ambiguity of slave status forming a backdrop, the music curriculum, with its emphasis on the ideals of freedom, could be supportive of abolitionist sentiment without difficulty. Thus, the racial distinctions operating in school songs served contradictory political and social aims. The French historian De Tocqueville had written,

> The particular pride of [Americans] will always seek to escape the common level . . . In aristocracies, men are separated from one another by high, immovable barriers; in democracies, they are divided by multitudes of small threads that are broken at every moment and are constantly changed.
>
> *(De Tocqueville, 2000, p. 578)*

The performative nature of singing traversed this terrain of social abjection and mobility, inequality, and racial animosity, providing sound spaces for the cross-fertilization of musical cultures and dreams of freedom. Radiating rhizome-like from the singular stem of social abjection, school music also nurtured new hopes for opportunity and equality in those, like Irish Americans, whose status was marginal.

Part III: New Technologies

Whereas the music curriculum in the early 19th century focused primarily on vocal music, the early 1900s' stepwise curriculum of listening to recorded orchestral music normalized and prescribed classical music as an indication of the advanced or delayed psychological state of listeners. One of the hallmarks of early 20th-century education was the proliferation of psychological categories through which future citizens were compared and judged worthy. The American psychologist-educator G. Stanley Hall had formulated a system of developmental stages of childhood and adolescence expressly for public school music teachers. His work fabricated higher levels of emotional and intellectual growth for people who listened to classical music. Jazz fans risked classification as antisocial. "Music Appreciation," as this developmentally organized school curriculum was called, judged schoolchildren by aesthetic taste and bodily responses to music. Many nationally distributed texts spawned the large enterprise of recording and cultural programs on radio. For public school music educators, the large number of children and regions taking part in music memory contests reflected national progress. For industry, it was the size of radio audiences and the sales of the music appreciation curriculum (with corresponding recordings) from the Victor Talking Machine Company. A 1920s graph from Victor claimed that more than 10,000 school districts had purchased phonographs.

In a typical music listening manual, building the nation meant teaching concert etiquette to the lower class:

> Music is something to think about, something more than entertainment. . . . An eighth grade class . . . from the poorest district . . . [gained] acquaintance with the phonograph from cheap playhouses, restaurants, and from open doors of saloons [bars]. Imagine my surprise when the children began to giggle and laugh [when I played Handel's *Hallelujah Chorus*]. . . . We must learn to listen, and it is regrettable that so few have acquired the habit.
>
> *(Fryberger, 1925, pp. 213–214)*

Another manual identified mental types of children as auditory minded, visual minded, and motor minded. This taxonomy was a recapitulation of racial destiny in which the early state of motor mindedness—that is, rhythmic movement—was a sign of the child's infantilism.

Many prominent music educators focused on differences in musical taste as signs of racial inferiority. In this atmosphere, music appreciation served as a pragmatic system for identifying superior personhood. The radio-phonograph-school nexus that had built a national "music appreciation" curriculum also made it possible for people from all walks of life to participate in regular symphony broadcasts, precipitating pressures on elites to offer free concert venues for all comers. Radio concerts, music appreciation courses, and "Red Label" classical recordings articulated an important aspect of the ambitions of some African Americans and the White middle class, for whom there was a significant overlap of consumption of jazz, blues, and classical music. This overlap precipitated change in the status of African American music and in the cross-fertilization of musical genres occurring between the 1880s and the early 20th century. During this time, African American and White composers began to use classical idioms to create new hybrid forms of expression, blending popular genres within the formal structures of the symphony and concerto. Just as singing in the early period of the Republic performed the ideals of freedom and happiness, music educators responded to this democratization of music by including African American spirituals in the curriculum. There are numerous accounts that some Black African American musicians, including the composer William Grant Still, learned Negro spirituals from family and church while also absorbing classical music from the Victor Red Seal recordings taught at school and individually purchased for home use. As a result, Still's music combines two formally distinct musical cultures, the classical (White) and the African American, each necessitating the other to identify difference. These and other musical hybrids created a unique American regional style. While the school curriculum stressed comparisons of the child's racial and social inheritance, music appreciation on radio and records disseminated the fundamental building blocks for the production of particular forms of cultural capital. In the language of social progressives, John Dewey wrote, "It [music and visual art] breaks barriers, impermeable in ordinary association . . . the artist, as social experimenter, made individual experience relevant to the common and public world" (Dewey, 1934, p. 144). The notion of a "common and public world" also became part of the language of progressive curriculum change. The ubiquitous vehicles of gramophone and radio turned the pedestrian nature of music pedagogy into the precious metal of Dewey's democracy. Publicity related to the famous conductor Toscanini, for example, broadened audiences for classical music radio through the popular view of him as an Italian immigrant, a "common man," who was transformed from "low" social status into "high." The strategy of mixed programming and spotlighting immigrant musicians in the first half of the 20th century resembled the lowbrow/highbrow conglomerations of the theatre, each racial, ethnic, and religious stereotype emerging from and producing Whiteness. Productions of high and low value were not only commercially useful to radio and recording industries but also pedagogically in tune with the mission of saving the nation from racial degeneration.

Breaking cultural barriers between village and city through wired technology, however, meant that some local communities felt threatened by a new, cosmopolitan social class who would usurp the authority of the rest of America. Broadcasters often took their own line of flight from the school music prescriptions by interspersing "high" culture with the "low," as well as promoting swing versions of the classics. In all levels of education, the curricular schema of an American musical canon that featured European "greats" emerged from the joint partnership of the Victor Company and music teachers. Belief in social progress along with opportunity for social mobility enhanced the support for classical music on radio. The more convincing "the belief in the redemptive . . . powers of classical music, the more compelling was the case for wanting larger numbers of people to share in them" (Goodman, 2011, p. 128). If classical music was a redeemer of an Italian immigrant such as Toscanini, his erudition exemplified the redemption of masses. Thus, a measure of social inclusion was purchased at a price of social abjection.

Public school music instruction had a large hand in drawing boundaries of social exclusion, but it also contributed to the dissemination of music to overturn social barriers. That is to say, new inscriptions of personhood produced in the larger discursive environment were not simply reproductions of musical ordinances. The social prescriptions in the alchemy of the music curriculum and its rhizomic lines of flight played an important role in organizing different citizen-ideals. By the 1930s, music supervisors stipulated the inclusion of African American song as a form of folk music, inscribing a new logic value for regional and ethnic musical expression. Harsh racial exclusions continued in music with contention in the concert hall and theatre, especially regarding the rule of segregating audiences, and in labor, education, and housing. While there is no doubt that high court decisions played a central role in the mobilization of the civil rights movement of the 1960s, the vocal traditions of African Americans forged powerful links between biblical and constitutional promises of freedom in songs such as "Joshua Fought the Battle of Jericho" and "Go Down Moses." The musical performance of civil rights comprised an aesthetic politics, dovetailing with American traditions of personal freedom. The admiration for the Negro spiritual expressed in the curriculum, although conditional, gathered sentiment against restrictions of freedom for African Americans and later underpinned support for civil rights. As such, familiarity with African American spiritual singing made it part of a broader, national culture, illustrating the vibrant role of school music in the repartitioning of resources in the mid 20th century. One historian has described this phenomenon as "a strategy that insists on conceiving dissent as loyal opposition . . . a recovery of a conformity with principles (liberty, justice, happiness) on which all are in a priori agreement" (Fliegelman, 1993, p. 69).

Part IV: Music Education, Multiculturalism, and the Digital Revolution

In the late 20th century, music educators promoted a "multicultural" curriculum. In general terms, music educators incorporated knowledge of a "global" musical community. The political atmosphere of the 1960s and 1970s civil rights movement made these reforms consistent with the mission of curing the ills of social and cultural inequality. Somewhat later educators prescribed multiculturalism in music as knowledge necessary to launch students on marketable careers. Moreover, the semantic features of multicultural reforms promised a remedy for the anxiety of global economic competition.

The alchemy of what are broadly called "multicultural reforms," however, produces distinctions between dispositions and competencies. The Euro-American disposition reasserted its transcendence of the ordinary through comparisons of the "other," that is, multicultural forms of musical expression with the Western canon. By using categories such as "authenticity and professional knowledge," the latest reforms prescribe standards for a typical course of multicultural study. These standards divide students by prior musical study and aesthetic disposition. The overlapping of race with musical practices marginalizes the sensibilities of broad sectors of the public school population. Fluency in electronic media, recording devices, and the use of synthesizers for composition of music are, in large part, elements of the cultural capital of families. However, on closer examination, the use of electronic technology and media in the music classroom, when available, produces lines of flight that contest a straightforward partitioning of the sensible world in terms of socio-economic class (Rancière, 2006). For example, electronic media allow an instantaneous mixing of musical traditions beyond the fixed notions of global cultures, authenticity, and professionalism inscribed in the music curriculum of the turn of the present century. This does not mean that using digital equipment reverses the hierarchy of specialized knowledge but rather that self-instruction and the dissemination of recordings proliferate to form new avenues of participation previously available to comparatively few. In effect, the global communications repertoire recently made part of the pedagogy in some music classrooms and academic venues operates as a "traveling library" (Popkewitz, 2005, p. ix), a mobile source of "high" culture that makes technical study of the Western canon unnecessary for its alteration or reproduction. This new hierarchy of skills challenges the established canon as a discreet domain. With the manipulation of manual phonographs, synthesizers, and cell phones, students are able to construct new aesthetic rankings from what they hear and perform on electronic media. Reordering skills and knowledge does not ensure democracy. Rather, it provides a way to understand how the alchemy of music reforms spawns contradictory and complex effects, serving a repartition of resources and a new configuration of social inclusion and exclusion.

Thus, while it is evident that the use of electronic media has reconfigured participatory boundaries in the music industry along the lines of high and low aesthetic dispositions, it is more difficult to trace the lines of social fracture in this hierarchical ordering of capabilities. These have the capacity to be instantly transnational and recombinant in the manner of chat rooms and blog sites. Nevertheless, some music researchers have documented the way in which the use of digital technology in the classroom is changing the definitions of music and musical competence to redefine notions of merit and broaden participation. Adria Hoffman and Bruce Carter (2013) write:

> Providing our students with a creative [digital] music-making experience necessitates the transfer of ownership to the learners. . . . Many of our students are more technologically savvy than we are, having grown up with [electronic] tools around them. . . . Students write one or more multiple parts, play them back . . . and post online for others . . . editing them to create layered professional recordings.
>
> *(p. 60)*

What is implicit in this work is that the alchemic mix of instruction and the socioeconomic prescriptions that highlight the global marketability of the knowledge in the curriculum produces effects at two levels. There is a production of social abjection for those who do not possess the dispositions to engage with the technology, but there are also diverse ways in which many students who do take up digital devices may participate in music classrooms. For example, the use of the cell phone can turn the marginal participant into a "sender" or producer of new musical combinations. This is not to characterize electronic communication as a utopian field of social equality but to draw attention to the way in which the school music curriculum not only generates evaluative schemes producing social boundaries but also proliferates, rhizome-like, new possibilities through its promotion of new technologies. In this sense, electronic devices and communication in the classroom are analogous to the varied effects of the Music Appreciation curriculum with its dissemination of musical knowledge and the reordering of social hierarchies.

Conclusion

The twists and turns in the constitution of "music" from the ancient Greeks to today's digital communications underscore the difficulty of locating a stable essence for music as an object of study in music education. The historiography of music education has serious sociological limitations, since it provides no entry point for theorizing changing patterns of abjection and merit. It has also lacked the theoretical tools to analyze the mutual fabrication of notions Blackness, Whiteness, and high versus low musical tastes. I have argued that music education in the United States emerges from an uneven topography in which different plateaus and seepages produce new forms of worthiness or disqualification. Music, as a form of social power, has an uncanny ability to build social barriers but also to bring about a repartitioning of resources through the very instability of its classification of compositions and audiences. From Plato to the medieval church, the Renaissance, and the modern era, notions of social differentiation in music pedagogy have authorized different patterns of social/aesthetic exclusion. These prescriptions have diverse effects as they combine with historical events. What I have sought to argue is that the dynamism and unpredictability of the movement of knowledge as it rearranges the partitioning of resources among social groups in concert with changing social conditions.

My exemplars of music history and the music curriculum from the 1840s illustrate only partially the double operations of the alchemy and rhizome, focusing on how the imaginaries of freedom, happiness, regional exceptionalism, and sublimity produce both exclusion and visions of social equality rather than a singular effect. In the early 19th century, the alchemy combined anxieties over immigration and comparisons between citizens' health and industriousness to fabricate the "gold" pedagogical system as a social template for citizenship. At the same time, the propagation of multiples lines of flight from the rhizome helps us think about the way songs generate ambitions of inclusion in context of the national "common sense of democratic reason" (Fliegelman, 1993, p. 45). The double movement of the music curriculum distinguishes the enlightened citizen from the unworthy. Yet this very division produces aspirations to overturn social limitations. Through the intimate relation between songs and the embodiment of political ideals, both listener and/or performer may overturn the aesthetic and social codes upon which any particular division of resources rests. The discussion of the early 20th century, for example, shows that teaching the population to listen to classical music spawned new valuations of American regional cultures. By the mid-20th century, the civil rights movement strategically deployed the idea of musical transcendence, or rising above worldly values, in African American spirituals to enhance social equality. At the turn of the last century, a multicultural curriculum fabricates different competencies for global marketability and notions of authenticity to rank students. In the meantime, some music classrooms foster a reconfiguration of musical authority through technology that allows students to alter music themselves and to reorder the aesthetic valuation of what they are hearing.

In each of the four parts of this chapter, the discussion treated the music curriculum as an alchemic process in which contingent social anxieties and aesthetic ideals would recognize the worthy citizen. I have also attempted to convey how a redistribution of material and repartitioning of symbolic resources emerges from the curricular plateau. While this double action of the curriculum articulates the boundaries of social inclusion and exclusion, it also activates challenges to those boundaries as they emerge from the ambitions of marginalized groups.

References

Boston School Committee. (1837/1982). Report. In M. Mark (Ed.), *Source readings in music education* (pp. 134–143). New York: Schirmer Books.

Bradbury, W., & Sanders, C. (1831). *The young choir.* New York: Ivison and Finney.

Deleuze, G., & Guattari, F. (1987). *A thousand plateaus: Capitalism and schizophrenia.* Minneapolis: University of Minnesota Press.

De Tocqueville, A. (2000). *Democracy in America* (H. Mansfield & D. Winthrop, Trans.). Chicago: University of Chicago Press.

Dewey, J. (1934). *Art as experience.* New York: Linton, Balch and Co.

Fitz, A. (1846). *The American school songbook.* Boston: Fowle and Capen.

Fliegelman, J. (1993). *Declaring independence: Jefferson, natural language, and the culture of performance.* Palo Alto, CA: Stanford University Press.

Fryberger, A. (1925). *Listening lessons in music graded for schools.* New York: Silver Burdett.

Goodman, D. C. (2011). *Radio's civic ambitions: American broadcasting and democracy in the 1930s.* New York: Oxford University Press.

Gustafson, R. (2009). *Race and curriculum: Music in childhood education.* New York: Palgrave Macmillan.

Hoffman, A. R., & Carter, B. A. (2013). A virtual composer in every classroom. *Music Educators Journal 99*(3), 59–62.

James, H. (1878). Americans abroad. *The Nation, xxvii,* 208–209.

Mann, H. (1844). Vocal music in the schools. In M. Mark (Ed.), *Source readings in music education* (pp. 144–154). New York: Schirmer.

Popkewitz, T. S. (2005). Preface. In T. S. Popkewitz (Ed.), *Inventing the modern self and John Dewey: Modernities and the traveling of pragmatism* (pp. vii–xii). New York: Palgrave Macmillan.

Popkewitz, T. S., & Gustafson, R. (2002). Standards of music education and the easily administered child/citizen: The alchemy of pedagogy and social inclusion/exclusion. *Philosophy of Music Education Review, 10*(2), 80–91.

Rancière, J. (2006). *The politics of aesthetics* (G. Rockhill, Trans.). New York: Continuum.

Schultz, S. (1973). *The culture factory: Boston Public Schools, 1789–1860.* New York: Oxford University Press.

Wald, P. (1995). *Constituting Americans: Cultural anxiety and narrative form.* Durham, NC: Duke University Press.

Wood, G. S. (1991). *The radicalism of the American revolution.* New York: Vintage Books.

15

THE PROBLEM

Historicizing the Guatemalan Projection and Protection of the "Indian"

Ligia (Licho) López López

This chapter is an intertwined analysis of educational policy documents and visuality. Emerging out of a larger inquiry over the difference of what is indigenous constituted as a scientific object, the chapter engages with the reasoning of the problem. An analytics of moments of intensity in indigenous making points to the emergence and prominence of the problematic indian[1] as a project of projection and protection. The "Indian problem" as a way to continue making up what is indigenous as an educational (s)object[2] has been in circulation from around the end of the 19th century and into the 20th and 21st centuries. Although the language of the indian as a problem is no longer employed in current political-educational discourses, the style of reasoning that makes it possible is ever present. The problem reasoning permeates even the most progressive policies, laws, and accords employed to justify respect for diversity in the name of equity and equality. Analytically, the chapter takes up Jaques Derrida's analytics of *problēma* as projection and protection. The task is to question the reasoning of the indian as a protection of all that has gone wrong in Guatemalan "modern" history and as a projection of the desirable aspirations anchored in the same violent systems of reason that were at the inception of the Indian-Other in the first place. Historicizing "the problem" was possible through an examination of Guatemalan archives from the turn of the 20th century that include photographs, policy documents, interviews, and classroom observations. The style the chapter follows is spiral. In taking a point and retuning to it in a fractal fashion, it aims to show the layers of complex dynamics of border drawing that projects and ostensibly plans the future of indigenous youth.

PHOTO 15.1 Region Kaqchiquel—Chimaltenango or San Juan Sacatepéquez
(Photo courtesy of the Valedavellano Collection, Academia de Geografía e Historia de Guatemala)

The Subject-ivity of Photographs and Gestures of "Modern" Configurations

Alberto G. Valdeavellano's (1861–1928) and Tomás Zanotti's (1898–1950) photography circulated widely. Portraits like these gave contours to the retina[3] in the making of *lo indígena*. Valdeavellano was Guatemalan, a fact that breathes pride into the development of Guatemalan photography (López Cuat, 2005; Luján Muñoz, 1987). His father was from the Iberian Peninsula and his mother from Guatemala. Valdeavellano's quiet introduction of images in the late 19th to early 20th centuries visually spoke for what is called rural Guatemala today. He travelled the country extensively documenting "rural" *and* "urban" life. His voluminous body of work also visually documents what is known today as pre-Hispanic Guatemala. These visual representations travelled as postcards through and out of the Guatemalan borders at the same time that they participated in the constitution of such borders.

The photographing of the "indian" and the "rural," among other things (and binaries, perhaps), highlighted the "indian's" anthropological distance from the "non-indian." This distance is the temporal relation that anthropological activities have created to define the world of the savage, the primitive, an Other. This world is a temporal state, a stage, and a condition—of backwardness, under-development, mental death. Anthropological distance is marked by temporal sequences enshrined in evolutionist time where the indian lives in another time, an undesirable past (a past of misery inflicted by colonization, as opposed to a victorious past of pre-Hispanic Mayan intellectual production; Fabian, 1983; Mitchell, 2011). This distance served as the framework on which the project of nation was mounted as exemplified in the words of Batres Jáuregui and Asturias in what follows.

The photographs have travelled to museums, made their way to personal col-lections, and were also in conversation with the literary production of Miguel Angel Asturias. In Asturias (1923, 2007), the indian was innocent, dirty, barefoot, rural, in need, and a problem. The picture of the "Region Kaqchiquel"[4] helps to visually activate this characterization. The image of the indian child barefoot and dressed in scruffy clothes came to epitomize what the nation needed to surpass if it were to progress and modernize.

> How far does this difference go? The Indian represents a past civilization and the *mestizo*, or *ladino* as we call him, a civilization that is to come. The Indian comprises the majority of our population, lost his strength in the time of slavery to which he was subjected, he is not interested in anything [. . .] he represents the mental, moral, and material poverty of the country: he is humble, dirty, dresses differently and suffers without batting an eye. The ladino makes up the third part, lives in a different historical moment, with desires of ambition and romanticism, aspires, wishes and is, in the end, the living part of the Guatemalan nation. Brave nation that has two-thirds of its population dead to intelligent life!
>
> *(Asturias, 1923, p. 12)*

It would be important to underline that Miguel Angel Asturias has been very influential in educational matters. Among other things, he founded and directed the Universidad del Popular in 1922, an institution whose aim was to "eradicate" illiteracy. His works *Hombres de Maíz, Mulata de Tal*, and others can be found in teacher education schools today and are read by indigenous youth who come to Guatemala City to receive an education and are expected to return to their communities to teach in elementary schools where most of the students are indigenous.[5]

While Valdeavellano photographed "indians" in rural life, Zanotti photo-graphed them in a studio. Unlike his predecessor Santiago K. Piggott, for whom indigenous clients were almost nonexistent, Zanotti photographed Maya-K'iche' people from Quetzaltenango City and its surroundings. This is the most prominent theme in the Zanotti collection housed in the Center for Mesoamerican Research (CIRMA). Zanotti was born in Mexico to an Italian father and a Mexican mother

PHOTO 15.2 Portrait in a First Communion

(Photo courtesy of the Tomás Zanotti Collection, Centro de Investigaciones Regionales de Meso-américa CIRMA)

and came to Guatemala in 1898. There seems to be a popular sentiment that Zanotti's portraits, in contrast to 19th-century European imperialistic practices such as anthropology and travel writing, give the viewer the sense of dignified Maya-K'iche "men, women and children," who "looking at the camera project a lovely, dignified sense of self" (Lock, 2000). According to Greg Grandin, it was the Maya-K'iche's *themselves* that "sought and consumed the images shot by Zanotti" (Grandin, 2004, p. 86). To enter the photography studio and consume photography would then speak of the Mayas' market *freedom* to choose and participate in a local practice previously consecrated to few.

Portrait in a First Communion is a rich entanglement of elements that invite the participant viewer to venture into questions of religiosity and a vision of modernity. The first communion is an occasion to be commemorated in Roman Catholic cultures. It is a life cycle event that arguably served as a checkpoint in the progressive development of one's Christianity and for civil control by the Catholic

Church (Rionda, 2012).[6] The choice of props, the Victorian furniture inspire elegance and sophistication and take one to the times of Darwin, his practices of observation and of classifying, a rather important reflection if one puts photography in conversation with such practices, especially on the subject of making up people. The pearl necklace, the rosary, the veil, the candle, and the Renaissance-like painting of St. Peter and Jesus in the background relate to the sophistication of materiality via "Europe"—a temporal and spatial location of aspiration. They are discursive elements of transition, enlightenment, and modernizing in which the "indian" is allowed to participate via her presence both in the photographic studio and in schools.[7]

> [I]n September 1797, [the Economic Society of Friends of the Country] offer[ed] a gold medal and meritorious membership, to whoever wrote the best essay on the following subject: "Demonstrate solidly and clearly the advantages that would result for the State if all Indians and *ladinos* of this kingdom put on shoes and dressed in Spanish styles, and they experienced for themselves the physical, moral and political benefits; proposing the most smooth, simple and practicable means to reduce them to the use of these things, without violence, coercion or mandate.
>
> . . . one of the most important social problems was about, as you can see, no other than to propose the means to make the aboriginal class and the other large portion of the less privileged social class, to enter civil life and participate of its benefits.
>
> Let's just say it straight. Primary and educational practical instruction is what we need for those masses of struggling Indians, that constitute a real hindrance for the development of the country.
>
> *(Batres Jáuregui, 1894, pp. 168, 188)*

The sober *Portrait of Ladino Boy*, with clean suit, tie, and shoes,[8] invites the retina to the *mappaemundi* and the alphabetical text in print to books and literacy. This distinct logocentric and phonocentric global making (Derrida, 1982; Goodman, 1978) privileges reading the printed text as the practice *par excellence* for development. Literacy of the kind suggested in this image secures Guatemala a prominent and historical second place in illiteracy rates in Latin America. The book, in connection to the globe, inserts this young reader in a three-dimensional world projection philosophically and mathematically located in the "West"[9] that is separate from the rest (Said, 1979). The thisworldly that he points at makes him, at the beginning of the 20th century, a Guatemalan citizen and, in the 21st century, a "global" and "cosmopolitan" citizen. The notion of cosmopolitanism here is one that, as Thomas Popkewitz asserts, organizes difference at the "divide of those who are enlightened and civilized and those who do not have those qualities— the backward, the savage, and the barbarian of the 19th century . . ." (Popkewitz, 2007). Sitting outside the global, with the globe at his fingertips, framed in an

PHOTO 15.3 Portrait of Ladino Boy

(Photo courtesy of the Tomás Zanotti Collection, Centro de Investigaciones Regionales de Meso-américa CIRMA)

Olympian perspective, "the world becomes an abstract form held in the mind, hand and eye of a sovereign, imperial intelligence" (Mitchell, 2011) of a Guate-malan citizen no longer a problem of the otherworldly inhabited by the "indian." This split of the thisworldly and otherworldly verifiable via science (mathematical) and literacy (Judeo-Christian) is fundamental for the unquestioned grounds on which intercultural and inclusive educational projects are designed and instructed via educational policies.

El problema del indio and Indian Making

The logic of *"El problema del indio"* in Guatemala (and the other places in the Americas) has historically travelled around "urban" corners and inside govern-ment cubicles, staging the "indio" in the past, premodern, and thus a problem for development. The act of naming and pointing to "el indio" is an orientalist philosophical performance to which Edward Said (1979) alluded as a form of radical realism in which the phrase makes an Other—that is being talked about—as having acquired reality or *be reality*. This discourse also enables the language of multiplicity that permeates public and educational policies and how they are discussed in bilingual education classrooms today. Consider this statement from a

Maya-Kaqchikel teacher educator in a bilingual-intercultural education class for in-service and preservice teachers at a university in Guatemala City:

> When we speak of the multilingual, multiethnic, we are talking about a concrete matter, if we say that Guatemala is multilingual, why? Because there are 25 languages, right? It is not an ideological matter, it is a reality, we can go and count, we can survey, we can keep an account of how many people there are by language.
>
> *(Class observation, August 18, 2012)*

"*El problema del indio*" is enunciated from an "us–them" relation in which, as Derrida says,

> the "this side" as a point of departure *must* remain *here, on this side,* undecided, that is to say, decided without any theoretical question, before any theoretical question: without proof. It must remain this way because **one cannot do otherwise,** it is necessary; and it must remain this way because, as soon as one cannot do otherwise, one must do it this way, it is better to do it this way: *here, in any case.*
>
> *(Derrida, 1993, pp. 53–54, emphasis added)*

The here is the "us" that defines the template on which the indian is inserted as a "reality." In this template, the indian, as radical reality, becomes a project, a task, a kind of division that allows for protection in case of danger, a *problēma*. At the same time, the indian "them" becomes the problem for "us" in "our" reality.

Problēma, as Derrida explains, is a Greek word that can signify projection or protection. As projection, *problēma* is "that which one poses or throws in front of oneself, either as a projection of a project or as a task to accomplish" (1993, p. 11). As protection, *problēma* is "a substitute, a prothesis, that we put forth in order to represent, replace, shelter, or dissimulate ourselves, or as to hide something unavowable" (Derrida, 1993, p. 11).

In what follows, I highlight how this *problēmatic* mode of thinking plays out in the planning of education through educational policies and laws contiguous to education. Let me begin by stating that modern, formal, and public education, through educational legislation, has always been tasked with the resolution of the "Indian problem." In the 1962 National Education Organic Law, the National Indigenist Institute (IIN) was a "technical" division. As such, the IIN was an "organization whose fundamental goals [were] to research the *indigenous problems and to cooperate in solving them.*" The IIN was charged with carrying out tasks, planning, and advising education on concrete matters related to indigenous peoples. One of the functions the IIN had was "to propose to the Ministry of Public Education the necessary recommendations that it considers appropriate for the *solution of the Indian problems in the country.*" These solutions were to be informed by the anthropological knowledge gathered from the extensive fieldwork the IIN conducted in most rural areas of Guatemala. Ultimately the IIN's activities were to "lead to *accelerating the process of ladinization and contribute to the culturization of the indigenous communities.*"

The National Education Organic Law engages with indigenous matters more openly than previous iterations of it.[10] The law, although seemingly an afterthought to the analytics and concerns raised in the chapter, is important in highlighting one of the noticeable moments when the Indian problem becomes a legal matter and thus relevant to educational demands. The law constructs an important part of the linguistic and philosophical heritages that fund educational preoccupations for working on the "Indian subject" as a task to be accomplished in favor of the advancement of the nation that, post–1996, signifies a "peaceful nation."

Policies and "Post"-War Problem Solving

The most influential text in educational legislation and reform in recent years is the Accords for a Firm and Durable Peace signed in 1996. The Accords serve as a strong marker in public spaces to support arguments for a "better" education for indigenous youth. The document is used as a starting point for the analysis of current policies and serves to authorize particular claims for a future national project—at least in what concerns public education, especially *vis-à-vis* bilingual and intercultural education that in many cases points to "indigenous themes." The text is and is not about education.

The Accords serve as a projection of the peace project that concludes a painful historical time to never again repeat it. The document aims to mark a passage from the painful past into a peaceful present that can serve as a pillar for future political action—an invitation for educational reform. The first lines draw a *problĕmatic* closure around times of atrocities and throw in front of the nation the illusion of a durable peace. The document rhetorically serves as protection or shelter against the dangers that wars re/present. Wars derived from the "agrarian problem and rural development," no longer the Indian problem but a "situation" of the "majority of the population that live in rural environments" (Acuerdo de Paz Firme y Duradera, 1996). The Accords state that

> The state and the organized sectors of society should join forces for the solution of the *agrarian problem and rural development* which are fundamental to respond to *the situation of the majority of the population* that lives in rural environments, and which is the most affected by poverty, inequity and the weakness of state institutions.
>
> *(Acuerdo de Paz Firme y Duradera, 1996, emphasis added)*

In Batres's words, "population [. . .] in rural environments" translates into "the aboriginal class and the other large portion of the less privileged social class"

(Batres Jáuregui 1894, p. 168), and which in Asturias's words means "the majority of our population . . . two thirds dead for intelligent life!" (Asturias, 1923, p. 12).

The document suggests that peace comes through paths of "economic growth," "solving the agrarian problem," and "rural development" toward a generalized "common good" of the "entire" or "majority of the population" for "national unity."

> Firm and durable peace should be cemented in socioeconomic *participative development* oriented towards *common good,* which should respond to the necessities of *the entire population.* Such development requires social justice as one of the pillars of *national unity* and solidarity, and sustainable *economic growth* as a condition to respond to the social demands of the population.
>
> *(Acuerdo de Paz Firme y Duradera, 1996, emphasis added)*

The paths for growth emerge from a *homogeneous* conception of materiality (embedded in national unity) and *linear time* (suggested in development of the rural), both modern notions, and through a struggle for a uniformity that is not present, a presence. It is precisely this homogenizing logic—perhaps not in what pertains to economics but in relationship to ways of being and knowing—one of the triggers for (armed) conflicts in Guatemala. It also emerges in sophisticated discriminating and alienating relations within this "participative development" framework inside government offices as demonstrated by Claudia Dary's recent study in *Trabajando desde Adentro* (Dary, 2011). These are government offices in the ministry of education that are indeed designated to "perfecting a democratic system without exclusion" by looking after the education of indigenous peoples.

The Accords invite a gaze over "rural environments," which, by default, recreates the opposition to the nonrural. Here the gesture within linear time and a stagist frame is likely a transition from the rural or not-yet-modern stage to the nonrural or modern. Recall, in Asturia's work, the evolutionist time that inserted the indian in the stage of "a past civilization" and the "*ladino*" in the stage of a "civilization that is to come." The terms of *what* is to move from stage/point A to B are diverse and complex and are not the same from the beginning of the 20th century to the end of the century or what is discussed during the second decade of the 21st century. However, the evolutionist and developmental aspirations prevail. Education, through "official programs," is charged with the duty to widely disseminate the Accords.

The project of the Peace Accords is announced and takes shapes in other laws such as the Educational Advancement Against Discrimination Law (EADL) of 2002, the National Languages Law, and the Accord for the Creation of the Vice-Ministry of Bilingual Intercultural Education. All of these engage with the dynamics of anthropological border drawing through education that relates to indigenous making. The EADL puts forth the formation of a "new citizen" who can be made through certain "knowledge, attitudes, and values." These, as described in curricula that have emanated from these policies such as the National

Based Curriculum (CNB), refer to, for example, scientific and linguistic knowledge, intercultural attitudes, and moral values.

The CNB is the largest curriculum reform in Guatemala post–Peace Accords. Some of the notions the CNB officializes are precisely interculturality in the curriculum and moral values pro diversity. The CNB also extends the century-long concern for scientific education and the linguistic preoccupation in that it "[p]romotes an education of excellence, adequate for the advancement of science and technology." The preoccupation over the linguistic is a suggested shift in orientation pro identity of indigenous peoples, self-determination, and respect for the diverse nation, which is to counter assimilationist linguistic orientations such as castilinization from the 1920s on.

Although elaborate notions of interculturality were in the making in Zanotti's photography from 1900, the elements that make possible the image of *Portrait of a First Communion* relate to the "new citizen" suggested in the lines of the 2006 CNB. Zanotti opened a conversation between the commercial photography lens of a foreigner, not "indian" and Maya K'iche' that, according to Greg Grandin, sought his services. Recall that the image includes elements of indigeneity, religiosity, and scientific and linguistic knowledge, all of which were central to educational discourses in Manuel Estrada Cabrera's administration (1898–1920). The *Minervalias* were "festivals of instruction" during Estrada Cabrera's 22-year dictatorship. As very popular spaces for educating the populace on how education should be thought about and carried out, they were successful in orienting the compass of education to the North, science, and the notions of progress I have discussed so far. *Minervalias* were celebrations of science, "progresses of human reason," and language. Poems of "Homeric" qualities were recited in this event that took place at the end of the academic year in Minerva temples scattered throughout the nation. Minerva albums, printed for the time of the event, were voluminous texts that included messages/letters written in English, French, and Spanish by "enlightened" people from other countries to commemorate the festival and the ideals it represented. It also included images of portraits of "advanced" people, poems by students, and of course "the sublime words of the benefactor of the Patria." In a speech given at one of the festivals and reprinted in a Minerva Album, Estrada Cabrera said, "Oh! Sublime Minerva Temple . . . always remain as eternal/enduring as the science of which you are an emblem. And you, oh noble Guatemalan nation, venerate in your Minerva Temple the love for study and progress . . ." (Estrada Cabrera, 1977).[11]

The language knowledge advocated within this discourse of progress is that of what in today's policies is called L2—the national language, or otherwise Spanish—and L3—foreign languages (i.e., English, French, German). The stress on learning an L3 at the turn of the 20th century is founded on "interculturalism" and "modernity," ideologies/discourses Guatemala has come to (and allegedly needs to) be in contact with. This is better expressed in an excerpt from Felipe Estrada Paniagua's commissioned speech given at the Minerva Temple in 1907:

Yes, Gentleman, the civilizations of the Old world and the vigor of the far Orient already touch our two seas and, through the railroad that joins us, converge to the heart of Guatemala, to cure it from the anemia of more than three centuries of atavism, and the intake of oxygenated and new blood make it throb with the heartbeat of interculturalism and modern sentiment.[12]

The interculturalism notion announced here is arguably rather different from how it has been constructed in more recent policies, for it engages not only with the global, which in this excerpt refers to the "West" (Western Europe and the United States particularly), but also the "multiplicity" of groups (defined by Western knowledges as anthropological and sociological) that live within the Guatemalan national borders. This is the acknowledgement made in the Accord of the Identity and Rights of Indigenous Peoples (AIRIP, 1995) discussed next.

Similarly to the Peace Accords, the AIRIP relies on the educational system as the "most important" technology in its operationalization. The document makes explicit the "linguistic [and ethno] diversity" of the nation in a way that was not available in most of the first half of the 20th century. The document, with the political and academic discourses that made it possible, arguably can and has been able to open participatory spaces for the "maya, garífuna, and xinca" indigenous groups that have been historically excluded from "the unity of the Guatemalan nation."

> The identity of the *maya* peoples is recognized as well as *the identities* of the *garífuna* and *xinca* peoples within *the unity of the Guatemalan nation*, and the government is committed to promoting a reform to the Political Constitution to this end before the Congress of the Republic.
>
> *(Acuerdo sobre Identidad y Derechos de los Pueblos Indígenas, 1995, emphasis added)*

The Accord arguably crystallizes the historical struggles for indigenous participation.[13] It does so by defining and patrolling the conceptual border of indigenous identity (Maya, Garífuna, Xinca), demanding a reform of the constitution that would open the anthropological borders of territories, languages, and cultures of the Guatemalan nation. Indigenous identity is put forth as a prothesis in order to represent a kind of *probléma* as protection of people and also represent what is not indigenous. Indigenous shelters both "us" and "them" under an appeal for unity that can hide things unavowable and perhaps unspeakable but yet responsive to a sense of duty. The appeal for unity reinscribes a way of Othering that continues to fabricate differences.

In the AIRIP, Garífuna, for instance, is retained within anthropological demarcations; the anthropological reasoning here classifies and orders "people," their "identity," and "values," but Garífuna is also mobilized to open the Guatemala conceptual and anthropological demarcation as a "nonindigenous nation." This border-crossing and border-opening dynamic can challenge limits guarded by traditions in which education was conceivable only through Spanish-medium instruction and only within the "dominant" culture. The ethical duty that policies carry aims to both patrol some borders and open others.

By demanding to "[i]ntegrate the educational maya conceptions and of other indigenous peoples, in the philosophical, scientific, artistic, pedagogic, historical, linguistic and socio-political components [of the educational system], as a source of integral educational reform" as in article 1c, the AIRIP continues the century-long efforts toward indigenous making. However, with the backdrop of indigenous revival and revitalization of the 1980s, the terms of such making have shifted to "recognizing and strengthening indigenous cultural identity, maya values and educational systems," as stated in article 1 on educational reform.

The policies I have discussed thus far are "fragile" and "hardly ever implemented;" "we are going from bad to worse." These arguments can be heard from classroom teachers to bilingual and intercultural education officials to parents. The main point of the arguments refers to the lack of budget allocation for the implementation of this educational reform. Hardly ever are questions posed on *what is indigenous*—and the logics that produce it—that serve as a protection of all that has gone wrong in Guatemalan "modern" history and as a projection of the desirable aspirations anchored in the same violent systems of reason that were at the inception of the indigenous as an Other in the first place. Leaving the foundations unquestioned that *problēm*atically keep *what is indigenous* under closure may no longer be a viable "solution."

> The philosophy of Bilingual and Intercultural Education is based on *the coexistence of various cultures and languages* in the country, oriented toward strengthening *unity in the diversity* of the Guatemalan nation.
>   *Develop a stable social bilingualism for the Maya-speaking student population and a harmonious coexistence among peoples and cultures.*
>   *(Dirección General de Educación Bilingüe Intercultural (DIGEBI),*
>   *Accuerdo Gubernativo No. 726–95, emphasis added)*

The Direction of Bilingual and Intercultural Education (DIGEBI Accord No. 726–95) is understood as the most concrete iteration of the efforts to physically open up an indigenous space within the ministry of education. As an office within the buildings of the ministry of education, the DIGEBI aims to redraw borders with a dotted line that allows for "coexistence of various cultures and languages," otherwise known as interculturality, while following the transnational folklore of "unity in diversity." This universalized desire gives a sense of porosity to the anthropological borders of the Maya, Xinca, and Garífuna cultures enunciated in the texts I have already discussed. Paradoxically, there is a solid line of closure of the same borders in "develop[ing] a *stable* social bilingualism for the *Maya speaking student population.*" A "harmonious life" is to be achieved through that unifying slogan that disciplines the indigenous "peoples" to live "harmoniously" as opposed to in a warlike, (counter)insurgent reality, in a backward state of exploitation or mental death.

Article 11 of the accord states that "[t]he Regional and Departmental Directors and the leader-technicians of DIGEBI must recognize, respect and promote *the culture of the place.*" There is a sense of decentralization in delegating responsibilities to the regions to imperatively respond to the "culture of the place." This decentralization is in tension with the notion of "coexistence of various cultures" in article 3. The "culture of the place" draws a territorial boundary that reduces the possibilities to responsibly and substantively recognize the "multilinguistic," "pluricultural," and unstable dynamics of "cultures" especially given that the DIGEBI is responding to "post-"war internal and transnational migratory populations that challenge stable socio-spatial configurations. This is the case of the multilingual region Ixcán, for instance, where small villages of a few inhabitants, who have migrated from several geographic locations in Guatemala, use multiple languages. Another complex case is that of Guatemala City itself. "The culture of the place" invites a distancing, spatial, under the shadow of the temporal, that creates a divide and a projected difference, a reinstated Otherness, a kind of arborescent relationship (Deleuze & Guattari, 1987).

With the duty of responding to the "culture" and "multiethnicity themes" in the nation, the Vice-Ministry of Bilingual Education (Government Accord 626–2003) is embraced as a celebrated space of indigenous participation within the state apparatus. However, more recently voices of concern for little educational change may be expressing disenchantment in the project. Nonetheless, it is highly regarded as a marker of success of indigenous struggles in education to hole the rigid walls of a hostile Guatemalan state. Its specific duty, as Article 1d states, is to work for "development of indigenous peoples, based on their own languages and cultures." Underdevelopment is an undesirable condition. The locale of enunciation for this duty seems to be *us*, which is anything other than the underdeveloped, distant, rural village. The development project is thus dutifully indebted to *them*, "their own languages and cultures." We continue to see the repeated themes in these policy documents; the stagist reasoning, the anthropological distance, the border demarcations between us and them.

Both the DIGEBI Accord and the Vice-Ministry of Bilingual and Intercultural Education demarcate, open, and relocate boundaries, make them porous, and are boundaries themselves, open and closed boundaries.

Thus far I have been referring to the duty and the project of policies as a task to accomplish, a duty that has a debt to pay back to those who have been *problēmatized* historically, who have suffered the most dehumanizing atrocities of necropolitical decisions (Mbembé, 2003), a duty within *problēmatic* closure—that is, a constant problem posing. The creation of DIGEBI is the deployment of a program, a technical application of a rule or a norm "to protect the decision of responsibility by knowledge, by some technical assurance, or by the certainty of being right, of being on the side of science, of consciousness, or of reason" (Derrida, 1993, p. 19). All these, Derrida warns us, must never be abandoned, "but as such, are only the guardrail of a responsibility to whose calling they remain radically heterogeneous" (Derrida, 1993, p. 19).

A final document in this analysis and also a highly referenced text by teacher educators and other educationists aware of critical politics in Guatemala is the National Languages Law, decree number 19–2003.

Language has been an important construct for indigenous making. The law specifies that "[t]he official language in Guatemala is Spanish" and that "[t]he state recognizes, promotes and respects the languages of the Maya, Garífuna and Xinka[14] peoples." This highlights the borderline redrawn between the colonial language—Spanish—and others—Mayas, Garífuna, and Xinka. The former is "official" and the latter "recognized, promoted, and respected." What both kinds of descriptors suggest is not clear. What seems clear, however, is their separation. The gesture is toward the historical separation in a linear line of historical development. This separation stages Spanish as a *language* and the others as *lenguas* [tongues] in need of "advancement" and "development" to become languages. Phonocentric linguistic reasoning and logics of separability and enumerability make possible the naming of "Xinka," "Garífuna," and "Maya," as well as counting the various Mayan languages,[15] thus turning them into items and making them more manageable and readily available to be inserted into grids such as policies, laws, and accords like the ones analyzed in this chapter.

As a language, Spanish is at the center, and Mayas, Garífuna, and Xinka, as *lenguas*, continue to be a project of indigenous making—a project that, in turn and through the struggles that made this languages law possible, is meant to challenge such center.

> *Identity.* The Mayas, Garífuna y Xinka languages are essential elements in *national* identity; their recognition, respect, *advancement, development* and usage in the public and private spheres are oriented toward *national unity* in diversity and are meant to strengthen interculturalism among *co-nationals.*
> *(Ley de Idiomas Nacionales, Decreto Número 19–2003, emphasis added)*

The law is also enshrined in stagist ("advancement," "development"), essentializing (languages), and totalizing (national unity) theories. Languages suggest an instrumental developmentalizing task for the peoples affiliated to Maya, Xinca, or Garífuna. They and their languages are essential and matter as long as they can be inserted in the project of "national unity." The motion toward national unity here suggests a prestage of nationhood and a desirable one that can come about if that which is *not national* passes to the seat of becoming a "co-national." Similarly to other texts in the chapter, the Languages Law continues to make anthropological (languages and language communities, Mayas, Garífuna, and Xinka) borders official.

> *Usage.* In the Guatemalan territory Maya, Garífuna y Xinka languages can be used in the *languages communities in which they correspond,* in all their forms, without restrictions in public or private spaces, in educational, academic, social, economic, political and cultural activities.
>
> *(Ley de Idiomas Nacionales, Decreto Número 19–2003, emphasis added)*

Finally, "Maya, Garífuna and Xinka languages can be used in the communities," *there,* "where they correspond" suggests their acceptance in certain places (for example, the villages where they are spoken) and not on in others (for instance, the capital city and other urban centers). This is similar spatializing and linguistic territorializing logic to what we have seen in previous excerpts.

The National Languages Law (as well as the other policies discussed) are popularly known as battles won by the indigenous peoples after several years of struggle to open the anthropological border of the Guatemalan state. While the passing of this law is at times celebrated within the feelings of *presence—and inclusion—*that it affords for indigenous peoples and advocates, it is paradoxically necessary and insufficient, as both Derrida and Chakrabarty (2000) warn us, to break through the problematic and/or *problēma*tic heritages from which it is written.

Conclusion

Images do not simply reflect a subject but constitute it. The photographs with which I introduced the chapter "functioned as clues in terms of the specific theoretical schemes that orient 'the historian's effort to shape an intelligible and usable past'" (Coronil, 2004, p. 4). They also served as clues for specific schemes that orient a reading of how the Indian problem has been defined philosophically. Such terms that define the indian as a social, political, and even ontological problem have shifted in the course of the late 19th, 20th, and beginning of the 21st centuries. The crafting of the policies shows complex dynamics of border drawing, location of centers, temporalizations, and spatializations. Educational aspirations have been installed in a *problēma*tic logic where *lo indígena* is perpetually problematized, posed as a problem to be solved, as a task to be accomplished for more just education, as a project to protect the nation and the self (both us and them) from their own past and more atrocities.

Historicizing a past that is intelligible and usable is crucial for engaging with questions—generated from within education—on why things don't change. Why does Guatemalan education not move forward? Why do indigenous peoples not progress if we have (educational) policies in place that are to serve precisely the indigenous peoples' cause? The thesis, assumptions, logics, and history behind these very questions are hardly ever held in abeyance even in the face of closure when the desire is openings.

Notes

1. "Indian" (and indigenous, and *indígena*) is often not capitalized in Spanish. In some historical texts it appears capitalized. The lower case "indians" in English can also signal the difference with Indians from India—Columbus's initial destination.
2. The textual play in (s)object here suggest a sensitivity to the distinctions made (from the 18th but more so in the 19th century) between "object" and "subject" which are linked to the discussions in the history of science as elucidated by Lorraine J. Daston and Peter Galison, *Objectivity* (Zone Books, 2010). In contexts such as the long struggle within the rights discourse for indigenous peoples' self determination and positioning as subjects, the linguistic difference—between being an object as the recipient of action from a more powerful subject, and vice versa—matters. The analytical work I lounge here recognizes that such difference matters politically. The latent preoccupation in this dissertation, however, is beyond any subject-object dichotomy which, colonial to certain extent, "posited that objects of study did not produce knowledge in their own right." Sonia E. Alvarez, Arturo Arias, and Charles R. Hale, "Re-visioning Latin American Studies," *Cultural Anthropology* 26, no. 2 (2011): 228. The preoccupation lies indeed on how something/someone—a (s)object—gets constituted and ordered through the educational.
3. W. J. T. Mitchell argues that "we live in a culture of images, a society of the spectacle, a world of semblances and simulacra," where such images are "a complex interplay between visuality, apparatus, institutions, discourses, bodies, and frugality" (Mitchell, 1995, pp. 5, 6). And in such a culture of images, Nicholas Mirzoeff states, we are visual subjects, "agents of sight (regardless of our capacity to see) and as the objects of certain discourses of visuality" (Mirzoeff, 2005) educated in particular regimes of appearance, as Inés Dussel would warn us, and instructed by ways in which one should look and what is to be made of the visual encounter (Dussel, 2001). For more on visuality of classroom and schooling specifically, see Grosvenor (1999, 2007); and for some initial efforts on visuality and images in Guatemalan museums, see, for example, Cesaús Arzú (2012).
4. This caption can be found on the back of the photograph, and it is believed to be handwritten by historian Luis Lujan Muñoz, who owned the collection of which this photograph is part.
5. For critical perspectives on Asturias's work *vis-à-vis* indigenous matters, see, for example, Pinto Soria (2007) and Preble-Niemi Oralia (2006).
6. See also Martínez Peláez (1970) and Argueta Hernández (2011a, 2011b).
7. See, for example, Bienvenido Argueta's research on the modernization project in Guatemala via schools for indigenous peoples and pedagogy in 1885 to 1899 (Argueta Hernández, 2011, 2011b).
8. According to Batres Jáuregui, in the 1799 contest, "part of the project to regenerate the nation was to try to persuade the utility and means so that the indians and ladinos dress and wear shoes the Spanish way" (Batres Jáuregui, 1894, p. 170).
9. The *mappaemundi* in this image is one of the methods of map projection. Its heritage goes back to dominant types of maps before the Renaissance, T-O maps, and others (Snyder, 1997).
10. For an account of Guatemalan educational laws from 1831 to 1991, see Argueta Hernández (n.d.).
11. For more on Minervalias, see Luján Muñoz (1992), Rendón (2000, 2002), and Carrera Mejía (2009).
12. Felipe Estrada Paniagua, 1907, speech given at the Minerva Temple on the name of the government at the Fiestas Escolares. CIRMA Taracena Arriola Collection 495 Guatemala.
13. On the peace process, see, for example, Sandoval (2013).
14. The spelling varies. Sometimes it is spelled Xinka, and others Xinca.

15. This is the complete list of Mayan languages according to the Mayan Languages Academy: Poqomchi', Achi', Q'eqchi', Ch'orti', Kaqchikel, Poqomam, Sipakapense, Tz'utujil, Mam, Ixil, Sakapulteka, Uspanteka· Awakateka, Chalchiteka, Akateka, Chuj, Jakalteka, Q'anjob'al, Tektiteka, Kíché, Itza', Mopan. See www.almg.org.gt/comun idades-lingueisticas.html.

References

Alvarez, S. E., Arias, A., & Hale, C. R. (2011). Re-visioning Latin American studies. *Cultural Anthropology, 26*(2), 225–246.

Argueta Hernández, B. (2011a). *El nacimiento del racismo en el discurso pedagógico.* Guatemala City: PACE-GIZ.

Argueta Hernández, B. (2011b). La pedagogía del Doctor Darío González. *Revista Education, 7,* 27–58.

Argueta Hernández, B. (n.d.). Una perspectiva histórica de las leyes de educación en Guatemala y los desafios actuals para una nueva ley de educación nacional. In *Memoria X Encuentro Nacional de Investigadores Educativos de Guatemala: Legislación e Investigación Educativa* (pp. 7–75). Guatemala: Universidad Rafael Landivar.

Asturias, M. A. (1923). *El problema social del Indio.* B. A. Thesis Lilcenciatura en Derecho, Universidad de San Carlos de Guatemala.

Asturias, M. A. (2007). *Sociología Guatemalteca: El problema social del Indio* (Julio César Pinto Soria, ed.). Guatemala: Editorial Universitaria, Universidad de San Carlos de Guatemala.

Batres Jáuregui, A. (1894). *Los Indios, su historia y su civilización.* Guatemala: Tipografía la Unión.

Carrera Mejía, M. (2009). Las fiestas de Minerva en Guatemala, 1899–1919: El ansia de progreso y de civilización de los liberals. *Portal Historia Centroamericana,* 1–13. www.hcentroamerica.fcs.ucr.ac.cr/Contenidos/hca/cong/mesas/cong6/docs/HistCult/mcarr.doc.

Casaús Arzu, M. E. (2012). Museo nacional y museos privados en Guatemala: Patrimonio y patrimonialización. Un siglo de intentos y frustraciones. *Revista de Indias, 72*(254), 93–130.

Chakrabarty, D. (2000). *Provincializing Europe: Postcolonial thought and historical difference.* Princeton, NJ: Princeton University Press.

Coronil, F. (2004). Seeing history. *Hispanic American Review, 84*(1), 1–4.

Dary, C. (2011). *Trabajando desde adentro: De activistas a funcionarios: Los mayas frente a los desafíos de la multiculturalización del estado (2000–2010).* Guatemala: Instituto de Estyudios Interétnicos, Universidad de San Carlos de Guatemala.

Daston, L., & Galison, P. (2010). *Objectivity.* Hereford, MD: Zone.

Deleuze, G., & Guattari, F. (1987). *A thousand plateaus: Capitalism and schizophrenia* (B. Massumi, tran., 1st ed.). Minneapolis: University of Minnesota Press.

Derrida, J. (1982). *Margins of philosophy.* Chicago: University of Chicago Press.

Derrida, J. (1993). *Aporias.* Stanford, CA: Stanford University Press.

Dussel, I. (2001). *School uniforms and the disciplining of appearances: Towards a comparative history of regulation of bodies in early modern France, Argentina, and the United States.* Ph.D. Dissertation, University of Wisconsin–Madison.

Estrada Cabrera, M. (1977). *La construcción del temple de Minerva y su destrucción.* Guatemala: La Hora [newspaper] archives.

Fabian, J. (1983). *Time and the other: How anthropology makes its object.* New York: Columbia University Press.

Goodman, N. (1978). *Ways of worldmaking.* Indianapolis, IN: Hackett.

Grandin, G. (2004). Can the subaltern be seen? Photography and the affects of nationalism. *Hispanic American Review, 84*(1), 83–111.

Grosvenor, I. (Ed.). (1999). *Silences and images: The social history of the classroom.* Oxford, Great Britain: Peter Lang Ltd.

Grosvenor, I. (2007). From the "eye of history" to "a second gaze": The visual archive and the marginalized in the history of education. *History of Education, 36,* 607–622.

Lock, M. (2000). A strong silent gaze, no matter what. *The New York Times* (January 20). www.nytimes.com/2000/01/28/arts/photography-review-a-strong-silent-gaze-no-matter-what.html

López Cuat, C. G. (2005). *Análisis semiótico del mensaje estético de la fotografía Artística del Guatemalteco Alan Benchoam.* B. A. Thesis Licenciatura en Ciencias de la comunicación, Universidad de San Carlos de Guatemala.

Luján Muñoz, J. (1987). *Los indígenas de Guatemala vistos por el fotógrafo Alberto G. Valdeavellano (1861–1928).* Guatemala: INGUAT/Academia de Geografía e Historia.

Luján Muñoz, J. (1992). Un ejemplo de uso de la tradición clásica en Guatemala: Las "Minervalias" establecidas por el Presidente Manuel Estrada Cabrera. *Revista de la Universidad del Valle de Guatemala, 2,* 25–33.

Martinez Peláez, S. (1970). *La patria del criollo: Ensayo de interpretación de la realidad colonial Guatemalteca.* Guatemala: Editorial Universitaria.

Mbembé, A. (2003). Necropolitics. *Public Culture, 15,* 11–40.

Mirzoeff, N. (2005). *Watching Babylon: The war in Iraq and global visual culture.* New York: Routledge.

Mitchell, W. J. T. (1995). *Picture theory: Essays on verbal and visual representation* (new ed.). Chicago: University of Chicago Press.

Mitchell, W. J. T. (2011). World pictures: Globalization and visual culture. In J. Harris (Ed.), *Globalization and contemporary art* (pp. 135–169). Malden, MA: Wiley-Blackwell.

Oralia, P. N. (Ed.). (2006). *Cien Años de magia: Ensayos Críticos sobre la obra de Miguel Ángel Asturias.* Guatemala: F&G Editores.

Pinto Soria, J. C. (2007). Introduction. In M. A. Asturias (Ed.), *Sociología Guatemalteca: El Problema Social del Indio.* Guatemala City: Editorial Universitaria, Universidad de San Carlos de Guatemala.

Popkewitz, T. S. (2007). *Cosmopolitanism and the age of school reform: Science, education, and making society by making the child.* New York: Routledge.

Rendón, C. (2000). *Minerva y la palma: El enigma de Don Manuel Estrada Cabrera.* Mexico City: Artemis Edinter.

Rendón, C. (2002). Temples of tribute and illusion. *Americas, 54*(4), 16–23.

Rionda, J. I. (2012). Los conflictos gobierno-iglesia. *El Heraldo,* August 28. http://heraldo delbajio.com/los-conflictos-gobierno-iglesia-28-ago-2012/

Said, E. (1979). *Orientalism.* New York: Vintage Books.

Sandoval, M. A. (2013). El Sueño de la paz: El inicio del diálogo Gobierno-Guerrila. Guatemala: F&G Editores.

Snyder, J. P. (1997). *Flattening the earth: Two thousand years of map projections.* Chicago: University of Chicago Press.

CONTRIBUTORS

Lars Bang is a PhD Fellow/Student in the Institute of Learning & Philosophy at Aalborg University, Denmark. He has a background as a teacher in special education and a Master in Education (Psychology). His current research and teaching interests include science education, educational research, history, and the philosophy of science. Email: lbj@learning.aau.dk

Ezequiel Gomez Caride, the Pontifical Catholic University of Argentina. He earned his PhD in the Department Curriculum and Instruction in the School of Education at the University of Wisconsin–Madison. He has published several articles from a comparative perspective and presented his research in a variety of international conferences. He was a Fulbright Scholar (2008–2010) and a Weinstein Distinguished Graduate Fellowship (2012–2013) of the UW-Madison. He is currently working as a researcher at the Pontifical Catholic University of Argentina. His research is concerned with issues of national identity, religion, educational policy, and cultural studies. Email: ezequielgomezc@hotmail.com

Jennie D. Diaz is a doctoral graduate in the Department of Curriculum and Instruction at the University of Wisconsin–Madison. She is interested in raising questions about the politics, history, and culture of schooling. Her current research examines how reforms aimed at *math for all* entangle with issues of equality, inclusion, and representation to shape foundational theories/practices of elementary math education. Email: jennieddiaz@gmail.com

Daniel Friedrich is Assistant Professor of Curriculum at Teachers College, Columbia University. Prof. Friedrich is currently interested in the system of thought behind the travelling of teacher education reforms around the world. He has published in the Journal of Curriculum Theorizing, Education Policy Analysis Archives, and the Journal of Curriculum and Pedagogy among others. His book *Democratic Education as a Curricular Problem* was published by Routledge in 2014. Email: friedrich@tc.edu

Ruth I. Gustafson is an independent scholar. Her research is about racial boundaries of participation in music education as a school subject. She is currently working on the period between the 1920 and 1970, the years of African American emigration to the northern industrial states of the US from the South. She is the author of Race and Curriculum: Music in Early Childhood Education (2009) and is currently working on a new book, *Fateful Songs: Music Education, Race, and Social Change.* Email: rigustaf@gmail.com

Jamie A. Kowalczyk is adjunct professor at Loyola University, Chicago. Her research interests include education reforms related to immigration and integration, intercultural and civic education, and the translation of globally circulating discourses within particular contexts. E-mail: jkowalczyk1@luc.edu

John B. Krejsler is an Associate Professor at the Department of Education, Aarhus University, Denmark. He sits on the boards of the Nordic Educational Research Association as well as of the European Educational Research Association. He recently had a visiting professorship at Kristianstad University in Sweden as academic leader of the research group "Work in Schools". His research covers transnational and national education policy, professional development and power relations in relation to the fields of school policy, teacher education and higher education reform. John has strong interests in epistemology and theory development, poststructural theory (Deleuze, Foucault) and critical theory. Email: jok@edu.au.dk

Nancy Lesko is Maxine Greene Professor at Teachers College, Columbia University and teaches in the areas of curriculum, social theory, gender studies, and youth studies. Her research interests focus on youth, affect theory in curriculum studies, and gender and sexualities in school. Recent publications include: *Act your age! The social construction of adolescence* (2nd ed), *Keywords in youth studies* (with Susan Talburt), and Pink brains and education: A postfeminist analysis of neuroscience and neurosexism. *Revista Brasileira de História da Educação,* special issue on the history of childhood and youth (with Stephanie McCall). Email: lesko@exchange.tc.columbia.edu

Ligia (Licho) López López is a graduate student in the department of Curriculum and Instruction at the University of Wisconsin–Madison where she focuses on curriculum history and theory. Ligia's research concerns transnational curriculum inquiry in teacher education, post foundational approaches to education and educational research, and concerns with difference and diversity. Her current project questions the making-up of difference as an object of scientific inquiry in Guatemalan indigenous education in the 20th century. The historical study addresses the limits of the practices of education to correct social wrongs that paradoxically recapitulates and continues to order the 'colonial'. Email: lllopez2@ wisc.edu

Catarina Silva Martins is Professor at the Faculty of Fine Arts, Oporto University, and researcher at i2ADS-Institute of Research in Art, Design, and Society, University of Oporto, in which she coordinates the Research Group in Arts Education. She is the Link Convenor of Network 29: Research on Arts Education at the European Educational Research Association. Her research interest lies in rethinking arts education curriculum studies in the present from a historical approach focusing on the systems of reason that govern policy and research. Email: csmartins@fba.up.pt

Ulf Olsson is Associate Professor at the Department of Education, Stockholm University, Sweden. His research interest is about the history of present knowledge/ rationality that governs international politics of education, educational politics and research. Email: ulf.olsson@edu.su.se

Kenneth Petersson is Associate Professor at the Department of Social and Welfare Studies, Linkoping University, Sweden. His main research interest is about the history of present knowledge that governs national and international politics of education, educational politics and research. Email: kenneth.petersson@liu.se

Thomas S. Popkewitz, Professor in the Department of Curriculum and Instruction, The University of Wisconsin–Madison, USA. His studies focus on the systems of reason that govern pedagogical and curriculum reforms, educational research, and teacher education. Central are the historical paradoxes of school reforms and sciences that exclude and abjection in the impulse to include; and the principles of stability and conservation in educational theories of change. Recent publications include *Cosmopolitanism and the Age of Reform* (2008); and *Rethinking the History of Education* (Ed., 2013). Currently he is writing a book about the impracticality of "practical" and "useful knowledge" as a strategy of change in the education sciences. Email: popkewitz@education.wisc.edu

Amy Sloane is Director of the Undergraduate Research Scholars Program at the University of Wisconsin–Madison, USA. She holds a joint PhD in Curriculum and Instruction, and Forest and Wildlife Ecology. She teaches environmental education and philosophy of education. Her research interests are history and philosophy of environmental thought, and equity and access in education. Email: alsloane@wisc.edu

Daniel Tröhler is Professor of Education and Director of the Doctoral School in Educational Sciences at the University of Luxembourg and visiting Professor of Comparative Education at the University of Granada, Spain. His latest publications include *Languages of Education: Protestant Legacies, National Identities, and Global Aspirations* (Routledge 2011) (AERA Outstanding Book of the Year Award), *Pestalozzi and the Educationalization of the World* (Palgrave, 2013), and he served as guest editor for the Special Issue *Historicising Jean-Jacques Rousseau: Four ways to commemorate his 300th anniversary* (2012) (*Studies in Philosophy and Education*). Email: daniel.troehler@uni.lu

Paola Valero is Professor at the Department of Learning and Philosophy at Aalborg University, Denmark. Her research explores the socio-cultural-political constitution of mathematics and science education practices as a central contributor of school curricula to the project of Modernity in the 20th century. She works across different national contexts, in particular Denmark and Colombia. Her research is part of the Nordic Center of Excellence in Education Justice through Education. Email: paola@learning.aau.dk

Weili Zhao is a PhD Candidate at the Department of Curriculum and Instruction in the University of Wisconsin–Madison, USA. Her research mainly explores the issues of language, body, and difference in contemporary Chinese education from a cross-cultural and historical perspective. Email: wzhao6@wisc.edu

INDEX

Page numbers in italics indicate figures and photographs.